Medical Anthropology

About the Editor

Prof. B.V. Sharma is a trained Anthropologist with research interests in Medical Anthropology, Anthropology of Education and Community Participation in Development. He obtained his Master's Degree from University of Pune and M.Phil. and Ph.D. Degrees from University of Hyderabad. Currently he is associated with the Department of Anthropology at University of Hyderabad. He teaches Medical Anthropology to the students of Masters programme in Anthropology and to the students of Master of Public Health in the University of Hyderabad.

Besides publishing and guiding many students in the areas of his interest for M.Phil. and Ph.D. Degree, Prof. Sharma conducted research projects for several International bodies like W.H.O. (Geneva & New Delhi), World Bank (New Delhi), DFIDI (New Delhi) and F.A.O. (Rome). He is currently working on 'Production and social distribution of ethnomedical knowledge', 'Uniformity and divergence in ethnomedical treatment', 'Therapy Management in Chronic Illnesses' and 'Internet use and health decision making'.

MEDICAL ANTHROPOLOGY

Tradition and Change

Edited by

B.V. SHARMA

CONCEPT PUBLISHING COMPANY PVT. LTD.

NEW DELHI-110059

ISBN-13: 978-93-5125-252-8

First Published 2016

Published and Printed by

Concept
Since 1974

Concept Publishing Company Pvt. Ltd.
Regd. Office:
A/15-16, Commercial Block, Mohan Garden,
New Delhi-110059 (INDIA)
Phones : 25351460, 25351794, *Fax* : 091-11-25357109
Email : publishing@conceptpub.com
Website: www.conceptpub.com

Editorial Office: H-13, Bali Nagar, New Delhi-110 015, India.

Cataloging in Publication Data—DK Courtesy: D.K. Agencies (P) Ltd. <docinfo@dkagencies.com>

National Seminar on 'Health Cultures and Tribal Communities: Emerging Research Agenda and Policy Shifts' (2013 : Hyderabad, India)

Medical anthropology : tradition and change / edited by B.V. Sharma.
pages cm
Papers presented at the National Seminar on 'Health Cultures and Tribal Communities: Emerging Research Agenda and Policy Shifts' during January 2-4, 2013 at Hyderabad, India, organized by Department of Anthropology, University of Hyderabad.Includes bibliographical references and index.
Includes bibliographical references and index.
ISBN 9789351252528

1. Medical anthropology—India—Congresses. 2. Public health—India—Congresses. 3. Health behavior—India—Congresses. I. Sharma, B. V., editor. II. University of Hyderabad. Department of Anthropology, organizer. III. Title.

GN296.5.I4N38 2013 DDC 306.4610954 23

Contents

Preface

Research interest in Medical Anthropology is gaining momentum in India. Several publications relating to health cultures among tribal and other non-tribal communities are being published in several professional anthropology as well as other journals, in edited volumes and anthologies. Further, multidisciplinary, interdisciplinary and transdisciplinary perspectives are being applied to the various areas of concern by medical anthropologists, like healing symbolism, spirit possession, placebo effects, social aspects of medical systems, therapy management, coping with illness etc. The initial interest in Applied Medical Anthropology and Ethnomedicine did not fade away; but the concern for theoretical discourses connecting to anthropological theories and methods is, however, on the rise.

The essays in this book covered aspects relating to Tradition and Change. The question of how illness and suffering are seen as consequences of social disruptions and how decisions of seeking cure from healers and sorceress are seen as 'rational' and 'appropriate' are dealt with in some essays more explicitly. The politics of medicine is elaborated in one chapter while dealing with Ayurveda, Unani and Allopathy in India, and two other chapters in this volume dealt with explanatory models dealing with two specific illness categories. The other chapters have dealt with policy and programmes of health care delivery. The aspect of tradition are largely referred to illness etiologies, utilization of services of healers and other traditional health care service providers, while change referred to the 'changed logic' and 'conflicting logic' to change.

As stated in the introductory note, some of the papers presented in a national seminar organized by me are selected for this edited book. Papers presented in the Seminar on 'Ethnomedicine' are excluded as they may not contribute to the exiting body of literature in that area. The papers selected for the book do not fall under one theme, but many share a common trait in terms of qualitative research methodology. The studies are based on primary data and attempted to contribute a new dimension to the understanding of the chosen issue. I hope the essays in the book serve as reference materials and also for critical discussion on the issues raised.

B.V. Sharma

Acknowledgements

Publication of this book would not have been possible but for the help and backing from several persons in various forms. I am not venturing to mention here my thanks to all those persons individually due to space constraints. However, I must mention some individuals and organizations whose support is really very valuable.

I thank the University of Hyderabad for the wonderful opportunity provided to me to organize the National Seminar on '*Health Cultures and Tribal Communities: Emerging Research Agenda and Policy Shifts*' during January 2-4, 2013 as part of UGC-SAP programme of the Department of Anthropology. The Seminar could be successfully organized because of the whole hearted support—academic and otherwise—of all my colleagues in the Department, namely Prof. K.K. Misra, Prof. P.Venkata Rao, Prof. N. Sudhakar Rao, Prof. R. Siva Prasad, Dr. George Tharakan, C., Dr. Romesh Singh, Mr. S.A. Munaf and Dr. Ratheesh Kumar (who was then associated with our department at the University of Hyderabad). The critical comments of Prof. N. Sudhakar Rao, Prof. R. Siva Prasad and Prof. P.Venkata Rao helped me to revise the drafts of my introductory note to this volume. I once again place on record my gratitude to them.

The contributors to this volume need special thanks for the encouragement they provided to me. In view of my responsibilities in the University as Dean, Students Welfare (D.S.W.) till April 2014, I could not work seriously on the publication of this book for a while and then the Publishers too have taken some time for genuine reasons. I greatly appreciate the patience of all the contributors and I place on record my gratefulness to them. My special thanks to my guru,

Prof. R.K. Mutatkar who had readily accepted to give the key note address for the Seminar and for revising that address for inclusion in this book.

My wife, Kusuma and my son, Rakshith swallowed all the glitches caused to them and always compassionately supported me. My students helped me in various stages of this book in a number of ways, and especially in typing and editing. I remember of having sought help at odd times and sometimes they postponed their work for my sake. I am particularly grateful to Mr. Gonnabattula Mohan, Dr. Alok Pandey, Dr. Udita Rathi, Mr. Sipoy Sarveswar and Ms. Deepti Bapat for all the assistance they provided in the completion of this task.

Finally, I am profoundly obliged to M/s. Concept Publishing Company (P) Limited, New Delhi, for accepting to publish this book without any hesitation and for taking the trouble to bring it in printable form.

B.V. Sharma

Contributors List

Girija, K.P., Centre for the Study of Culture and Society [CSCS], 194, 2nd Cross, Domulur, Bangaluru. girijakp@gmail.com

Goyal, Jaya, Tata Institute of Social Sciences (TISS), V.N. Purav Marg, Deonar Mumbai. Jaya.goyal@gmail.com.

Haripriya, Narasimhan, Department of Liberal Arts, Indian Institute of Technology (IITH), Hyderabad. haripriya@iith.ac.in.

Kaur, Reetinder, Department of Anthropology, Punjab University, Chandigarh. reetinder1986@gmail.com.

Mutatkar, R.K., Former Dean, School of Health Sciences, University of Pune & Chairman, INCAA & President, MAAS, 64, Anand Park, Aundh, Pune. rkmutatkar@gmail.com.

Nuckolls, Charles W., Department of Anthropology, Brigham Young University, Provo, UT 84602. charles_nuckolls@byu.edu.

Reddy, K.S., National AIDS Research Institute (NARI), Bhosari, Pune. ksreddy.nari@gmail.com.

Shubha, Ranganathan, Department of Liberal Arts, Indian Institute of Technology (IITH), Hyderabad. shubha@iith.ac.in.

Sahay, S., National AIDS Research Institute (NARI), Bhosari, Pune. seemasahay@yahoo.com.

Sharma, B.V., Department of Anthropology, University of Hyderabad, Hyderabad. sharmabhallamudi@gmail.com.

Sharma, Priyam, Department of Sociology, University of Hyderabad, Hyderabad. priyam07sharma@gmail.com.

Sinha, A.K., Department of Anthropology, Punjab University, Chandigarh. ksinhaanil@yahoo.com.

Sumathi, S., Department of Anthropology, University of Madras, Chennai. sumathirajesh2004@yahoo.com

Introduction

I

This book Medical Anthropology is an outcome of the National Seminar organized by the Department of Anthropology, University of Hyderabad during January 2-4, 2013 on the broad theme of 'Health Cultures' under the Special Assistance Programme (SAP) of University Grants Commission to the Department. Only 10 papers including the Keynote address delivered by Prof. R.K. Mutatkar have been chosen for this book, though many have presented papers in the seminar and some have even revised their papers for inclusion in this book. It was planned to publish this book within a short time, yet some delay has occurred due to my 'non-academic' commitments in the University. I apologize to the contributors to this volume for this delay and appreciate their patience.

The seminar was conceived to showcase the divergent interests of Anthropologists and other anthropologically oriented social science scholars working in the areas of health, illness and healing. India owing to the presence of variety of ethnic communities and multiplicity of medical traditions offered a grand opportunity for Indians as well as foreign scholars committed to ethnographic research to contribute immensely both in the area of anthropology of medicine and anthropology in medicine. The engagement of scholars with health cultures or with specific aspects of health cultures of tribal communities may be striking; at the same time the concern shown for the study of such aspects among social groups in semi-urban and urban neighbourhoods is no less. The interface of local, regional and national health cultures has been explored from different perspectives. The issue of continuity and change of local health cultures under the impact of rapidly changing medical technologies, improved access to health information due primarily to electronic revolution, displacement and rehabilitation, weakening of traditional institutions responsible for transfer of indigenous knowledge and skills relating to health care etc., was of course a priority. The shift in the recent past to discourses on contexts of medical syncretism, networking of medical practitioners, changing roles of family and community in therapy management is, however, noteworthy. Similarly, subjects of medicalization and changing notions of body and human nature under the influence of biomedicine too received attention, though scantily. The identification of anthropologists with people—the patients their families and also their communities—as well as their sympathy for the people resulted in approaching the culture bound syndromes, medical care and health behaviour issues in a different manner. The non-acceptance of medical authority as a norm permitted the anthropologists to pose the research questions with emphasis on asymmetrical power relations in the context of acceptance of biomedical practices.

Apropos to the aim of the conference the papers presented reflected different themes and diverse perspectives. Thus, the papers in the book too are not really focused on any single theme. The Keynote address of Prof. Mutatkar has set the tone for the discussions in the Conference. The growing significance for 'anthropological approach'—the qualitative interpretative approach—for the understanding of health and illness and exposing the limitations of 'quantitative' approaches that dominate the health research generally, is perhaps what is common to most of the papers in the volume. While the first three chapters in the book fall under the broad head of 'Popular Health Cultures', the two chapters that followed them focus on the 'Indian Medical Systems'. The common theme for these two chapters is the relationship of different medical systems. The next two chapters dealt with the 'Health Care Delivery', examining the private-public partnership and community participation in health care. The last three chapters fall under the theme of 'Explanatory Models and Health Behaviour'.

II

Almost every study conducted among the tribal communities in India which focused on health and illness paid some attention to the human agents in disease causation and the magico-religious healing. Vijayendra and Bhat (2004), while describing the two techniques of sorcery employed by Jenu Kuruba—*datu* and *chilluhodeyuvadu*—for instance noted that 'sorcery, locally called *mata* is no less important in illness etiology of Jenu Kuruba'. Nilanjan Khatua (2005) observed that among the Hill Korwas of Chhattisgarh sorcery is conducted by *dasia* (female sorcerer) and *dain* (male sorcerer). The *dasia* cause illness by casting evil eye, a power which they acquire due to their birth on a no moon day and the *dain* implants dirt, hair, stone, bone piece, fish scale etc. of the dead into the body a person to cause acute disease. *Dain* and in some cases *dasia* too acquire the power by worshipping evil spirits and offering some sacrifices. However, Gardner (1995) makes an interesting observation in case of Paliyans, the south Indian foragers; that sorcery is seldom applied among the Paliyans though the techniques of sorcery are known. Sinha and Banerjee (2004) published on the basis of secondary data on "Tribal Witchcraft and Personalistic Disease Theory: Concepts and Issue". This article first dealt extensively on the meanings of witchcraft and sorcery and how these subjects have been studied by different scholars, more particularly in African context. The 'reintegrating functions' of sorcery and witchcraft have been critically examined. Subsequently, the authors briefly reviewed tribal witchcraft beliefs in India citing the works of Roy on Birhor (1978), Oraon (1985), Kharia (1937), Griffith's work on Kols (1946), Fuchus (1950) work on Balahis (a low caste community), Chaudhury's work on Santhals (1984), Deb Burman's work on Santhals (1986), Saha's work on Dublas of Gujarat (1986), Rizvi's work on Jaunsaris (1986), and Backon's work on Kurumba (1995). Recognizing the abundance of literature on sorcery in the context of tribals in India, Joshi (2004) in a paper on "*World of Tribal Healers*" observed that anthropologists and others by and large focused on sorcers though there are other different kinds of healers. Some of these studies which dealt in some detail with the role of witchcraft and sorcery in illness explanations and the significance of magico-religious specialists in providing health care, of course, had to deal with social aspects of medical systems. Raj Pramukhi and Palkumar (2006), for instance, dealt with ethnomedical beliefs and practices among the tribes of Eastern Ghats in Andhra Pradesh. They say that the specialists of magico-religious healing look at cure for illness also located in the very supernatural beings that cause them. It is also pointed out that reference to sorcery is common as it is believed that fortune provokes envy. The shaman seeks to restore patient's relationship to the physical, metaphysical, and social worlds to correct the imbalance that is root cause of illness.

The chapters of Dr. Subha and Dr. Haripriya in this book deal with magico-religious healing in Indian context. Both deal with the question of 'rationality' in the use of services of healers/sorcerers, besides the question of tradition and modernity. Subha's paper "tried to demonstrate on the one hand, the complex ways by which the patients and monks frame temple healing as simultaneously spiritual and scientific and on the other to see how the broader socio-political trends in the state of Maharashtra are related to the monks? narratives about scientific healing." The essay of Dr. Haripriya which focuses on rural and tribal women's encounters with magic and sorcery in Tamil Nadu attempts to answer the question of why do women approach a sorcerer. She discusses on why sorcery accusations formed a significant part of women' discourse about health in two of her selected villages, though most of them expressed their doubts in the efficacy of sorcery examinations. Women attended *kami* sessions, as long as it offered them an explanation they already suspected, or something they could not get from consulting other health care practitioners. She also points out that women feel a lack of agency when interacting with biomedical specialists while sorcery allows them more involvement in health care decision-making.

The chapter by Nicholas, based on his fieldwork among the Jalaris, the fishermen caste in Andhra Pradesh, is not directly on magico-religious healing of any specific illness. However, relevance of this chapter lies in the fact that Jalari employ divination (e.g. spirit possession) to determine the causes of events, from illness to the failure to catch fish, but also to identify the reason a goddess would manifest her power in the sudden eruption of a snake mound. He observes that "all divinations, whatever their immediate concern, reduce to some kind of social disruption. That is, the goddess is angry because of a dispute within the family that worships her, and she afflicts family members in order to call attention to the dispute and coerce them into solving it." Similarly, he also observes that "the Jalaris generally do not tell anyone to do anything.... The individuals are brought to a realization of their responsibility by the manifestation of the divine in their life, possibly through miraculous visitations, but probably through misfortune in *illness and suffering* (emphasis added). Then they would seek confirmation in the *pati* and finally would do what was necessary." These observations have many implications for illness etiologies and health seeking among the *jalari*.

III

The medical pluralism in India offered social scientists a variety of research opportunities. Three scholarly papers in Social Science and Medicine on medical pluralism by Indians published in 1980s by Bharadwaj (1980), Minocha (1980), and Bhattacharya (1983) triggered a variety of research interests. More generally, this context was used for studies on illness behaviour; to explain the choice of a system of medicine. The issues of simultaneous use of different systems of medicine, the hierarchy of resort, and the question of forced and free choice were the points of debate and discussion. On the other hand there are also studies of Sociology of Medicine; study of nature of relationships between the different systems of medicine, the power equations and the 'politics of medicine'. The claims of antiquity, the identity markers for the brand of 'classical tradition', the historical processes that have contributed to the visibility and authenticity etc. were researched. Ms. Girija in her chapter in this book looked at "the process through which a pure Ayurveda is historicized as the classical tradition of Kerala at the cost of a variety of practices or Ayurvedas." Further, she attempted to: "unravel the process of rendering certain knowledge forms more visible and hence authentic at the cost of certain other knowledges"; "point out a few continuities and ruptures in the reconfiguration of *nattuvaidyam*. Taking note of the arguments of scholars that the reconfiguration of Ayurveda has happened through the selection and rejection of modern elements (Panikkar, 2007; Sivaramakrishnan, 2001; Alavi, 2007), it is pointed out that "the selective choice of colonial modernity in its interaction with and administration of indigenous practice is equally relevant in rendering visibility and authenticity to certain practices."

The chapter by Ms. Priyam Sharma in this book is a contribution to the medical pluralism in India. The chapter dealt with, in her own words, Does co-existence of different medical system mean simply co-option? How does a particular medical systems gain certain degree of authority to claim itself superior with respect to 'other' medical systems? And in this construction of the 'other', how other medical systems are affected by this power dynamics that operate in plural medical system? How do power relations influence this hiatus between the medical systems?

IV

The Public-Private-Partnership (PPP) has become a buzz word now in discourses relating to development and governance. In the field of health care, the discussion of this received greater attention as the State is gradually withdrawing from the health care and the health care is highly privatized. Different models of PPP are evolved, piloted and tested for replication in different contexts. Most PPP initiatives in India are to achieve improved access, affordability, quality and equity in health services (Institute for Health Sector). The PPP experiments for implementation of reproductive and child health programmes, perhaps-out numbered others that dealt with other national disease control or elimination programmes. However, the models shared some common features and also differed in many respects. The rural and urban contexts, the number of organizations partnering, the strengths and weaknesses of these partnering organizations and others influenced the final organizational structures of the PPP models. The chapter by Ms. Jaya Goyal in this book is a detailed analysis of three PPP models in RCH. The study analysed them on institutional assessment criteria as suggested by the existing literature on PPPs. The chapter deals with stakeholders in the partnerships, their contribution and the conducive environment that led to the partnerships. The chapter attempted to contribute to Public Policy on health drawing attention to the determinants of successful PPPs and factors leading to failures of PPPs. The author observes that most states lack policies to interact with private health sector and also to engage them in any partnership and that locally applicable model of partnership are more likely to be successful.

Like Public-Private-Partnership, the idea of "community participation" also gained currency in recent years. Guidelines for community participation are issued virtually for all areas of development like health, education, agriculture, irrigation, forest management, watershed, ground water management, gender equity etc. Community participation in health, however, was formally introduced long ago at the Alma Ata Declaration in 1978. Since then, it has become a growing theme in healthcare reforms in many societies. The concept along side received a detailed and critical examination by many scholars. Such an examination resulted in appreciating that it is a complex entity and that it is a means and also as an end in itself.

The need for community participation in health has been realised for the disease control programmes like Tuberculosis, Leprosy, Malaria, Blindness etc. and also for the RCH programmes. The importance of a community based care approach for successful implementation of Directly Observed Therapy Short course (DOTS) for control of TB, perhaps received a greater attention recently (Sharma, 2002). Like in the case of PPP, different models of community based TB care were evolved and tested in different countries. The chapter by Srikanth and Sahay in this book examines the factors that influence the community participation in HIV/AIDS health care delivery. The explanatory models of illness in case of HIV/AIDS pose many challenges for realization of successful community participation. The chapter details these challenges in terms of demographic, social, cultural, economic, psychological and other factors. Rightly, it stresses that "community participation is not an instrumental means, but a dynamic process, which passes through different stages of cooperation and conflicts. These stages are shaped not by a single factor, but as a cumulative result of interaction between several factors."

V

"Explanatory models are the notions about an episode of sickness and its treatment that is employed by all those engaged in the clinical process. The interaction between the explanatory models of patients and practitioners is a central component of health care"—Kleinman (1980:105). As Fabrega has pointed out, "disease" in its generic sense is a linguistic term used to refer to a certain class of phenomena that members of all social groups, at all times in the history of man, have been exposed to. "When people of various intellectual and cultural persuasions use terms analogous to 'disease', they have in mind, among other things, that phenomena in question involve a person-centred, harmful, and undesirable deviation or discontinuity... associated with impairment or discomfort" (Fabrega, 1972:1501). Since, the condition is not desired it gives rise to a need for corrective actions. The later involve beliefs and explanations about disease as well as rules of conduct to rationalize treatment actions. These constitute socially adaptive devices to resolve, for the society in which the sick person lives, the crises and uncertainties surrounding disease. Such culturally derived belief systems about disease also constitute models, but they are not scientific models. These may be referred to as popular or folk models. As efforts at social adaptation, they contrast with scientific models, which are primarily designed to promote scientific investigation. The historical fact we have to face is that in modern Western society biomedicine not only has provided a basis for the scientific study of disease; it has also become our own culturally specific perspective about disease, that is, our folk model. Indeed the biomedical model is now the dominant folk model of disease in the Western World" (Engel, 1977:130). Explanatory models are sets of beliefs or understandings that specify for an illness episode its cause, time, and mode of onset of symptoms, pathophysiology, course of sickness, and treatment. Explanatory models are "formed and employed to cope with a specific health problem, and consequently they need to be analyzed in *that* concrete setting" (Kleinman, 1980:106, emphasis added).

Beginning in the late 1970s with Kleinman's work, explanatory models emerged as a new approach in the understanding of health, culture and medicine. Unlike earlier approaches which focused more on ethno-medical terms and collection of ethno-medical knowledge base, interpretative anthropology placed culture and illness as the centre of its analytic interest. EMs cannot be confused with general beliefs about sickness and health care. General beliefs exist independent and even prior to illness episodes or experiences. EMs through drawing from these belief systems get clearly defined in respect to the specific illness episodes.

Kleinman's works, and that of many others influenced by his approach, however, fail to specify in any detail the extent to which individual explanatory models are shaped by culture and the extent to which they are idiosyncratic formulations. A major innovative effort to analyze this important issue is found in a study of the Canadian Ojibway (Garro, 1987).

Paul Farmer studying 'Move San' a 'folk-illness' in a Haitian village discusses the EMs of practitioners patient and family. He emphasizes that the EMs of herbal practitioner, patient and family are close to each other, but the EMs of the patient and institutionalized practitioner have very little in common. Farmer in his book "*Infections and Inequalities*" (1999) also brings to notice the change over a period of time in the understanding of HIV/AIDS and its aetiology as well as EMs held by laypersons in a Haitian village.

Though EMs have been discussed by many scholars like Jennifer King (1982), Steffensen and Colker (1982), Greenwood (1981) etc., the limitation of this model to inform us about the links between illness and social context has not been so much discussed. It is Good who on the basis of fieldwork in the Iranian city of Maragheh, examined the complaint of heat distress in its social and cultural context. Bibeau (1981) similarly attempted to contextualize verbalized medical categories and forge links between them and the social settings in which they occur. Reid and Reynolds (1990) have documented the 1980s 'epidemic' of repetition strain injury (RSI), an occupational illness involving musculoskeletal pain of uncertain etiology. In their study, they seek to understand the diverse and contradictory explanatory models (EMs) of RSI forwarded by state agencies, industrial managers, clinicians, lawyers, and workers themselves, arguing that these disparate EMs reveal many of the structural tensions inherent in the Australian workplace and in Australian society at large.

The study of EM, as is shown by many, undertakes many aspects into accounts. These can be enlisted as perceptions of aetiology, responsibility *versus* self-blame, cultural contextualisation of illness, prototype culture model and variation therein, the political, economic and ecological context of illness, schema, syncretism and narratives in the general domain of illness and also specific to chronic diseases like TB and AIDS (Sharma, 2008).

The chapters by Sumathi on maternal anaemia and Sinha and Ritheender Kaur's on breast cancer dealt with explanatory models of illness and illness behaviour. The work of Sumathi which is essentially to inform the public health practitioners, points out that the community people consider the various observable characteristics of anaemia, and then categorize the affected people accordingly into types. The ethnographic approach enabled the researcher not only to list out the criteria for categorizing anaemia among the communities, but also to identify that the community's system of risk classification, as compared with allopathic criteria, has a high threshold for what constitutes risk with the pregnant mothers. Thus, the chapter recommended that, "as such, the challenge for public health professionals now becomes one of promoting the seriousness of the disease and perceiving it as a disease become a frame or constitution, as an important determinant of public health in a locally relevant way."

Sinha and Kaur reported differences in description and terminology used for breast cancer. The various factors that resulted in the delay in sharing the initial symptoms with family members were elicited from cases. The explanatory models for cancer contained views that: cancer is caused due to past *karmā* and *kismet;* cancer is a contagious disease and spreads from one person to another; cancer is incurable and a fatal disease; cancer grows faster after surgery or any attempt made to remove the cancerous mass. The study also points out that the body image concern in relation to breast cancer was not in relation to public appearance, but a concern related to women themselves. Authors consider that breast cancer is stigmatising illness as it represents potential physical limitations and is also associated with particular negative images and myths, and therefore, take a symbolic meaning.

VI

Though not all chapters in this book are written by anthropologists as such, they are nevertheless important contributions to the discipline of Medical Anthropology in India, as all of them dealt with study of health, illness and healing in different communities and, as noted by Janzen (2002) while clarifying the nature of medical anthropology, "with an emphasis on how members of the community direct their behaviours, articulate their ideas, and organize their resources in these realms." The roots of medical anthropology in India lie in descriptive accounts of medical beliefs, magico-religious healing, myths relating to origin and spread of diseases etc. For instance, the work of Bodding (1925) on Santhal Medicine and its connected folklore, William Crooke's (1926) work on "*Religion and Folklore in Northern India*" referring to health beliefs, Aiyappan (1931) publication of paper on "*Myth of Origin of the Small Pox*" in Folklore (London), Mahaboob (1950) inventory of medicines among Gonds, Kolams and Chenchus, works of Harper (1957) and Rudolf (1959) on shamanism in south India and northern and middle India, Maheswar Neog's (1951) account of 'AI, the small pox goddess of Assam' and Mandelbaum's publication in 1960 on "*Curing and Religion in South Asia*", Choudhury's work on '*Traditional methods of treatment of disease among the Juangs of Dhenkanal*' and '*Magic and Medicine*' are important contributions. However, Hasan and Prasad in 1959 brought to the notice of the biomedical practitioners in the country the potential of anthropology to medical sciences by a brief note in the *Journal of the Indian Medical Association*. Incidentally, the major category of anthropological studies in health fields in India since then is "why an individual belonging to a peasant culture does not accept western medicine?" (Sahu, 1987: 23). The problems of institutional transfer and technological transfer are addressed.

Owing to multiplicity of influences, the research agenda for medical anthropology in India is changing. The effects of globalization, increasing privatization of health care and medicalization, shifts in policy and others demand research in newer areas. However, the traditional areas cannot be ignored as they have potential to contribute to anthropological concepts, theory and methods.

References

Aiyappan, A. 1931. "Myth of the Origin of the Small Pox". *Folklore* (London) 42: 291-293.

Arthur Kleinman, 1980, *Patients and healers in the context of culture. An exploration of the borderland between anthropology, medicine and psychiatry*. University of California Press, California.

Bharadwaj, S.M. 1980. Medical Pluralism and Homoeopathy: A Geographical Perspective. *Social Sciences and Medicine*. 14 B (4): 209-16.

Bhatacharya, D.P. 1983. Psychiatric pluralism in Bengal, India. *Social Sciences and Medicine*. 17 (14): 947-56.

Bodding, P.O. 1925. *Santal Medicine*. Memoir of Asiatic Society of Bengal 10.

Bibeau, 1981. The Circular Semantic Network in Ngbandi Disease Nosology. *Social Science and Medicine*, 15B: 295-307.

Early Evelyn, A. 1982. The Logic of Well-Being: Therapeutic Narratives in Cairo, Egypt. *Social Science and Medicine*, 16:1491-97.

Elwin Varrier. 1941. Dreams of Indian aboriginal Lepers, *Man*, 41 (21), 55-60.

Engel George, L. The need for a new medical model: a challenge for biomedicine. *Science*, 8th April, Vol. 196, number 4286, pp. 129 to 136.

Fabrega, H. 1972. Medical Anthropology, *Biennial Review of Anthropology*; 167-229.

Gardner, P.M. 1995. Illness and Response among South Indian Foragers. *Medical Anthropology*, February 16 (2); 119-39.

GarroLinda, C. Explaining High Blood Pressure: Variation in Knowledge about Illness. *American Ethnologist,* 1987, pp. 98 to 119.

Greenwood, Bernard, 1981 "Cold or spirit? Choice and ambiguity in Morocco's pluralistic medical system", *Social Science and Medicine*, Vol. 15B, pp. 219 to 235, Pergamon Press, Great Britain.

Hussain, Syed Khaja Mahaboob. 1950. "Medicines among Gonds, Kolams and Chenchus". Vol. 51. *Man in India*.

Janzen, M. John. 2002. *The Social Fabric of Health: An Introduction to Medical Anthropology*, New York, McGraw Hill.

Joshi, P.C. 2004. The World of Tribal Healers. In Joshi P.C. and A.K. Kalla (Ed.) *Tribal Health and Medicines*. New Delhi. Concept Publishing Company.

Khatua Niranjan, 2001. "Sickness and healing among the Hill Korwa". *Man in India,* 54(1), 51-62.

King Jennifer, B. 1982. "The impact of patients' perceptions of high blood pressure and attendance at screening", *Social Science and Medicine*, Vol. 16, pp. 1079 to 1091, Pergamon Press, Great Britain.

Maheswar, Neog, 1951. "AI, the Small Pox Goddess of Assam"; Vol. 31: 74-87. *Man in India*.

Minocha, Anita. 1980. Medical Pluralism and health services in India. *Social Sciences and Medicine*, 14 B (4): 217-23.

Paul, Farmer, 1999, *Infections and Inequalities*, University of California Press, California.

Raj Pramukh, K.E. and PDS. Pal Kumar 2006. "Indigenous Knowledge: Implications in Tribal Health and Disease", Studies in Tribes and Tribals, 4 (1): 1-6.

Reid, Janice, and Lyn Reynolds. 1990. Requiem for RSI: The explanation and Control of an Occupational Epidemic. *Medical Anthropology Quarterly*, 4(2): 162-91.

Sahu, S.K. 1987. "Medical Anthropology in India: Issues and Perspectives." *Man and Life*, 13 (1 and 2).

Sinha, A.K. and Banerjee, B.G. 2004. "Tribal Witchcraft and Pesonalistic Disease Theory. Concepts and Issues." In Joshi P.C. and A.K. Kalla (Ed.) *Tribal Health and Medicines*. New Delhi. Concept Publishing Company.

Sharma, B.V. 2008. Implications of Explanatory Models for TB and HIV among the slum dwellers of Hyderabad towards response to treatment under RNTCP. Unpublished Mid-term Report of UGC Major Research Project submitted to UGC, New Delhi.

Sharma, B.V. 2002. *Community-based T.B. Care: Asian Experience*, Geneva: World Health Organisation.

Steffensen, Margaret S. and Larry Colker. 1982. Intercultural misunderstandings about health care. Recall of descriptions of illness and treatment, *Social Science and Medicine,* Vol. 16, pp. 1949 to 1954.

Vijayendra, B.R. and Bhat, H.K. 2004. "Ethnomedicine among the Jenu Kuruba of Karnataka". In Joshi P.C. and A.K. Kalla (Ed.) *Tribal Health and Medicines*. New Delhi. Concept Publishing Company.

POPULAR HEALTH CULTURE

1
Practicing Medical Anthropology for Policy Shifts

R.K. Mutatkar

Let me first congratulate the Department of Anthropology, University of Hyderabad for choosing the topic relating to wider issues of health research focusing on tribal communities. The key words are—'Health Cultures, Tribal Communities, Research Agenda and Policy Shifts'. The role of Anthropology in establishing the links on these key words is a challenging task.

I am aware that I have been invited here since we happened to be the first department in the country at Pune to start teaching of medical anthropology in India in 1974. We got an opportunity to organize the Post International Congress symposia on Medical Anthropology in December 1978. The proceedings of one session on Medical Pluralism came out as a special number of the International Journal, '*Social Science and Medicine*'. We also had the privilege of establishing Indian Association for the Study of Traditional Asian Medicine (IASTAM) under the aegis of our Department in 1980 under the leadership of the doyen of Ayurved, Pandit Shiv Sharma and the great Indologist Prof. A.L. Basham, whose book '*The Wonder that was India*' continues to be an unparallel classic.

In classical anthropological monographs on isolated indigenous communities, there is no focused ethnography about health. However, issues relating to health such as birth, initiation, death, medicine man, shamans, diet etc. and the rituals thereof have been described under relevant chapters. Health has not been specifically referred as an aspect of culture in Malinowski's discussion about the needs doctrine in functional theory. We have the publications by William Caudill in 1953 on '*Applied Anthropology in Medicine*' in Kroeber's '*Anthropology Today*' and from Benjamin D. Paul and Margaret Mead on health issues from anthropological perspectives in 1955.

Anthropology as a discipline is known for holistic studies of man and his works, for field work tradition which provides us the emic, i.e. insider micro-level situation and the qualitative research methods which provide us the answer to 'Why and not how many people respond to our questions?' That makes us strong to study the processes of change. Disciplines professing measurement want to quantify impact from the etic, that is, outsider perspective, but cannot analyze the processes. Ethnography has been our strength which came out with the classical dictum of 18 months of fieldwork and 18 years of writing. Another strength has been called 'going native' or looking through their specs, through their eyes; in short, understanding the people's perspectives, emic perspectives, to the issues under examination. Gandhi had gone 'native' in his dress and living style in a hut, to win the confidence of '*daridranarayana*' in his political, and socio-economic-health agenda of constructive programmes.

What is the health management scenario in the country and in the world? We are guided by WHO and pay lip sympathy to the International slogans like 'Health for All', 'Primary Health Care Approach' and 'Intersectoral Coordination' or 'Think Globally, Act Locally'. Unmindful of WHO's comprehensive definition of health and the definitions of health given by our sixth century B.C. ayurvedic pundits like Sushruta and Charaka, we are governed by the patient oriented, disease control programmes and all our medical education, medical institutions and the latest documents such as the Universal Health Coverage by the Planning Commission for the XII Five Year Plan, focus on medicalization of health. India may be the only country with two national policies about health, approved by Parliament in 2002; the National Health Policy and National ISMH Policy now referred to as AYUSH. At the political level, governments and political parties keep on giving election promises about universal health care delivery to the people, which is translated into budgets for providing more hospital beds, more medical colleges and more drugs. We do not find any discussion in the government documents or major committee reports about how people have been taking care of their health through centuries. Anthropologists on the other hand, give ethnographic accounts of the health beliefs and practices of the people and about the local traditional professionals. Anthropologists do not discuss the statistics of infant or maternal mortality or morbidities due to Malaria, Tuberculosis, Leprosy and now HIV and AIDS. The national surveys reflected in Census, NFHS, NSS etc., compute the figures for the administrative and political categories such as ST, SC, OBC and others, which are actually not the research categories. If we go by these categories, even undernourished tribals would have sizeable prevalence of life style disorders like diabetes and cardio-vascular problems among S.Ts. since several S.Ts. are pseudo-tribals. We have to keep on advising our ICMR institutes across the country not to use these reservation categories for research, but use the ethnic identities of the people.

As a result of influence of Mahatma Gandhi and Jawaharlal Nehru, in dialogue with Verrier Elwin, it has been recognized that the tribal communities need special attention with reference to their development issues. Tribal development funds flow from tribal sub-plan. However, there are no special policies about tribal health. In fact, there is as yet no national tribal policy approved by the parliament although draft policy documents have been made. Very few anthropologists are consulted with reference to issues on tribal welfare or tribal development or tribal health, as all these fall in the domain of civil services. There have been committees headed by Verrier Elwin and S.C. Dube, L.P. Vidyarthi has been a member of such committees. B.K. Roy Burman also participated in such committees. His association with the census produced village monographs, but hardly anything worthwhile about health has been reported. Rarely the recommendations of these committees have been translated into programmes except Dhebar Commission report drafted by Verrier Elwin. Anthropologists continue to be associated with the committees which adjudicate on the issues about the pseudo-tribals claiming scheduled tribe status.

I would like to mention a report by a British Civil Servant, Symington, submitted in 1938 about the backward areas which after 60 years was formed into a tribal district of Nandurbar in Maharashtra with 75 per cent tribal rural population. According to government human development indicators, the district ranks lowest amongst 35 districts in 2002 and continues so in 2012. Is this a coincidence that a tribal district should continue to rank lowest according to HDI? Symington observed in 1938, "It has hitherto been usually assumed that whatever measures were suitable for the country at large were suitable also for the tribal areas.... the common law of the land is in many respects highly unsuitable for the tribal areas and produces serious oppression and exploitation."

Anthropologists have to set their research agenda on health issues in the context of the functioning of tribal development programmes. I once asked a Minister as to what were the development schemes in his department, as I could see there were only survival schemes. What are our research questions about high infant mortality and undernutrition? If anthropologists do not proactively study these issues and make recommendations, who else will do it?

The deprivation of tribal communities has increased due to the policy of treating forest as a source of revenue to the government which has made the minor forest produce inaccessible to the tribals. Ethnic disparities within the tribal communities are linked with the ownership of land as is also the case with caste disparities and disparities within scheduled castes. Seasonal migration of landless and marginal farmer tribal groups for survival and for earning extra cash amongst those who have production to last for the whole year for consumption, are also determinants of health. PDS is not available to the migrant families. Additions of the family members by marriage or by birth is denied to the *Antyodaya* card holders asking them to wait till the next decennial census.

In spite of the 73rd Amendment giving powers to *gram sabhas* in scheduled area, general practice of group *gram panchayats* in tribal areas make the *gram panchayats* and *gram sabhas* non-functional. The recommendations of S.C. Dube Committee of 1972 recommending hamlet as the unit of action has been upheld by the PESA Act of Central Government, but ignored by several State Government Acts, including Maharashtra. Our research agenda, therefore, about health does not limit us only to the health issues, but should extend to issues of general administration of the tribal sub-plan which also includes governance about health. Actually, the administration of tribal sub-plan through the tribal development department makes a mockery of Nehru's *Panchsheel* about tribal development, since the department only functions as a post office to disburse the budgets to the sector departments or line departments without having any authority to monitor the functioning of the respective departments about tribal development, in this case the health department. The media debate as to who is responsible for undernutrition of tribal children, the tribal development or health department and to which Ministers should be made to resign is a ludicrous matter.

We tried practicing anthropology in a project on malnutrition of tribal children in tribal population dominated taluks and blocks all over Maharashtra in all tribal ethnic groups. The interventions included feeding the children in the age group of 6 months to 3 years with local culture specific protein rich precooked *Sattu* (combination of roasted Wheat and Bengal gram). The lactating women were fed with *Sattu* fortified with Ayurvedic tonics which are known as Lactogens. The pregnant women were fed with once square meal a day to increase the birth weight of the babies. In tune with the anthropological concept of integration of culture, interventions were also made in other aspects of culture such as education, leadership, cultural activities and gender specific activities. The measurable results in terms of increase of weight, reduction of malnutrition grades and increase in birth weights have been documented. The project was conceptualized as 'Comprehensive and Sustainable Human Development of the Tribal People of Maharashtra'. All the interventions were carried out by about 500 male and female tribal volunteers from 250 villages covering a population of 1,50,000. The capacity building of these volunteers is expected to sustain the activities after the expiry of the project. The confidence building activities included the delivery of Allopathic and Ayurvedic drugs at the hamlet level free of charge. Recently, these 500 volunteers were brought together on 22 November, 2012 at Nasik for them to express their qualitative quotes about impact, on the *dias* addressing to the Minister, Tribal Commissioner and Media. The tribal men and women who had not travelled beyond 20 km in their lifetime travelled in chartered buses, distances ranging from 200 km to 800 km. Never before these ethnic group had heard of each other or had met although fired with the same mission in the programme. The lasting impact on their personalities and vision could be understood by anthropologists.

As mentioned earlier there are two national health policies. The ISMH Policy has led to the establishment of a separate department of AYUSH at the Centre and the renaming of the Departments of Ayurved into Departments of AYUSH in the States. In some states like Himachal and Chhattisgarh, there are parallel systems of AYUSH and Health Services. That means, there are distinct Ayurvedic Health Centres (AHCs) under District Ayurved Officer apart from the Primary Health Centres and the Sub-centres under District Health Officer. All of them have to participate in the administration of National Health and Disease Control Programmes. But, AHCs do not have any extension activities in the community except the OPD. In states like Maharashtra, Ayurvedic graduates are employed in the Primary Health Centres (PHCs) under the district level control of DHO unlike the DAO in States with AHC. That means, in States like Maharashtra, Ayurvedic Physicians in the PHC Systems are dispensing Allopathic medicine. There is a total gap between the supply of Ayurvedic medicine in the PHC and the positioning of the Ayurvedic doctors. We have done a situation analysis in three districts about these gaps. In Himachal Pradesh, AHCs are more than double the PHCs. The number of patients in the OPD is not sizeable as to warrant the high salaries of the doctors at the AHC according to health bureaucrats. I had pointed out to the Chief Minister of Himachal Pradesh, as to why the performance of AHC should be linked with a number of patients at the OPD? If OPD was the only function of the doctors, whose responsibility was it to look after the pregnant women and the children in the villages? In Chhattisgarh, the Department of AYUSH has mooted the concept of Ayurved Gram, whereby the AHC doctors have to initiate the extension activities in the village with community participation. In a study of four States—Himachal Pradesh, Chhattisgarh, Madhya Pradesh and Maharashtra, we were asked to find out the grassroots level situation in the States about utilization of AYUSH. We selected a proper research model to cover the district from village to block level and using the anthropological model of covering the universe of the village. We found out that the women in the house had knowledge of several herbs and were using their preparations for common ailments. The local herbalist knew much more in some cases about 300 herbs which they were administering to the people as a first line of treatment. These documentation of the people's sector earned us Centre of Excellence: AYUSH in Public Health. The Secretary of AYUSH realized that we as students of Anthropology had better knowledge of public and their perceptions and practices and we could comprehend health in its totality. Actually, public health is a social science. Once I asked the President of All India Public Health Association, as to where was public in Public Health and where was health apart from disease? The very fact that there are plural systems of medicine catering to the health and treatment requirements of people clearly indicates that medicine is not a natural science. Having realized that all systems of medicine have their respective strengths, NRHM advocated and budgeted for collocation of health institutions of plural systems in one institution. However, this has met with failure except probably with some success at the CGHS. In fact, the collocation of the systems within AYUSH also does not work. This may not be possible unless the knowledge of plural systems is woven into the medical education of all systems.

The current intervention in the AYUSH Project in the three States of Himachal Pradesh, Chhattisgarh and Maharashtra includes training of AYUSH doctors in Epidemiology and Research Methods in order to equip them to undertake public health activities with scientific documentation. If the patient based approach and activities have to be oriented to the people based approach and activities, it is necessary to understand as to whether the health issue or a disease condition is a public health problem in their block or not. The national health policy needs to address the concerns of the people and to prioritize the preventive and promotive care of the majority of population and some specific groups like children, adolescents, women including mothers and people in geriatric age group. No disease has ever been and can be controlled by chemotherapy.

The disease control programmes have to address the concerns of people and not the issues of prevalence, with the hypothesis that it would automatically bring down the incidence. In leprosy for example, people's concern is threat of social death, as a result of a person being labelled having leprosy. The English word 'leprosy' or the Government term '*kushtha*' in India and in Indonesia, connote different meanings. In the Ayurvedic text, *kushtha* denotes several skin conditions, leprosy being one of them. In biomedical terms, the issue of concern in leprosy for the people is nerve damage which causes deformity, while the leprosy control programmes concentrate on chemotherapy to kill the bacilli to bring down the prevalence. I had asked Dr. R.V. Wardekar, the Founder Director of Gandhi Memorial Leprosy Foundation (GMLF) and an eminent Pathologist in 1965, as to what was the problem of leprosy; he immediately said, "Case finding and case holding", which are not medical terms. From the anthropological point of view, I had recommended to WHO in 1981 that the medical research in leprosy control should concentrate on nerve damage. This led to changing the objectives of leprosy control at the WHO, to include 'preventing deformities' as the third objective in addition to the objectives of diagnosis and treatment. Similarly, the definition of the case of leprosy was revised to include the leprosy afflicted who needed social rehabilitation. What I am proposing is that the anthropological understanding of the perceptions and concerns of the people are needed to formulate the policies about the disease control and such issues as population control.

Proverbs and the terms used by people which are a subject matter of linguistic anthropology provide us with hard core of cultural values about an issue. We made a historical review of words used for what we now call commercial sex workers, sex workers or in the feminist expression, only workers who are forced to sell their flesh as commodity. The words provide us with the cultural expressions, the abuses which stigmatizes the woman, who is a victim of poverty or lust.

Recently, rape of a young woman has been denigrated as national shame. What of rape of a living woman, even a foetus is not safe in her mother's womb. Sonography is directly related to female foeticide. How come number of Sonography machines have a direct statistical correlation with female foeticide? Sugarcane rich district of Kolhapur in Maharashtra has shown this due to Collector's crusade about female foeticide. On behalf of UNFPA, we had investigated the matter couple of years ago.

I had once asked the villagers in a Gwalior village on which I have an anthropological village monograph, as to from where they got the brides while they were involved in female infanticide, they showed me two women whom they had purchased for ₹ 300 each while a journalist had 'purchased' Kamala for ₹ 1500 at Dholpur, in the Chambal region to create public debate in Parliament.

Why a tribal woman is never raped or molested by a tribal man? Why there is no female foeticide among tribal community and there is bride price instead of dowry? These are research questions.

Similarly, the expression HIV/AIDS used in scientific writing gives a message to people that HIV and AIDS are synonyms while our counsellors tell HIV + persons that AIDS could be kept at bay for 20 years by following healthy life style. Vasectomy was projected as castration by the opposition leaders to defeat Congress and Indira Gandhi in election. These emic perspectives are in the domain of anthropological research.

Farmer's suicide requires anthropological qualitative studies. The chronically poor do not commit suicide. But entrepreneurs who are probably attracted and trapped by commercial advertisers of pesticides, fertilizers and seeds promising doubling or trebling production take loans to become transient poor, have a risk of committing suicide when crops fail and the bank goons start troubling for repayment.

The terms health care delivery, provider-beneficiary, and the patient or the respondent to the interview as subject, and the term like compliance clearly brings out the techno-centric top-down approach about health. Animal experimentation tried on human subjects particularly the patients in hospital set-up through clinical trials, when administered as a programme bring out the problems of delivery. The research shots fired by the programme, lead to operational research, in which many of us are engaged. Operational research is aimed at improving the services and supplies in the given drug oriented health care delivery systems from the providers management perspective. It is very rarely that the patients and their families are asked about the difficulties in accessing the services. The solutions are usually discovered in terms of monetary incentives to the patients and service providers. I cannot anticipate what kind of *Bhasmasur* is being created with cash transfer which would be made applicable to health care. All these years, the culprits for diseases were identified as bacilli and viruses, the agents in the epidemiological triad. Now, the therapy has been found for several chronic ailments, which does not claim with confidence to cure the disease, but the patients are released from the treatment as per programme registers.

The recent culprit for the deficiencies in programme outcomes is branded as 'social stigma'. That means that the people or the beneficiaries and the society at large are at fault for not accessing the drug therapy which as scientific marvels would cure the ailments. The therapy for social stigma has been Health Education; later termed as Information Education Communication (IEC) and now christened as Behavioural Change Communication (BCC). It, therefore, surmises that the victim of the techno-centric system, that is, the patient and his family are to be educated to comply with the system. Several research papers on compliance in leprosy have been published. George Foster in his Malinowski's Oration in 1982, has discussed these issues:

> "A generation ago physicians and anthropologists alike defined the problem of providing better health care for traditional peoples as how to persuade them to accept scientific medicine. As anthropologists, our fundamental research task was to learn those things about the health beliefs and practices of these peoples that would enable health care providers to convince them of superiority of modern medicine over their traditional therapies. Our practical goal was to further effective cross-cultural communication, which, we assumed, would lead to scientifically acceptable health beliefs and behaviour."
>
> "The striking thing about these questions is that almost all assume that effective health care can be achieved only when members of traditional communities change their health behaviour. Rarely if ever is the question asked, 'How can anthropologists help to change bureaucratic behaviour that inhibits the design and operation of the best possible health care systems'?"

I have myself dealt on this issue in my Editorial "The Social Responsibility of Social Scientists" in *Social Science and Medicine* (1994):

> "Social scientists were drafted in an attempt to convince the illiterate about the scientific efficacy of modern health

> concepts. As with the training of paramedics, health education was conceived that would miraculously change people's behaviour in favour of modern medicine. The help of social scientists was therefore sought to increase compliance to technological interventions in modern medicine."

The demand for social science interventions have come from the field of Disease Control Programmes, thus making Social Scientists react to the research questions of health administration.

Now, that a separate Department of AYUSH has been created at the Government of India level with equivalent institutional infrastructure on lines of Indian Council of Medical Research and national institutes for the respective AYUSH systems, there is indeed a necessity for operational research about the role of AYUSH in public health. As yet, there are no health education cells or significant health education material on AYUSH for the lay people. There are no paramedics in the AYUSH systems. However, since AYUSH practices are followed in the homes as traditional home remedies and there are *Dais* and traditional local herbalists with indigenous knowledge, particularly in the tribal areas, it is necessary to document the ground level practices through Ethnography. However, this focused Ethnography has to be used for establishing a link with the professionally trained AYUSH physicians using the concept of little tradition, great tradition interaction of Robert Redfield. We have documented a list of about 350 herbs known to the local herbalists. We have experimented to train these herbalists to make the Ayurvedic drugs on lines of what is commercially available in the market. We are now trying to orient them to the *Panchamahabhuta* and *Tridosha* theory available in Ayurvedic texts. The ethnographic data can be used for preparing health education material for the masses and training material for the paramedics. An ANM in Himachal Pradesh, said, "My kitchen is my dispensary. If it does not work, I take my medicine provided by the Government." However, as we are trying to use the numbers of AYUSH trained personnel for carrying out national health programmes based on western models, we are also being innovative in using the trust that lay people have in traditional healers to push forward drug therapies through them. Health Minister of Himachal, himself an Ayurvedic physician asked us as to how to mainstream the home remedies in the Government system. We have found through ethnographic interviews that all lady doctors of all systems of medicine follow traditional practices based on Ayurvedic, Unani or Siddha system when they become mothers themselves. But our Ayurvedic hospitals do not have maternity wards. Have we studied these phenomena as students of anthropology? Why not?

Medical Anthropology can develop as a professional discipline. The sub-disciplines like Ethno-botany and Ethno-physiology have developed with which we have closer academic links. Our task has become easier as a result of advocacy about bio-diversity and preservation of environment. Our friends in modern medicine are the preventive and social medicine and psychiatry departments. We have to understand the epidemiology and develop social epidemiology further. Now, the social determinants of health are being widely discussed, although the emphasis is only on equity. The UGC model curriculum of Anthropology provides for a post-graduate diploma on medical anthropology. The MPH syllabus of National Institute of Epidemiology, Chennai based ICMR apex institute of Epidemiology has as many credits for social sciences as for epidemiology.

In the context of holistic nature of anthropology, I am proposing the research agenda, which would cover the issues having direct and indirect bearing on health. Actually, the slogan "Health for All by the Year 2000" which had advocated primary health care approach through inter-sectoral coordination has been the anthropological approach. Another slogan "Think Globally and Act Locally" has been the holistic approach of bringing together the emic and etic perspectives in an integrated fashion. Although, academic anthropologists need not become activists themselves or may not undertake interventions in the University Departments, they could become Friend, Philosopher and Guide to the social and health activists to help them do advocacy on the basis of our research data. We may not undertake intervention projects ourselves, but we can do that through our academic associations or other voluntary organizations and study the dynamics and processes of change. Networking of university academics with the voluntary sector or NGOs, is as much important as of Science with industry.

Let us dedicate ourselves to Article 21 of the Constitution of India about Right to live with human dignity which includes right to livelihood and right to health. In short, let us rededicate ourselves to the classical anthropological model of pro-people or people-centric perspectives.

It is high time anthropologists with their strength of fieldwork tradition take a proactive stand and frame people-centric research questions. Theory building in culture and social change is not possible without applied anthropology, as also advocated by Malinowski. The debate on value neutrality of anthropology is over, in the post-colonial era of participatory development, since, value neutrality tacitly supports establishment which could be anti-people. Anthropologists as citizens and also upholding the universal values enshrined in the UN Charter of Human Rights, which was drafted by an Anthropologist, expects us to work for human good with the use of indigenous knowledge and modern science.

We are aware about Gandhi's Talisman:

> "I will give you a talisman. Whenever you are in doubt, or when the self will become too much with you, try the following expedient: Recall the face of the poorest and most helpless man you may have seen and ask yourself—if the step you contemplate is going to be of any use to him. Will he be able to gain anything by it? Will it restore him to a control over his own life and destiny? Then you will find your doubts and yourself melting away." (*Gandhi*, 1969, Vol. VI, p. 535)

I would like to add to it. We should take up the research questions which would impact people-centric, pro-people policies for health and development. Our theory and research techniques of qualitative methods for collecting primary data are most suitable for analyzing the processes of change, fortified by the available quantitative secondary data. But let us shoot the research questions ourselves in a proactive mode, instead of following the shots fired by multinational pharmaceutical industry for curative programmes. Good Luck.

2
Hierophantic Crisis and Divination in a South Indian Fishing Village

Charles W. Nuckolls

The starting point for this discussion is the phenomenon Eliade called "hierophanies," physical manifestations of the sacred. Hierophanies are always paradoxical, according to Eliade, because the act of giving religious value to a material thing makes the transcendent and eternal dependent on the immanent and historically particular.[1] A hierophany represents a "paradoxical coming-together of the sacred and profane, being and non-being absolute and relative, the eternal and the becoming."[2] The best example of hierophantic paradox, Eliade claims, is the Incarnation: a being both timeless and perfectly free (God) is manifested in the physical reality of transitory existence. While hierophanies may be characteristic of all religious experience, Elide assumes a definite position on their evolution, since all represent 'prefigurations' of the one complete Incarnation (Christ). It is not necessary, however, to agree with Eliade's premise (that hierophanies can be ranked developmentally) or his conclusion (that hierophanies, other than the Christian, represent 'abortive' attempts to reveal the mystery of the coming together of God and man). Instead, we can start from Eliade's theoretically more tractable observation that hierophanies are historically contingent and that they contain, or emerge from values and attitudes that are strongly contradictory to each other.

Let us, following Eliade, define 'hierophany' as a culturally postulated physical manifestation of the sacred, where 'sacred' is understood as that category of objects construed in the mind of the believer as both real and other with respect to the profane/material world.[3] A 'hierophantic crisis'—not Eliade's term, but mine—refers to the process of recognition: a thing is a hierophany when believers recognize in the object or person the presence of contradictory alternatives and their resolution in material form. Recognition need not be conscious; in fact, in most cases, it probably isn't, and the object only functions the way it does because of its capacity to act as a projection. For this to be true, however, the contradictory elements must possess deep emotional salience, and the opposition between them must be problematic, even unresolvable. The hierophany operates something in the manner of a Hegelian *Aufhebung*, temporarily reconciling the opposition while keeping intact the internal contradiction.

Consider the Incarnation of Christ. From the moment of his birth Christ represents the concatenation of opposites: God and man, the timeless and the temporal, the spiritual and the material. The purpose is not to reveal simply that opposites can combine, but to manifest the unique power of this combination to perform the miracle of forgiveness, or in Christian terms, infinite atonement—something we are told could be not done in any other way. If, however, divine forgiveness is necessary in order for men to be saved, why couldn't God simply decree it by fiat? He is all-powerful, so presumably the capacity to forgive is one of the abilities he possesses. And God uses divine fiat in other contexts, most notably in the early chapters of Genesis, where he creates the world simply by decreeing that it exists. Why, then, must God, at least in the traditional Nicene view, incarnate himself in order to perform an act that could be achieved by divine fiat?

Views on this subject abound, and the purpose here is not to recount them. But one deserves mention. It is the view that God cannot forgive unless he understands the uniquely human travails of mortal life. The Incarnation enables God to provide understanding and forgiveness. There is no way to comprehend this transformation except by assuming that God is not (or does not remain) the omniscient being of the first several chapters of Genesis. Change is possible only for someone who can learn, and who is also not the same (on some scale) at the beginning as he is at the end. Christ makes possible the transformation of forgiveness into a knowing act of sympathetic understanding—a process whereby the creator puts himself in the role of the sinner and identifies with everything that has precipitated the act of transgression.

Even though, as I will argue, forgiveness is absent from the South Indian culture that is the focus of this study, there is still the postulation of hierophany, and of the juxtaposition of opposites that makes the manifestation of the divine relevant to the process of social change. Eliade maintained that any hierophany in a generic sense always reveals itself as paradoxical, because the manifestation of the sacred in normal reality must contradict its status as sacred. In other words, the manifestation of a snake mound remains itself (a mound of dirt) at the same time it participates in the realm of the ganz andere, the wholly 'other.' This makes the hierophany paradoxical, enhancing its status as something totally different. Eliade's view was shaped by his Christianity; it should not surprise us, therefore, that he considered Christ the supreme hierophany—a being simultaneously in the world, but not of it. Here, we have dispensed with the specific logic of this analysis, but preserved Eliade's central insight: the manifestation of the sacred is often correlated with irresolvable oppositions of some kind.

But first, some ethnographic details: The subject of this study is a Telugu-speaking fishing caste called Jalari, a community resident on the south-eastern coast of India in Andhra Pradesh state. Jalaripet, the village where this fieldwork was conducted, is a large coastal hamlet at the northern edge of the Visakhapatnam municipal area. The urban populations of this area is around 3 million. Until about 1980, the village was detached and somewhat isolated from the rest of the city. That has changed in the years since, and Jalaripet is now surrounded on three sides by the rapidly expanding boundaries of urban metropolis—a conurbation that is said (albeit mostly by Visakhapatnam residents themselves) to be the most rapidly growing port city in Asia. Jalaripet's population is around 7,000, and most of its people still support themselves by fishing in the Bay of Bengal. This, too, is changing, as mechanized fishing fleets from elsewhere in India, and even abroad, competes for diminishing fish stocks in coastal waters. As a result, increasing numbers of Jalaris (both men and women) have moved into the city's casual labour market, and work in construction, hauling, and domestic service.

Fig. 2.1: Jalaripet (at centre)—A fishing village near Visakhapatnam, Andhra Pradesh, India

Here, I am concerned with the manifestation of 'snake mounds' in various village domestic spaces over the last few years. The snake mound (*pamu putta*) is understood to represent the appearance of a goddess—usually the household goddess of a family. To anyone else, it looks like the mound of dirt created by termites when they swarm, and one does not usually see a snake anywhere in the vicinity. To the Jalaris, however, the 'snake mound' signifies that a goddess is angry and needs attention. The family whose house contains the mound must employ the services a diviner to find out how they have transgressed, and what must be done to set the matter right.

Can we compare Christian and Jalari hierophanies? What the two have in common is the fact that they temporally unite oppositions—in the case of Christ, between God and man, and in the case of the snake mound, between two kinship ideals (unity *vs.* separation). The first produces forgiveness that implicates the agent of forgiveness in the misdeed he did not commit, but is willing to understand. In effect, he becomes the sinner, and takes upon himself the full effects of transgression. Only a perfect being, we are told, can perform an act of such all-encompassing sympathetic transference. The snake mound does not involve transference of responsibility, understanding, or act of charity. It is about restoring balance, not between agents in a world of intentionality, but between different (and opposed) social imperatives concerning the relationship between brothers. Does this implicate forgiveness? It could be said that the hierophany of the snake mound results in an act of forgiveness, since the purpose of the manifestation is to call people to account for misdeeds they have committed. The goddess forgives the transgression once restitution is made. Restitution takes the form an offering to the goddess and the promise to undo the misdeed that led to her manifestation in the snake mound. 'Forgiveness,' however, might be the wrong word, since restitutive justice implies a balanced exchange whereby the agent of transgression directly compensates for his action. Forgiveness, however, usually means something more, at least in the Christian context: a transcendence of balance, whereby the forgiver voluntarily foregoes balanced exchange and instead 'makes up' the difference out of his own charity. Christ's forgiveness is not measured by how much men repent because total repentance is never enough, nor is it even possible. Rather, the atonement of Christ is said to be all sufficing because it is without limit, unbound by situational constraints or calculations of direct loss and recompense. The Jalari goddesses, on the other hand, operate more on a strict cost-accounting basis, and do not generally exemplify the quality of charitable forgiveness.

Jalaris employ divination (e.g., spirit possession) to determine the causes of events, from illness to the failure to catch fish, but also to identify the reason a goddess would manifest her power in the sudden eruption of a snake mound.[4] All divinations, whatever their immediate concern, reduce to some kind of social disruption. That is, the goddess is angry because of a dispute within the family that worships her, and she afflicts family members in order to call attention to the dispute and coerce them into solving it. The disruption is usually an argument that divides brothers against each other, and such a dispute can (and sometimes does) lead to their division and separation into separate families. Such a division is important because Jalari culture is patrilineal and extended, meaning descent is in the male line and the fundamental unit is the extended family consists of brothers, their wives, and children. Patrilineal solidarity is an anthropological term for the unity of a social group connected by bonds of descent in the male line. A group of brothers, for example, possesses patrilineal solidarity for as long as it remains united as a coparcenary (i.e. joint property-owning) and residential unit. While such groups can stick together for some time—two or three generations, if they are lucky—they invariably break down and divide, creating new groups that begin the process all over again. The pattern is not unique to patrilineal societies in India. However, Jalari men feel decidedly ambivalent about the structural inevitability of patrilineal fission. They know it will happen. But they wish it would not. They know it will happen because there is no such thing as a joint patrilineal household that consists of lineages united at any level of above the third ascending generation—meaning that by the time there are grandchildren a group descended from brothers will on the verge of separating. Why? Various reasons are cited, but usually it comes down to control over resources; descendants no longer want to submit to the authority of the senior-most male member. When they divide, they "fly away, as birds to separate branches," in the words of villagers—a fact that always carries more than just a note a regret and sadness. Their only solace is that in talking about it they usually blame their wives, as if to suggest that only the nagging and scolding (*tittadam*) of women led them to split up.

Hierophanies do not appear randomly. The Jalaris see them manifestations of the family goddess (*ammavaru*), but recognition is correlated with kinship tension. They signal that family affairs are seriously disturbed, and given the dynamics of the kinship system, their cause is likely in the fear of an approaching fission. The hierophany of the snake mound represents the collision of opposites—that is, the collision of opposed, but equally necessary kinship ideals. The first is the desire among brothers to remain together, and the second to divide and separate: all patrilineal organized groups experience both, but at certain times in their development the pressure to divide is especially acute. The first is when brothers marry, and the second when their own children are of marriageable age. Both moments intensify, in different ways, the brothers desire to separate and create their own independent families. The hierophany of the snake mound *at just these moments* signifies both the desire to remain joint and the fact that threats to unity are inevitable and intensifying. The meat of the issue is the fact that a crisis in the kinship dynamics of fraternal solidarity is also sometimes a hierophantic crisis—a moment when the opposition between continuity and schism 'erupts' in the sudden manifestation of the sacred.

A Case Study, or, How the Anthropologist Lead to the Eruption of a Snake Mound

The rest of this chapter is a case study in hierophany and fraternal crisis, and interesting because it involved the anthropologist. In 1980, I was adopted as a member of the Teddi patrilineal group, and as younger brother to Teddi Pentayya, a fisherman then about 45 years old. The events described below took place in the 1990s, but with effects that even today define the relationship between me and Pentayya.

When I arrived in the village in 1993, Pentayya said that the long-delayed goddess festival must be held. Two days later, an event confirmed this. A snake mound—*pamu putta*—suddenly appeared in the corner of the thatched hut next to Pentayya's main house. Pentayya said the Teddi clan household goddess, Ellamma, had noticed my arrival. The *pamu putta* meant that a festival in her honour, and on behalf of the ancestors, would have to take place. Pentayya's youngest daughter, Sankaramma, was the first to see the mound. She recounted the experience to my colleague, Krishnayya, as follows:

> Sankaramma: On the fifth night after our uncle's visit a snake mound rose up in our thatched hut.
> Krishnayya: Who is your uncle and where did he come from?
> Sankaramma: He came from America. He is Charles and he is our uncle. Our father's sister stays in the thatched hut.
> Krishnayya: What kind of stuff is kept there?
> Sankaramma: Cooking utensils and a wooden box used for selling fish.
> Krishnayya: When did you see the snake mound?

> Sankaramma: On Saturday night, Uncle Charles visited us. On Sunday morning I went into the house to get some stuff. While I was about to take them, I saw that huge snake mound behind the box.
> Krishnayya: It is a snake mound?
> Sankaramma: Yes. The snake mound is huge. I took the vessels, but the box would not move. Some tried to move the box, but it wouldn't budge.

The fact that the *pamu putta* appeared where it did, in a thatch hut adjacent to Pentayya's new concrete house, is significant. Like many, the new house was constructed with government loan money, shortly after a fire in 1984 destroyed most of the traditional palmyra leaf huts. Unlike the old round huts, the new house is square. Row after row of them have been built in a grid-like pattern, conforming to the Government's (and the Jalaris' own) view that modern urban dwellings should be arranged that way. Pentayya lives in his new house with his wife and three of his four children. There is only one room, with a small alcove to one side. This is the *ammavari gadi,* the "goddess room". It contains the *saduru,* a low platform (usually made of dirt, but now built of concrete) where lamps burn in homage to the goddess. In fact, the *sadaru* should be made of dirt scooped out directly from Ellamma's main snake mound/temple at the edge of the village. Pentayya's house is a *peddillu,* a "big house," which means that he is obligated to maintain a goddess shrine in his house. A big house with its consecrated *sadaru* is the ritual centre of a lineage group and the focus of group solidarity, but in Pentayya's case, the lineage consists only of him, his immediate family, and me.

Just outside the new concrete house is a low hut, just big enough for one or two people. It is a simple affair, barely sufficient to keep the sun and rain out. Pentayya's old mother and his younger sister sleep there at night. The younger sister, Goramma, is a leper, and never married. She sells fish during the day, but otherwise rarely appears in public. Although I know the family well, it was years after my first arrival that I first actually met Goramma. Pentayya and the others steered me away from her, mostly out of embarrassment, but also out of fear, since leprosy is a sign of spiritual displeasure and could signal worse disasters to follow. The fact that the goddess chose this hut, with its obvious defilement, as the place to manifest her power is odd, especially since, the big house next door already had a shrine to her.

On the day I first saw the snake mound, Goramma was in the hut, sleeping on a rope bed not far from the miraculous visitation. I asked her what she thought about it. She said that she had dreamed about the goddess just before the appearance of the mound, and that the mound signified that the goddess wanted something.

That was the last time I saw Goramma alive.

Pentayya's wife, Desamma, and I talked about the appearance of the snake mound. She said that she had also been surprised. After all, didn't they already have a special room prepared for the goddess in the new concrete house? It was a fine room, too. The walls were painted a shocking blue colour, and above the *sadaru,* there was a brilliant yellow and red paining of a cobra with its head raised. Neighbours often came over to look it at. But the goddess, in whose honour all of this had been done, did not like it. According to Desamma, there was a precedent for such an occurrence, and she described it in our conversation one day in her house.

> Charles: Did something like this ever happen before in a *peddillu?*
> Desamma: Yes, to lots of people.
> Charles: You mean a snake mound coming up like this?
> Desamma: Yes, it has happened a couple of time recently—in Kancumuttu Maratu's house and in ours.
> Charles: How long has there been one in Maratu's house?
> Desamma: From ancestral times.
> Charles: What's the story?
> Desamma: The whole village burned down in the fire. Maratu's house also burned. Then their household goddess thought, "Why should this be problem for me?" and she rose up in a snake mound.
> Charles: So, there was a snake mound even before the fire?
> Desamma: Yes. It has been there in their house from ancestral times. The old snake mound got burned in the fire. Later, the Government people bull-dozed the whole place. But the

mound popped up again in a week on the same site. We recognized the truth (*satyamu*) of the goddess then. The family left it alone. Afterwards Maratu's wife thought that the government will sanction money for the house construction. "Why should I leave the snake mound?" she asked herself. She decided to remove the snake mound and level it. But the goddess appeared to her in the night and warned her: "You, woman, how dare you remove snake mound! Have your eyes become white with arrogance? Watch out! See what I am going to do by morning." When she woke up and the dream, her second son had spots on his body. Like the patches of leprosy. She then went to a diviner to find out what was going on.

Charles: "To whom did she go?"

Desamma: "She went to a *pati* ('possession-medium'). The goddess told her, "I am the goddess of a thousand eyes. What have done to my snake mound? You dug it up. You are greedy for the government buildings. You don't want me even to have a spot in shade. You're so greedy. I am the goddess of a thousand eyes, so how proud (*ahankaram*) do you think I am." Then this woman pleaded with the goddess: "I realize my fault. I didn't think of the implications. Please forgive me and heal my son." Then the goddess cooled down and healed her son.

Charles: "What did they do then?"

Desamma: "The snake mound came up again. The woman made a *sadaru* on the concrete floor of her new house, but the goddess didn't like it. So, she went back to the spot where her old house used to be and set-up a shrine there. That's where the new snake mound appeared."

Charles: Now, you have a snake mound in the thatched hut adjacent to your new concrete house. What will you do now with the hut, since before you said you would tear it down?

Desamma: "We have to cover it with palm leaves."

Charles: "Is the hut is enough or do you have to construct a concrete building in the same place?"

Desamma: "No. The goddess won't like a concrete house. This is a concrete house, but she is saying that she will not

> stay here. She says that she wants to reside in the place of the ancestors. She needs the place improved, that's all, and made nice.
> Pentayya: "It is true but we must have money."
> Charles: "But if you keep the thatched hut, the goddess may get wet when it rains.
> Desamma: "It will not leak, not even a drop. That goddess will not get wet. There was a heavy rain yesterday and it didn't leak."
> Charles: "So will you make a *sadaru* in the old hut?"
> Desamma: "We've got to fix it up. The goddess will not feel good if we do not fix it."

I have quoted this conversation at length to show how Desamma uses precedent and case history to construct an expanation. Precedent is never obvious, since, it depends on recognizing commonalities across occurrences. To be sure, Desamma and the woman whose case she relates are both Jalaris. But they come from different surname groups (Desamma is a Teddi, while the other woman is Kantamutti), and they worship different Goddesses. One could just as easily point to these differences as to the similarity of their experience when the snake mound appeared. The point is that something had to happen, in order to make the commonality more relevant than the difference, and this was the fire. When the fire destroyed the village in 1984, it ushered in a new era with many surprising new features: one of these was a strong sense of common experience.

The experience was not simply the result of having faced disaster together. The fire completely erased the physical landmarks people used to measure and mark the limits of their cultural universe. For Jalaripet, despite its proximity to an urban metropolis (Visakhapatnam), was a remarkably self-contained unit before the fire. People would not think of leaving it for long, and when they did, they always tried to get back before nightfall. Space in the village was understood in terms of surname groups and their residential patterns, and these patterns had not changed much in the whole of the collective memory of the village. This was especially true with reference to the great *peddillus,* where clan goddesses were worshipped.

At the same time the fire destroyed all fixed reference points, it introduced something altogether new: the concept of the village as a political abstraction, which could be shaped and moulded by decision-making. There began to be a feeling that the village was not entirely cosmogenic entity, the creation of heroic beings who lived long ago—the traditional account—but an accident of time and circumstance. That meant it could be changed. Political and economic considerations could become as important to its design as the location of sacred sites—even more so, since the rebuilding process would be financed by outside agencies (Government agencies and banks), and they respected these considerations. For the Jalaris who wanted to participate in the urban system of power relations—and they were becoming an increasingly powerful segment—the fire was a perfect opportunity to effect the triumph of the modern. Within days, in fact, government officials descended on the village and began the process of assigning building plots based on individually sanctioned land titles—something unkown before, in this culture of clan-based ownership. Could a *peddillu* be located anywhere? Would it now be possible to sell one? Who would make these decisions?

When I speak, then, of shared experience in the aftermath of the fire, I refer to the collective sense of anxiety these questions provoked. No one knew the answers. In a place where, quite literally, all knowledge really is local, thinking about "the village" as such required a leap into a new cognitive environment. People felt the effort of making this leap, but they did not express it openly or directly. How could they? Moreover, there is a long tradition in Jalari culture of converting social unease into religious discourse, where it becomes the subject of divinatory explanation. That is what happened here. The eruption of the snake mounds, and the divination required to explain them, became a means to address a growing sense of anxiety over the issue of the village's rapid change.

To return to my brother Pentayya's snake mound: Pentayya and his family knew that something strange was happening, but they needed confirmation, and that is why they consulted Nukali, the village shaman, and went to the *pati* diviner. I was not present for the divination, but Nukali summarized the results:

A snake mound never came up in Pentayya's house before. On Friday, having paid homage to the goddess as usual, he was just going along as usual. Then Charles showed up after a long time. He came to our village on Saturday. The moment he arrived in our village the snake mound erupted. Pentayya's daugther, Sankaramma, first saw the mound. She was affraid and told her father. Pentayya looked at the mound, and then at an old wooden box that was in the corner. The mound had come up around this box, partially enveloping it, and Pentayya examined it closely.

Whenever a mound appears, people examine it to see if the snake that lives within is visible. It almost never is, but that does not matter. Since, the mound would not have appeared unless the goddesses were present, the real question is what to do next, and in a case like this there was only one answer. The goddess would have to be given a festival, and made to "come out" in the experience of *punakam*, or spirit possession.

After examining the mound, Nukali decided that the best thing to do was to consult a possession medium (*pati*). Manifestations of the sacred—whether as a snake mound, as here, or as illness or any misfortune—cannot be accepted without confirmation in a truth-testing forum. The medium—an old woman in her sixties—was known to be particularly adept, and worth the bus ride to visit her. Nukali, Pentayya, and Desamma (Pentayya's wife) made the trip, and confirmed that in fact the mound was a manifestation of the goddess Ellamma. Then they prayed to Ellamma and promised her that on the following Tuesday, her sacred day, they would pay homage to her. Still, this was not all they were seeking. It was important to link me to the manifestation, and confirm that without my participation in a grand festival the goddess would never be satisfied. So, they went to another *pati* in the fishing village of Bhimulipatnam.

Here is Nukali's account: "On Monday we went to Uppada, and then we went to Bhimuli. There we did a *pati*. We asked, "Mother, why did this snake mound come up?" She said, "Because several years ago the Englishman (Charles) promised to lift the *jangidi*. Then he left. Now, he has come back. Within three minutes of his arrival I took the form of a snake mound, anticipating that he would light the *jyoti*, lift the *jangidi*, and put a dot (*bottu*) on his forehead." I told the goddess that we celebrate her festival and do all she asked. "Please destroy your ant hill and leave," I said. The goddess replied, "No. I won't go. I am not ashamed of what I have done. Tell the Englishman

[Charles Nuckolls] to light the lamp for me. Then I will protect him and his country."

In his offer to the goddess Nukali refers to the main actions of the festival. The officiator must carry a basket, called a *jangidi,* on his head. The basket contains implements that represent the goddess. He must light a lamp (*jyoti*) and apply a dot of *kumkum* (vermillion) to his forehead. To confirm that the goddess meant what she said. Nukali returned to Pentayya's house and tried to lift the old wooden box around which the ant mound was growing. "Even ten people could not lift it up, so I prayed to her to let us lift the box, so that we could have faith in her. 'I am Ellamma,' the goddess said, and she allowed us to lift the box."

The spirits of the dead are also involved. In fact, the festival in honour of the goddess is simultaneously a funeral rite for Petnayya's long dead younger brother, Parasa. From what I can tell, Parasa died in the mid-1960s during the last smallpox epidemic. When family members die, they become associated with the family goddesses and eventually their identities become fused. The principal household goddess of Pentayya is the Teddi clan goddess, Ellamma, known elsewhere as Renuka and famous in mythology as the chaste wife who is beheaded by her rishi husband in a fit of jealous rage. The ghost of Parasa has not attacked or afflicted anyone with else—if he had, this would have been in keeping with Jalari understandings of spirits who have been denied their proper funerary rites. Even Ellamma, the goddess, has not hurt anyone. Instead, she caused the snake mound to come up, a particularly public way of making her wishes known to the Englishman. It is assumed she is acting not just on her own behalf, but as a representative of the dead Parasa. And, implicit in this is a threat: if the Englishman and Pentayya do not perform the required homages, the goddess and Parasa will attack them, either directly or—more likely—indirectly, by making their wives and children sick.

It is interesting that Pentayya and his family did not inform me immediately when the snake mound erupted in a dark corner of the thatched hut. When they did tell me, as in the conversation with Desamma reported earlier, no mention was made of my arrival or how it had triggered the eruption in the first place. Yet it was pretty obvious, from discussion of the festival that I was to be involved.

How, precisely, had the link been made? And how was I supposed to find out about it?

The reason this question interested me is that the Jalaris generally do not tell anyone to do anything. They do not expect the resolution of any social dispute to follow debate and discussion, or an act of forgiveness. Instead, the decision to act in a certain way follows conversion of a social issue into a discourse about the goddesses, with social action itself redefined as a religious rite. They need not "inform me". I would be brought to a realization of my responsibility by the manifestation of the divine in my life, possibly through miraculous visitations, but probably through misfortune in illness and suffering. Then I would seek confirmation in the *pati* and finally, I would do what was necessary—in this case, pay for and perform the festival in honour of the goddess and the ancestors. All important decisions are made this way, according to the Jalaris.

Consequently, the question was, how did Pentayya and Desamma themselves understand this sequence? I could not ask them myself. They had already described the eruption of the snake mound and the fact that is signalled the goddess's desire for a festival. The link between the two was me, of course, but this has to be demonstrated indirectly, in a spiritual idiom that is subject to verification in divination. One of my non-Jalari friends, Sugamma, visited Pentayya and Desamma one day and had this conversation:

> Sugamma: "It is now 14 days since the snake mound appeared. You are saying that it started as soon as your brother-in-law [Charles] came here. Then why did you not tell him?"
> Desamma: "He did not come for the last three days."
> Sugamma: "But it happened ten days before that! Why don't you tell him?"

This is exactly the sort of question that anyone not Jalari would ask. Why not be direct, in other words, and inform the relevant person that something has happened that must involve his participation? Again, Desamma cannot do this, not because she is deceptive or misleading. Doing so would directly violate the Jalari theory of action—more specifically, it would assume that another person could be motivated to respond simply because of personal reasons, goals, and aspirations. Explaining this to Sugamma is difficult, even for someone as practiced as Desamma in talking to outsiders:

> Desamma: "He came, but we did not feel like telling him. We didn't know how he would take it. Sugamma, I will tell you one thing. He came from far away, and recruited all of us for pay. If he is kind enough, he will give us money, otherwise he will not. We can't do anything if he feels that Pentayya and Desamma are trying to get more money."

The point here is that I should come to know of the snake mound by indirect means, in the same members of a Jalari family do. This would have the effect of making it a public issue and defining it as a religious event. It would thus be harder to ignore, and thus, in the Jalari view, would provide me with the motivation to act, since knowledge obtained in this way could only have one real source: the goddess. To be sure, we see Desamma's own calculations at work here. Ten years before I had paid Pentayya a small wage to help me transcribe some tapes, and I had also given him various gifts of money over the years. There is no doubt that he and his wife regarded me, not only as a family member, but also as a family resource. But, it would be wrong to assume that they had concocted the present event as simply a scheme to extort money. They had other ways of doing that, and indeed, it would take another chapter to describe all of them. The snake mound event was of another order altogether, and that is what Desamma wishes to convey in her answer to Sugamma. But Sugamma does not understand this, and still tries to pin Pentayya and Desamma down:

> Sugamma: "But why did you not tell him for ten days?"
> Pentayya: "That man [Charles] asked me, "You have a case in your house. You did not tell me about that." I replied: "If you stay for a minute in my house you will know. I need not tell you." He asked me how he would know the meaning. Then I said: "You will either know about that in your dream or it will come into your mind that on a particular day you should do something."

Now, this is an important point. Onc does not "inform" others of a spritual event, especially if it involves conflict between family members. They should find out through other means. I first found out about the snake mound from the village shaman, Nukali, who mentioned (almost in passing) that he had been called to perform a divination for Pentayya. I had been very surprised. Pentayya was not only my elder brother but my closest friend, and knew better than anyone that I had a long-standing interest in recording divinations. If there had been a divination in his house, he should have been the first to call me. But he did not, as Desamma said. I should find out through a dream, or some other event, such as a sudden high fever or an attack of diarrhoea. Sugamma then questions Desamma on the festival the goddess wants me to help perform:

> Sugamma: "So, to fix up the hut and perform the festival will cost several thousand rupees. Then will the goddess cool down?"
> Desamma: "We don't know. We must take the man [Charles] to the *pati.* Tomorrow is Thursday. We bring Nukali here and offer a small homage (*dandam*). We must take a bath, and then wash the area around the snake mound with coconut milk. Then we can move that box. We have to buy liquor for all the elders of the village. Somehow we'll borrow the money. Tomorrow morning we go to the *pati.* The Englishman did not listen."

The cultural logic at work is this: When the village shaman told me about the divination and the reason for it, I should have responded by agreeing to perform the festival. I did not refuse, but it is true that I did not accept either. In fact I did not know what to do, since all my years working in the village, such an event had never occurred before. As I saw it, I was trying to find out more about what was going on—asking quesitons, doing interviews, collecting information. I hadn't been in the village in almost three years, and there was a lot of catching up to do. How could I act without enough knowledge? But this sort of reasoning has no place in the Jalari theory of action. The eruption of the snake mound and the subsequent divination should have been enough, and if not—as Desamma says—then other means must be found, including more public divinations. My failing to take notice could not be excused on the grounds that I was considering my options, or trying to make up my mind, or simply confused. Jalaris define this in only one way, as an *addu* or "obstruction," which would have to be overcome by force of divine proof.

More to the point, proof depends on a demonstration of causality—one event linked to another event in an unbroken sequence. This is important, but to our minds somewhat legalistic; wouldn't another way have been simply to say, "take it on faith"? Christian thinking often resorts to this, especially when theologians announce that only through the faith (a gift of God) can one accept the divine order that includes both unpredictable happiness and suffering. A Christianized Teddi Pentayya, then, could have asked me to accept on the basis of our kinship, or our assumed faith in the goddess-created order of the universe, the fact that I had been chosen to perform the festival. The Jalaris would laugh at such an argument. They would consider it stupid, and wonder that anyone could be convinced by such trickery. There must be proof (*rujuvu*), and proof must always be causal and demonstrable. That is the purpose divination. It is not a religious act of worship, but a verifiable system of testing explanatory hypotheses.

Nevertheless, hypotheses are tightly constrained by distinctly Jalari criteria of causal relevance. These reduce the range of possible precipitating events. Spritual manifestations, like the snake mound, must be due to some kind of social dispute, either within or between households. In other words, a goddess is one's own household goddess, and is "showing herself" either to punish the members of her own household for some slight or wrong-doing. Or the goddess is somone else's, and is attacking because the victim household has comitted an offense against the goddess's household. One or the other must be true. In this case, because the manifestation was a snake mound, and only Ellamma is represented as a snake mound, the only explanation could be the first, i.e. an internal household problem. Moreover, this kind of problem is almost invariably the result of a dispute between brothers. Clearly Pentayya and Desamma saw it this way and acted in a traditional manner to "prove" their case through divination.

In her conversation with Desamma, Sugamma continues to draw out the details of this line of reasoning:

> Sugamma: What are the villagers saying about this snake mound?
> Desamma: All of this is surprising, from my brother-in-law's arrival to the appearance of the ant hill. Why is it not there earlier? Should it happen the very moment the brother-in-law came here? The goddess has desires (*asa*). Pentayya does not have any money. He does not go anywhere; he will not work. The goddess considers (Charles) Pentayya's younger brother. The goddess felt that these two brothers are her grandsons. She wants them to celebrate the festival for her. This is what people are saying.
> Sugamma: Now if you do not celebrate, who will be at a loss? You or the Charles?
> Desamma: For both of us. Whether or not there is actual harm, there will be shame (*anumanam*).

Here Desamma describes the causal sequence. First, it is understood by the village and the goddess herself that I am Pentayya's younger brother. Like any brother, therefore, I have obligations and responsibilities, chief among which is to share my resources with my extended household—in this case, my elder brother, Pentayya, and his family. To some extent I have done this, but not as fully or as often as my elder brother wishes. This has culminated in the failure to conduct the goddess festival, and since I am to blame, the goddess signals her attention to me by causing a snake mound to pop up just at the moment I "set foot" in the village for the first time in three years. No one will come to me and explain all of this. What would be the point, since human words, say the Jalaris, are flexible and fallible. Let the goddess show herself, and in divination, let her word be proved.

My relationship with Pentayya is key to an understanding of these events. I have been working in Jalaripet for more than twenty years, and in that time my status had gone from junior male family member to a senior householder, with all the responsibilities (ritual and financial) that go with it. One of those responsibilities was the performance of the household goddess festival, which should, by custom, take place every three years, but which because of the extended household's condition had been postponed for more than two decades. Pentayya has no other brother, his "real" (*sonta*) younger brother having died of smallpox decades ago. This means that his household is unusually small, and unable by itself to put up the money for a goddess festival and funerary ritual for the dead. The matter is not helped by Pentayya being a man who preferred to amuse himself in conversation and drink than go fishing. How did I become his other younger brother? It is a long story, and I summarize it here.

Many years ago, after I had known Pentayya for about three years, one of his younger sisters suddenly died. She died unmarried, and the expenses for her funeral had to be borne by Pentayya himself. His youngest daughter had just been born—the same daughter, Sankaramma, who found the snake mound. Pentayya already had a lot of expenses, and when he told me about them one evening I asked him if I could help. Up to then Pentayya and I had a shared a lot together, mostly time spent talking about the fishing and life in the village. In fact, we had first met on a boat, back when I visited Jalaripet for the first time and asked a man (it turned out to be Pentayya), if he would take me out for fishing. Intimacy is a culturally specific process, however, and in Jalaripet—as in many "traditional" places—it is usually mediated by kinship, either real or putative. It took me a long time to understand this in something other than a theoretical sense. I had to be brought within the logic of thing, and as in most things anthropological, it happened by accident, when I offered some money to help bury Pentayya's sister. "After all," I said, "am I not your younger brother?"

At that moment, suddenly, Pentayya grasped my hand and looked at me with a completely altered face. It was if I had said the magic word, and everything changed. One indication that something had changed happened later the same day. I was on my way into the village, and a Jalari woman I had known for years stopped with a grinning face and made a rather surprising suggestion about what we might do together later under cover of darkness. It was a joke, and like a lot of Jalari humor, sexually explicit. The point, however, is that such jokes are restricted to "joking relationships" between men and women who are, or might be, marriage partners to each other.

The joke only made sense in this context, and outside that relationship, it would be considered extremely inappropriate. This woman was Pentayya's (classificatory) cross-cousin, and related to him as a potential marriage partner in the traditional south Indian pattern. She joked with him this way, and he with her, even though both are married to other people. Now, she was doing the same with me, and that was because I was now classified as Pentayya's younger brother. In less than a day, in other words, I was part of the kin network, with all the joking and avoidance relationships that go with it.

The relationship between brothers is one of the most problematic in Jalari culture, and in many patrilineal societies for that matter. When the snake mound erupted, Pentayya and I entered a new phase in that relationship, one entirely congruent with the pattern of development in Jalari extended household. As brothers age, fraternal solidarity becomes harder and harder to maintain. Older brothers feel this most acutely, since, it is their power that is challenged until finally the extended family breaks down. Pentayya may have had no "extended family" in the traditional sense, but he had me, and the customary scenario would be enacted even with this somewhat unusual relationship. By this I mean that Pentayya had to act to exert his authority as my older brother, both to enhance his prestige in the village and to enforce the solidarity of our family which ritual worship of the goddess Ellamma and the spirits of the dead represented. No doubt Pentayya was also motivated by the benefits he knew would acrew to his family as a result of my participation. There would be more money, more food, and lots of new clothes. But it would be a mistake to assume Pentayya considered these more than secondary gains. After all, he had asked me for money and goods before (and generally received them), so an elaborate goddess festival preceded by signs and visitations, spirit divinations and shamanic consultations, was not really necessary. If I were really his brother, then he and I together must pay homage to the goddess, and this would constitute a crucial test of our sibling solidarity. Pentayya's logic came down to this: I now had a job, and was therefore "earning well". His children were growing up; one was already married, and the other three were soon to follow. He was getting older and the villagers were beginning to ridicule him for my lack of involvement in the family's ritual affairs. Family honour (*mariyada*) required it, and the goddess Ellamma, in her wisdom, had brought me to the village at this particular time in order to get it done.

Pentayya and I discussed just how the festival would be arranged. A fully performed ritual would take a long time to prepare and cost far more money than I could afford. What the Jalaris calls a *cinna pandagu,* a somewhat simpler version, would cost less, chiefly because we would not have to feed the whole village, but only the heads of its constituent families—about 600 people in all. In the end, that is what we agreed to do, and a "seeing stone" (*cupa rayi*) divination (Nuckolls, 1996) was performed to seek the goddess's approval. She gave us permission to proceed. We began collecting the required materials, from huge bags of rice to the new clothes that would be needed. By early July all the preparations for an elaborate goddess festival had been made. One of the Jalaris came to my door early the morning to bring me to the festival, or so I thought. He said something bad had happened. Pentayya's sister, Goramma, was dying, and I should come immediately, he said. I rushed to Pentayya's house, and found him on the porch, in the back, one of several people standing in a circle. In the middle of the circle was Goramma. She lay unconscious, her chest barely moving as she breathed. Her old mother was closest to her, and every time the flies would try to land on her daughter's face, she would brush them away. It was clear Goramma would be dead soon. I went back inside the house, where Desamma and Pentayya were sitting. It was the death watch.

I asked Desamma what had happened. Yesterday, when I had seen Goramma, she seemed perfectly well. Last night, Desamma said, she told Goramma that she was going to buy some things for the festival. Goramma told her to go ahead. Then this morning, Sankaramma went to the hut and found Goramma unconscious. She has been like that ever since. How was she last night, I asked? She was walking and talking, Desamma, but towards evening seemed to be a bit sick. She told Desamma that she would die the following day.

Pentayya's story followed next. As he spoke he was sitting against the wall of the house. His hands seemed to be trembling and he looked depressed. He said he went to the thatch hut about seven last night. Goramma was not exactly sick, but neither was she well. She asked him to get her some sleeping pills. He told her that that would be impossible, since that would require a doctor's prescription. She then told him that she would die by no later than the next day. Jokingly, he told her to go ahead and do it. At this point in his story, Pentayya got up and went to the hut, and tried to give his sister some water. It was no use. He came back crying, and went into the goddess room—apparently overcome with emotion. I had not seen him like this before. Very little phased him. He came and sat down next meet. I tried to persuade him to eat, but he wouldn't, and neither would any of his children.

At about noon, after sitting in silence for a couple of hours, I went back to a friend's house, telling Pentayya's son, Parasa, to come and tell me when Goramma died. He arrived at about 1:30 pm. I went back to Pentayya's house and saw that a large group of women had gathered around the hut and had set-up wailing. The village priest's younger brother had gone to town to fetch a new sari for the body. There was a long delay, during which several arguments took place on the question or whether or not to proceed without the new clothing. Some people felt that since she was diseased—no one said exactly by what—it was not wise to bathe the body or wait too long to bury it. But they waited anyway, and eventually the sari arrived.

The women brought the body out from the porch and put it on a wooden stretcher, a much less elaborate version of the magnificent palanquins used for people who die more auspiciously. This was just some wood, tied into a platform, with a palm mat on top. In fact, on the way to the burial ground, it just about gave way two or three times, throwing the body to one side. At about 4:40, we went to the burial ground. Pentayya of acted as *talakorivi* ("chief mourner") and held the basket containing parched rice, which he threw ever now and again backwards over his head. About half way down the hill, towards the beach, the women of the funeral procession stopped. A couple of them fell down and started wailing. The men proceeded to the burial ground.

The grave had already been dug. The procession moved around the grave three times, in clockwise direction. The grave-digger picked up Goramma and put her face down in the grave, a chicken egg on her left shoulder. She wore only the white *sari* that had been bought this afternoon. On her face was smeared tumeric paste. Pentayya threw in the first bit of earth, then the rest of us followed suit. In no time it was over. Pentayya then took a black earthen pot, filled with water, and walked around the grave three times. Then he repeated the circumambulations, but this time, each time he went around, the gravedigger poked another hole in the pot, and from each hole a stream of water poured. By the third time around, the pot was empty and Pentayya threw it off in the distance, where it broke into pieces. That was the end. We went from there to the beach, where Pentayya jumped in the water for a purificatory bath. The rest of us waded it and threw water on our heads three times, to remove the death pollution.

Everything had happened so quickly. Ellamma's hierophany in the form of the snake mound had touched off a mad run to the shamans and diviners, and culminated in my decision to sponsor the festival. Over the last few days, we had been busy collecting and preparing the ritual implements, buying food and liquor, and making arrangements to feed hundreds of people. Only one day remained before the festival. Now, it was all over, and I could only wonder: If Ellamma had signaled her wish for a festival by the appearance of the snake mound, what did the death of Pentayya's sister signify? Death is extremely inauspicious, and unless it is expected—as in the case of the very old—the Jalaris usually take it for granted that household goddesses are involved. Whatever the cause, of course, death automatically cancels all ritual activities except those connected with the funeral. There was no question of performing the goddess festival for at least forty days, and by then, as Pentayya knew, I would have returned to the United States. But the main question, I thought, would be what causes the sudden death in the first place.

As it turned out, I seemed to be the only one curious about this question. Pentayya refused to consider any but natural causes. After all, Goramma had been "sick" for some time. That is, she was a leper, and suffered the periodic infections and incapicitations that are typical of that disease. But the timing, I asked Pentayya—surely the timing of the death was significant, since it occurred just before our big festival? Perhaps the goddess had killed Goramma, not to punish her—she had been punished enough—but to punish someone else, or to make him do something. That was a logical possibility in the Jalari scheme of things. Or the goddess might have been dissatisfied with the festival arrangements, and killed Goramma in order to stop them. I did not pursue this line of inquiry very far with Pentayya. It was apparent that speculation on such questions was not in his interest, and that made sense.

The reason it made sense was that Jalaris do not undertake inquries into the causes of misfortune simply out of curiosity, especially when the cause may be related to their own misdeeds. Denial and avoidance are much better. That much is common even in American culture. But in the Jalari case, causal inquiry will take place when the goddess is suspected of attacking someone—not the intended victim, but always someone close to him or her. That way, the guilty party will feel shamed into acting. In this case, if the goddess had killed Goramma, the intended victim was not her, but could be Pentayya. And because her death had affected me, as chief celebrant of the goddess festival, it was up to me to consult a diviner and determine why, based on likely causal scenarios involving infractions of fraternal unity. In other words, if I blamed Pentayya for something, now was the time to prove that he was responsible for Goramma's death. That is one of the reasons Pentayya did not wish to consider the goddess-related antecedents of his sister's death, since, it might implicate him and undermine his relationship with me.

The logic might sound tortured and difficult to follow. For what could I have blamed Pentayya that the goddess would have chosen the death of Goramma to call attention to it? The list of possibilities is small, if tradition is any guide. All of them involve a failure on Pentayya's part to live up to his obligations to me as my older brother, such as the failure to arrange my marriage or to provide me the necessary means to support myself as a fisherman. In fact, the relationship had always worked the other way round, and I had always given more (in a material sense) than I received. This led to a perception, often voiced by others, that our relationship was upside down, and Pentayya was taking advantage of me. The same happens in Jalari kinship relations all the time. My being an American had nothing to do with it. The point is that the assymmetries in our relationship might have led me to resent it, and resentment, according to the Jalaris, "wakes up" the goddess. It causes her to take notice, and if the cause of resentment is just, she acts against the offender by causing him some kind of suffering. Pentayya was afraid I resented him, and if I choose to pursue the matter in divination, it is very likely Goramma's death would be blamed on him.

There are other reasons, too, for thinking Pentayya might have felt guilty about the death. The day after the funeral, I discussed his relationship. Goramma with a few of my village friends. One called attention. Goramma's request for sleeping pills and said that she probably wanted them to kill herself. I thought that was significant, too, since few Jalaris know about sleeping medications and even fewer have ever used them. It seemed unlikely to me that Goramma was one of them. Still, more interesting than her a typical knowledge was her asking for drugs the very night she died. She did not get the drugs; that we know. But could not she have used other means, if her goal was not simply to induce sleep but to kill herself? I asked Pentayya, in general terms, how a person who wanted to commit suicide might go about it. Drowning was one possibility—jumping into a well or walking into the sea. The difficulty, he said, was that one might be rescued. The best means was poison, and when I asked him the type, he said that was easy. The plant oleander grew in great abundance around the village, and ingesting a few leaves insured death within a few hours.

Other Jalaris pointed out that Pentayya had neglected Goramma and his mother until recently—in fact, until I had arrived. Goramma had never married, as I said before, because of her life-long history of leprosy. She never appeared in Pentayya's house, and I rarely caught a glimpse of her. In fact, I had known Pentayya for more than a year before I even discovered Goramma. It was not that she was hidden. She simply did not appear socially. Even though Pentayya had not done much for Goramma, she had given Pentayya plenty of support. For years, it was she and Pentayya's wife who supported the family, since Pentayya never earned enough. They would buy fish at the beach and take it to market, making a small profit on the transaction—just enough to keep the family going. At the same time, Goramma and her mother lived in the tiny hut next to Pentayya's much bigger house—the same hut in which the snake mound appeared.

No one connected the timing of the death and the timing of the goddess festival, but this, to me, was difficult to ignore. People had already said she might have died because of Pentayya's neglect, or because of his decision to hold the festival in the main house and not in the hut. One villager said that the decision to build the *sadaru* and enshrine the goddess in the new house should not have been made. The plan in the beginning had been to do it in the hut. When Pentayya changed the location—admittedly, with the goddess's approval, as validated in divination—it touched off a series of events that culminated in Goramma's death. In other words, the decision to change the site should not have been made, and Pentayya was, therefore, to blame for his sister's death. This was a valid interpretation, but only by assuming an intentional act on the part of Goramma. At the time, I wrote down my suspicion in my fieldnotes:

> But to speculate: Why would she have killed herself? Clearly the day could not have been better chosen—the very day of the festival that would celebrate the consecration of the *sadaru* in the new house. If the old hut had been selected—as, indeed, it was at the time of the homage—would this have altered Goramma's situation, even ameliorated it? After all, the hut was her domicile. If it had become the *peddillu,* wouldn't that have made a difference to her? It is possible now, with her death, that people will interpret the death as a sign from the goddess that in fact she prefers to have the *sadaru* in the hut. After all, the final decision to move it to the big house—decided in the divination—had been somewhat forced.

Goramma might have committed suicide, or she might have simply died of leprosy. We shall never know for sure.

In any case, Goramma' death, like the eruption of the snake mound, said something to the villagers about the relationship between Pentayya and his American younger brother. The mound was taken to mean that the relationship was out of balance in favour of the younger brother, and that corrective action (i.e., the performance of the goddess festival) needed to take place to restore the older brother to his position of hierarchical superiority. The sudden death of Goramma on the very day the festival was to take place implied the opposite: that Pentayya had neglected another family member—his sister—and exhibited the quality of *ahankaram* ("pride") in insisting that the festival take place in the new concrete house instead of the old thatched hut. All of this was taking place, too, at a time of heightened tension over the meaning of Jalaripet as a traditional village in the wake of the 1984 fire. The result was a return to the *status quo ante*—not exactly what Pentayya wanted, but still a situation in which I was involved in the extended family but not under my elder brother's control. It was best viewed a holding pattern. What is interesting is that this pattern has continued to the present day (2011), testament to the fact that the opposition between sibling solidarity and division need not be resolved, but can remain in a state of suspension over a longer period of time.

Conclusion

Eliade preferred to see hierophantic manifestations as numinous realizations of a religious consciousness beyond the power of social science to describe. The hierophany of the Incarnation resolves the contradiction between mortal and divine, and provides, through its mediation, the possible of infinite forgiveness. The present analysis has shown that social factors, and in particular the internal contradictions of Jalari kinship, set the stage for recognition of an event as a religious hierophany. The frame of reference is not forgiveness between people, or between people and their goddesses. Rather, it is sibling solidarity. The conclusion is that hierophany in Jalari culture is the physical embodiment of a kinship dialectic that pits two values against each other. One is the value of fraternal solidarity and the other is the value of separation and division. A hierophany is a crisis in the opposition of values—a representation, in physical form, of an uncomfortable juxtaposition, and it commands attention. The crisis, I have shown, need not be resolved in favour of either value, but can, at least for a while, exist in a state of temporary suspension.

3
Obtaining 'Fruit'
Sorcery and Illness in Rural Tamil Nadu

Haripriya Narasimhan

Introduction

They won't go (to a doctor). If something happens, they will do *kani* and see. Someone we know was given blood of a garden lizard! One human's blood does not match another's. How will garden lizard's blood match?—*Murugesan, Tirupattur*

The focus of this chapter is on rural and tribal women's encounters with magic and sorcery in Tamil Nadu. Women felt particularly vulnerable to attacks of jealousy and sorcery (*seyvinai*)[1] committed by relatives. They worried that their kin might impact their health adversely. While not all cases of suspicion point to kin, I will show through specific examples that more often than not, it was a kin who was suspected. How do women arrive at the conclusion that it is a kin who has affected their health? How do they manage the treatment process for such illness? Author hopes to answer these questions in this chapter. Data presented in this chapter are from Author's fieldwork research amongst women in Tirupattur and Yelagiri, in 2001-02.

Though ambivalent about the efficacy of sorcery rituals like *kani* (meaning—fruit) and of practitioners of such rituals, women in Yelagiri and Tirupattur approached them to find out what/who had caused their illness and why? Based on the inference, they proceed to take action. Women's discussion of *kani* is not a "destructive" act (Nabokov, 2000), but evidence of their sense of agency regarding their health. Author follows Laura Ahearn's definition of agency as a "socio-culturally mediated capacity to act" (Ahearn, 2001:112). Women were not necessarily confused by the fact that they had options available to them. For them, "the existence of alternatives does not appear to be problematic; in fact, lay medical culture is often surprisingly inclusive, readily integrating new elements" (Whyte, 1982: 2056). They only wanted to make use of all options available to find out the cause of ill health and to take remedial action. This chapter discusses in detail how women in rural Tamil Nadu deduced sorcery to be a cause of ill-health, and approached sorcerers/magicians to undo spells cast of them and improve their health.[2]

The Field Sites

Yelagiri is located in the district of Vellore, about 250 kilometres south-west of Chennai. It is considered to be a hill station due to its cool climate and elevation. There are fourteen villages or hamlets in the hills. A village is called an *ūr* and the village headman, *ūr cauntar*. A commonly accepted origin myth about Yelagiri refers to the presence of cardamom (*yelakāi*) on the mountain.[3] Human settlements are supposed to have appeared around two hundred to four hundred years ago. The natives are called 'Malayali', meaning 'one who lives in the mountains'. Malayali also refers to themselves as *kārālar*, 'the one who rules the clouds'. They claim to have come from the plains, escaping the warring soldiers of Tipu Sultan's army in the seventeenth century. The retreating Vellala cauntar (a caste group of cultivators) from the district of Kancheepuram made the plateau of Yelagiri their home.

There is some dispute about the "tribal" claims of the Malayali. It is generally believed that the Malayali are not tribals, but cultivators. The Malayali are found in many parts of the state.[4] They consider the Irula, another tribe considered native to Yelagiri, to be 'lower' in social hierarchy. When asked to name their *jāti,* a native of Yelagiri would say either 'Malayali' or 'Vellala'. While the former is classified as a scheduled tribe, the latter is the name of a forward caste group in Tamil Nadu.

The Malayalis are primarily agriculturalists. The main crop is millet (*sāmai*). Today they also grow paddy, corn and castor. The Malayalis hunt wild pigs and other small animals, and gather firewood from the mountains. Consumption of beef and fish is considered taboo. Pork is a favourite. A typical Malayali household lives in a thatched roof hut with a spacious room, kitchen, and a storage space. On the ceiling are built several wooden shelves to store grain. This type of housing is becoming rare. The Government-built house comprises a room with a partition for a kitchen, built of cement with asbestos roof.

A road was built connecting Tirupattur and Yelagiri in 1963-64. Until then, people had to walk down the hills to the town of Kodiyur, fourteen kilometres away, to buy essential items like food grain, and oil. With the road in place, bus transport was introduced. People began to go to Vellore, Tirupattur, and even to Bangalore in neighbouring Karnataka.

The Malayali women are known for their autonomous lifestyle, compared to those in the plains of Tirupattur. This conforms to the stereotypical image of the tribal woman. Because drinking alcohol is not taboo for women, people from other caste groups view them as lacking in morals. Marriage practices are also different. Bride price is the norm. Women have the right to terminate relationships and remarry.

Tirupattur is a town south east of Chennai, approximately 200 kilometres away. A majority of the people in Tirupattur are Hindus, while Muslim families, are concentrated in particular localities. In the village of Guddur where I did fieldwork, Kannada-speaking Kurubas live along with Telugu-speaking Reddiars and Yadavas, while the Tamil-speaking Vaniyar are the dominant caste in this region. Scheduled castes, or *Dalits* as they prefer to be called, live on the outskirts of the village, in a "colony", separated from the *ūr* or village. *Dalits* live in one-room clay huts, roofed with thatch. They work as wage labourers in the agricultural fields. When there is no work they migrate to other towns and cities.

The Believers

Domestic conflicts between blood kin, in-laws, lovers and co-wives usually revolve around the contradictions between kinship norms and individualistic conduct rather than legal codes. Alleged victims failed to follow customary rules of reciprocity or the moral order of kin relations, or they behaved selfishly by reneging on financial obligations or marital transactions or stealing a husband (Nabokov, 2000: 47).

Gulnar lived in a village in Tirupattur. A Muslim, she was married at the age of twelve to a relative much older to her. She had four sons and one daughter, all unmarried. In 2002, she was fifty years old. Her husband owned some land, and also ran a petty shop in the front yard of his house. She did not leave her house much, except to give food to labourers in the fields. Sometimes she attended the counter in their shop when her son was out. I met her briefly in 2001 and again in 2002. Gulnar complained of the torture (*citiravatai)* she underwent at home. She said, "If there is too much suffering, the body cannot withstand it." She complained of hip pain and heavy vaginal discharge. Biomedical doctors in Tirupattur recommended hysterectomy. But being anaemic, she could not undergo surgery immediately. She said that her inability to walk was due to a spell cast on her. At first she refused to speculate on who it could be. Later, when we were talking about her sister-in-law's daughter's death at childbirth recently, Gulnar's anger towards her husband's sister (*nāṯtanār)* became evident.

Gulnar's youngest child and only daughter Najma was studying in class eight. Insisting that she must study in an Urdu school, Gulnar's husband left Najma in his sister's care in the nearby town of Ambur.[5] Gulnar wanted Najma to finish class ten before she got married. But her sister-in-law wanted to get Najma married to her son-in-law. Gulnar's sister-in-law had lost her nineteen-year-old daughter at childbirth. Her sister-in-law was asked to take care of the two young children of her deceased daughter. The son-in-law of Gulnar's sister-in-law informed her that he would remarry soon. Fearing that he might either leave the children permanently in her care, or take them away and thus deny her access to her grandchildren, she came to her brother, Gulnar's husband, with a proposal. She wanted Najma to marry her son-in-law. Gulnar's refusal to give her daughter in marriage to her husband's sister's son-in-law became a point of contention between the two families.

When talking about her health issues, Gulnar declined to discuss about magician-healers. "I don't know all that" was her constant refrain to most of my queries on the subject. In what way did Gulnar think the spell works on her body? "It affects (one's) heart...hands and feet don't work. They become like wood." When I probed her further about how exactly someone would affect her health. Gulnar replied, "They do that only because we are doing well, is it not?" She has personally experienced the effect of such action. "Since yesterday I have been feeling like this. That's why I am now unable to walk." When I asked her if she knew who did it to her, she refused to speculate. "I don't know who did it". How did she conclude that someone had cast a spell on her? Did anyone in her family comment about it? "No one said anything. I feel that someone has done something to me."

Unlike Gulnar, Nagu, another informant, did admit to going to a sorcerer and even told me who she suspected of doing sorcery against her. The previous year, she had been very articulate and chatty. But this time, she seemed very worried. "I am worried about my daughter", she said again and again in my meeting with her for over two hours. She was contemplating returning to her natal village close by. The cause for worry for her cousin who was staying with her.

Her daughter Lakshmi was helping her in the fields one day when a grain of rice flew in the air and hit the pupil of her eye. The injury turned septic and Nagu rushed her daughter to a private doctor who referred her to the famous Aravind Eye Hospital in Madurai. The wound was infected by then and Lakshmi had to undergo immediate surgery, costing nine thousand rupees. She borrowed money from the women's self-help group's scheme and raised the rest of the amount from amongst her relatives. Repaying such a huge sum was a big financial burden. In addition, she was also plagued by stress because of her cousin's strange behaviour towards her.

Sometimes, when I just sit and think, my heart hurts that my daughter has become like this. I brought my uncle's daughter (*citappa pen)* to stay with me. I kept her well. I don't know why she scolds me. If I go alone to her house, she scolds me all the way back and forth. Then I get chest pain.

She used the word "tension" to indicate her mental status. Her husband did not pay attention to her complaints. Nagu suggested that he might even be having an affair with her cousin. She did not actually accuse her cousin of doing sorcery but strongly agreed that such actions by kin could cause harm. Though, it may seem like Nagu was accusing a patrikin of commissioning sorcery against her, it was actually her affinal kin that she was complaining against, hence, the lack of attention on her husband's part. Her husband is Nagu's second cousin on her father's side. So her first cousin on her father's side is also her husband's cousin. This cousin would also be eligible to marry Nagu's husband if she so desired.

On advice from neighbours, she went to a healer and got a talisman (*tāyattu)* made, consisting of a sheet with eight elements inside (*astapantaṇa takatu)*. The healer told her she had some *dosaḍm.*[6] Unsupportive husband, and a daughter critically injured at marriageable age, and an angry cousin all combined to make Nagu sorrowful (*vicanam)* and susceptible to sorcery.

Women in tribal hamlets of Yelagiri described sorcery as an external force. Prema, an informant, shared her experience. Some years ago, she was suddenly struck with diarrhoea. Allopathic medicines did not work. She was sure she was going to die and asked her husband to leave her at her mother's house. While on their way, the couple was approached by a stranger who offered a prophecy. Prema urged her husband to find out more. He was asked to return with Prema and her mother. When they went to the person concerned, he told them that someone had infused a spell to "yellow water" (i.e. water with turmeric) three months ago. "One man, two women" he said. On his advice, she proceeded to Chenji hills[7] and got a talisman (*kolu*) tied to her legs. When she returned to her in-laws' house, she ate the food cooked by her mother-in-law as usual. She soon fell ill again. Her husband expressed concern at her failing health and fetched her maternal uncle from Andhra Pradesh. Prema was very dear to this uncle. Her uncle told her after doing magic (*mantiram*), that the spell was cast by none other than her mother-in-law, her husband and his mistress. He then squeezed a lemon on top of her head, and removed the spell. Prema believed that she would certainly have died if her uncle had not intervened.

This narrative is important because while Prema accused her husband of collaborating with his mother and mistress in endangering her health, she also pointed out that it was he who brought her uncle, who presumably was trained in magic, to cure her. This story captures the tension in kin relations that many women in Tamil Nadu talked about. These tensions caused havoc to their health status. Allopathic medicine could not help them get out of this quagmire. The helplessness gets accentuated because women feel that their health problems will not be taken seriously by their family and particularly by biomedical health care practitioners. In the words of another Malayali woman, Parvati, problems in life cause tension, but "if we go to the hospital, they say 'no'... In cases of *seyvinai*, how can I explain that pain? What can I say?"

Belief in sorcery is not confined to the Malayali tribe alone. Lakshmi belonged to a scheduled caste community that migrated to the hills. She strongly believed her husband died because his relatives cast spell on him. The evidence came from threats and warnings that emerged during family fights. For instance, Lakshmi remembered her husband's kin threatening him, "You refused to give us land. We will make sure you don't live on this land for long." He soon started vomiting blood. Suspecting tuberculosis, they rushed him to a hospital where he was subjected to many tests. Finding the treatment unhelpful, Lakshmi consulted a magician who told her about the spell. She described her horror: "It was on his *veshti* (*dhoti*), his shirt, his slippers... he was soon drenched in blood... his shirt, slippers they were all wet and he died." Such instances strengthen fear and suspicion of sorcery causing illness, especially amongst women.

Many women accused their kin of committing sorcery. In fact, most people accused only kin. I rarely came across anyone accusing people other than their immediate kin of sorcery. Nor did I see "resignation" (Lambek, 1993 cf Nabokov, 2000) at this discovery. Women found it a "painful revelation" to see "what one suspected but could not accept or internalize" (Nabokov, 2000). But once they were sure that a kin had commanded a spell on them, women did not hesitate to take action, by consulting a sorcerer to remove the spell.

Doing Evil

I will now discuss in detail about the study done by Isabelle Nabokov (now known as Isabelle Clarke-Deces) in a town called Chengi, about 180 kilometres from Chennai, in the temple of Mel Malayanur where the famous Ankalaparamesvari cult is located. My own research areas were in the neighbouring district. In a thorough examination of a sorcery ritual in the Tamil context, Nabokov concludes that the meaning of sorcery is destruction, and not "pragmatism" as Bruce Kapferer alleges, from his analysis of the same in Sri Lanka.

Nabokov (2000, 2000a) critiques Bruce Kapferer for his phenomenological approach to the issue of sorcery. She accuses him of reducing "the personal aspect of sorcery for its sufferers" (2000:148). In her fourteen months of fieldwork, no one told her of their visit to a sorcerer to do evil to others. Nor did she meet a *mantirakārar*.[8] Because she could never find anyone who actually commissioned a spell, Nabokov argues that in Tamil Nadu, the only sorcery that exists is counter sorcery. The same could be said for the Nyole of Eastern Uganda. Susan Reynolds Whyte, who worked among the Nyole, proclaims that "the treatment of sorcery seldom involves direct confrontation with the suspected sorcerer, but rather the employment of a specialist who turns the sorcery medicine back on the sorcerer" in a form of counter-sorcery (Whyte, 1982: 2057).

The counter-sorcery ritual, *kalippu,* is similar to a death ritual in Tamil Nadu. A cause is found for a person's misfortune, such as a sudden or recurring illness. Once the perpetrator of the illness is identified, which could be a ghost, spirit, a relative or a deity, an effigy of the same is made with bones of a first-born male child. It is shaped in the same way that lower gods of the Hindu pantheon, usually village deities look. Rites resembling a funeral are performed to the effigy and then it is cremated. While the sorcerer concludes, in the one case that Nabokov discusses in detail, that the ceremony gave the sufferer a second lease of life, the person commissioning the ritual did not think so (Nabokov, 2000:49-53). Nabokov concluded that the ritual signified an end of ties to the woman's lover, with whom she had an affair, bore children and later found through sorcery that he and his wife were the reason for her inexplicable illness and death of three children.

While Nabokov is primarily focused on sorcery rituals in Tamil Nadu, my interest is not exclusively on the symbolic and ritualistic aspects of sorcery.[9] Rather, my focus is on how people who talk about sorcery as a case for ill-health respond to it. In other words, how do women decide which illness is caused by magic/sorcery/spell? What do they do about it? How do they talk about the process of seeking explanation through sorcery? There are some illnesses that everyone understands to be beyond the boundaries of biomedicine or indigenous medicine. It has to be dealt with only by another medium, i.e. a magician or *mantirakārar* (Nabokov, 2000: 50).

Like Nabokov, I too never found anyone who admitted to having approached a magician to do sorcery to another individual. Women only spoke about removing the spell. *Seyviṉai*[10] is caused by *vaippu* (deposit). An object, such as egg, lime, or a piece of human hair is placed in the vicinity of the victim, near his or her house in most cases. Women would tell me "*yāro veccitānka*" ("someone has 'deposited' something"). That object can transmit misfortune in the form of illness. I am not concerned with the ritual with which a sorcerer removes *ēval.*[11] My concern is how women translate the effect of *seyviṉai* onto their health. In Sri Lanka, *kodivina* (curses by 'evil people') is believed to block the capacity of a medicine to cure (Nichter and Nordstrom, 1989: 378). Similarly in Tamil Nadu, women felt that *seyvinai* will not allow biomedicine or herbal medicine to work. The only remedy was to perform a *kani.*

Nabokov does not see people seeking or performing counter sorcery ritual as actors. Her focus on the symbolic meanings of the ritual and the fact that it resembles death ceremonies in its form have made her see this process as destructive. But, seen from another angle, it does portray Lakshmi, the protagonist in Nabokov's article as an active agent.

Lakhsmi was a poor Paraya woman. She was married at a young age, but left her alcoholic husband and returned to her natal home. When she was about twenty years old, she started a relationship with another man who she claimed was her husband though she never "married him". After three of her four children died, the man left her and returned to his wife. It was then that Lakshmi started having convulsions. Though diagnosed with epilepsy and prescribed biomedicine, Lakshmi continued to suffer seizures and her parents decided to take her to "a man who would say *kuri*[12]", Nagaji. Lakshmi was ill, and she wanted to find out who had made her sick.

> First one must identify the cause. Is it a demon, an inauspicious astrological configuration, sorcery spell, the evil eye of an envious neighbour, sinful actions committed in past lives? (Nabokov, 2000: 50).

Once she found out the causal agents, in her lover and his wife, Lakshmi proceeded to perform *kalippu* (Nabokov, 2000: 56-59) which not only made her disconnect all ties she had with her former lover, but also made her healthy. Nabokov remarks that a few months later, when she met Lakshmi again, she found no sign of illness or remorse, nor any recollection of the ceremony.

Consulting sorcerers is not always a decision taken independently by women. The "therapy management group" (Janzen, 1978) was extensively involved. Nevertheless, what comes across is women's perseverance in taking action. A number of women were quite skeptical about the efficacy of sorcery rituals. However, they go through the process, so that, they can ensure they have done their part, while their health is still under their control.

In his discussion of the Hindu ideas of misfortune, Fuller talks about the effects caused by "malevolent people" (2004:236). One such character is the sorcerer, known as *mantirakārar* in the Tamil villages where I worked. I follow Van Hollen's definition here of a sorcerer as "someone who practices magic by reciting sacred hymns (*ma<u>n</u>tiram*[13]) and can remove and/or inflict spells" (Van Hollen, 2003: 252). As Fuller details, "these *mantras* may produce their effect directly if, for example, they are chanted as spells to cause or cure illness" (Fuller, 2004: 237). The sorcerer may also work his way through charms, and medicines.

Sorcerers can also do harm. The man I met in Yelagiri swore that he never did evil but he could if someone crossed him in the wrong way. Women rarely spoke about sorcerers. They were keen on those who for a small sum would perform some simple magic.[14] Some people are skeptical of such men and dismiss it as "it's all in the mind" (Fuller, 2004: 239).

Nabokov argues that contrary to anthropological literature that says such consultations reflect broader social discontent, her informants felt their problems were unique to each person. "They constituted painfully felt, immediate crises that confronted them with dramatic, threatening consequences" (2000:32). When the other options do not bear "fruit", people consult *cāmis*. *Cāmi*s maintain their authority by bullying their clients (2000: 41).

In grounding her analysis in anthropological theory, Nabokov acknowledges the contributions of various ancestors of the discipline.

Evans-Pritchard, Turner, Douglas and Redfield have all said what she has found about sorcery in Tamil Nadu, that it is a "social fact", indicates "failed social bonds", and thrive in times of rapid change (2000:48). But these ideas do not go far enough. In her view "in Tamil Nadu sorcery is first and foremost a *psychological* expression" (Nabokov, 2000:48). She explains further, "the ontology of Tamil sorcery is grounded in the subjective experiences of the sufferers; its cosmology and sociology depend on their psychology" (2000: 49).

Finding the Fruit

Kani literally means 'fruit'. 'Fruit' is the consequence of one's action, according to the *karma* theory (Fuller, 2004: 245). The consultations that people have with sorcerers is *kuri sollutal. Kuri* means several things—'sign', 'aim' or 'target'. Nabokov defines it thus: "*Kuri sollutal* can be generously defined as speech that decodes 'signs' whose referents are generally obscure to ordinary humans. In Tamil practice it specializes in identifying causes of personal affliction and misfortune..." (Nabokov, 2000:31). A session with a sorcerer results in people obtaining *kani* or fruit. Nabokov refers here to a similar inference by William Sax in his work among Himalayan Paharis (cf. Sax, 1985). *Kani* is expected to "offer solutions that are intended to transform ... existential predicaments" (Nabokov, 2000:32).

In Tirupattur and Yelagiri, the ritual is called *kolu potaratu.*[15] It involves animal sacrifice, either a goat or a chicken. It can be done on anything, e.g. coconut, a betel leaf. The person who does it will evoke the family deity and will predict what he sees in the leaf/coconut as to who could have cast the spell, where it is located and how it can be removed. *Kani* is used to find out causes for various unknown or unexplained events, such as locating a missing person, before starting a new career, marriage, or business, and to find out which system of health care is best suited for consultation for a particular disease/ illness.

People consulted sorcerers after their efforts to find solutions by other means became fruitless. But how do the sorcery sessions bear "fruit"? Nabokov illustrates using two examples. One involved a couple worried about the delay in fulfilling a vow that required an offering equal to the child's weight. The other involved a high caste woman in love with an untouchable man and threatening elopement. In both cases, the *cami*[16] they consulted provided them solutions that they could not have obtained elsewhere. The *cami's* job here is to "decode" sorcery powers (2000:43). *Kani* is the aim or target of *kuri* (2000:31). *Kani* or fruit is the result of the effort undertaken, similar to a pilgrimage, to transform one's life.[17]

The most disturbing aspect that people learn during a *kani* session is that "*someone* had tried to command them" (Nabokov, 2000:45; emphasis original). The command could be in the form of *vaciyam* or *ēval.* In Tirupattur and Yelagiri, women used the term *ketutal* (evil) to denote sorcery. *Vaciyam* refers to the binding power of ritual prestations (Nabokov, 2000: 46). *Eval* means command, i.e. that people are under a sorcery spell (Nabokov, 2000: 44).

The Irula, a tribe considered lower in the social hierarchy of the hills, act as magicians in Yelagiri. Stories of origin suggest that the Irula were created by Shiva and Parvati. The Irula were given a "coin" and asked to "drive out ghosts and spirits". Since then, the Irula have been practicing sorcery and magic in the area. Only men perform sorcery. I did not hear of any female sorcerers in Yelagiri or Tirupattur. According to information given by an Irula woman from Yelagiri, not everyone can become a sorcerer. A sorcerer cannot do anything unless asked. If someone approaches him to cure a fever, he would visit their house. If someone else had cast a spell on that house (i.e. *seyvinai*), he would remove the magic and cast his own on that house, and around the sick person. Usually, for such tasks, he would not be paid. The Irula charged eight hundred to three thousand rupees to remove possession by ghosts and spirits, in 2002. They do not perform *mantiram* for their own immediate family members, as it is believed to lack potency.

Reasons for Suffering Evil

Jealousy breeds "divisiveness" and threatens the notion of sharing (Gold and Gujar, 2002: 312). Raami, a Kuruba woman in Guddur said,

> I am a little weak *(sīku)*. I am not as strong *(tempu)* as I was before (marriage). If you think good in your heart, (I/we)

> will be good. If you are doing well, there are people who think 'these people are doing well'. There are people who think ill also (*keṭutal).* If you are doing well (*naḻlā poḻakara*), if you are wearing a good dress.... There is jealousy here....(*poṟamai*). If you wear some jewellery, a good dress... They will say "see how poor she was (*arapātu)...* now see how she is. She is wearing a good dress. Eating good food." If we continue to suffer (*avastai)* for *kanci* (gruel) and water, if we wear torn clothes, then they will say 'look how proud (*timiṟ)* she has become.... If we pin our sari, like you have done, we cannot do that, the have-nots (*illatavaka*). Those who have (*kiravaka)*[18] can do. We can't. They will talk amongst themselves, the haves."

This quote by a Kannada-speaking shepherd woman Raami brings out the class context. The poor are more afraid of being hurt by jealousy than the rich are, because amongst the poor those who do well, even if just by very little, arouse jealousy in other poor people. They then become victims of jealousy. She also noted that her health suffered after marriage and that she became weaker. After marriage, Raami lived with her husband's kin where she was more vulnerable to effects of envy and jealousy.

Fear of the evil eye or *dishti* in Tamil Nadu has been widely discussed (Fuller, 2004; Kapadia, 1995; Trawick, 1992; Van Hollen, 2003). A girl who has just attained puberty is at a great risk from *dirusti* (Kapadia, 1995:94). Sudden illnesses are generally blamed on *dirusti* cast by other humans than by supernatural beings (Kapadia, 1995: 127). New, born babies are in danger of attracting 'evil eye', sometimes from their own mothers (Trawick, 1992). As Trawick goes on to say, "anyone could gaze at anything with appreciation, without the slightest malice, and harm could come to that thing" (1992:93). Even gods and goddesses need to be protected from evil eye (Hancock, 1999: 80). If an affectionate look from a mother could harm a child, what then would become of an eye with a malicious intent? That seemed to be the logic women employed in expressing their feelings about evil eye in Rajasthan. Evil eye or *nazar* can be caused by evil winds (*hawa*) started by dangerous spirits (Unnithan-Kumar, 2002: 180). Evil eye is usually caused unconsciously (Fuller, 2004: 238). Women are more susceptible than men (2004: 240) and "any sort of weakness makes a person vulnerable to mystical harm" (2004: 239). For women, this is like a double-edged sword. They are weak in body and mind because they are women and are therefore, more likely to be affected by sorcery which renders them weaker.[19]

Jealousy operated in various ways on health. For some women, it came through the eyes of someone who looked at them with envy. For others, the envy actually had its origin in one's stomach (*vayiṟu)* which burns (*ericcal)*. In Latin America, the heat produced by envy makes a person cast *mal de ojo* or evil eye upon another (Strathern and Stewart, 1999:21). Some others told me that envy could occur in one's mind and could affect another's body.

Kokila, belonging to the barber community in Tirupattur, said her health could be affected if someone thought "look, how well she is." Jealousy worked in the following manner; "it is all in our thoughts. When we know (that someone has become jealous), we get ill." Kokila had three sons, two of whom had established their own hair saloons (as a barber shop is called) and earned reasonably well. One son was in the army. In addition to an affectionate and caring husband, she also earned respect from her sons, who she claimed, never went against her word. Her sons were also doing well financially. So, she had every reason to be envied. Therefore, if someone said "look how well she is", Kokila believed that it could affect her physically.

A woman who looked young for her age, had healthy children who were doing well in life, and a husband who was attentive to her, like in Kokila's case, expects people to be jealous. She also expected that jealousy to have an effect. The moment it was acknowledged that someone was jealous, an illness (whether it was chronic or sudden) was explained on those terms. I also noticed that some women interpreted the opposite, that is, if they became unwell, depending on the illness, they began analyzing if it was caused by jealousy.

The Skeptics

"If our time is right, everything will go well. If our time is bad, whatever has to come to us will stop half way." This was Vasantha's response to my question whether "time" (*nēram)* plays a role in determining health. Diseases will 'come' *(varum)*[20] if a person is going through a "bad time" *(keṯṯa nēram)*. Not everyone buys this theory. Dhanam dismissed it outright as a cause for her mother's sudden death. "My mother was ill. If we had money and had looked after her, she would not have died. That is what I think." Vasantha's mother-in-law explained the concept of time. "If it is bad time, it will be spent somehow. Even if you are at home. That is what we mean by time." 'Bad time' will follow a person even if he/she does not stir out of his/her house. Again, the disease/ailment is seen as external to the body. If one is going through a tough time, the body is susceptible to illnesses.

It can also strike a person when he/she goes out. Vasantha continued "we cannot say (when we will fall sick). Our body is not with us. We go to the forest. If a snake bites, we cannot say it is because of us. It is fate." The body and one's health is not in our control, implied Vasantha. This is especially the case when a person is going through a bad phase. Good health was not a permanent state of being.

Rangam of Mallapalli village, Tirupattur, did not believe in *kani*, which people frequently resorted to, to find out causes for theft, robbery, missing persons or property, and disease. "I don't like it. It's all superstition. No one is jealous of me", said Rangam, adding that even when she did not conceive after ten years of marriage, she did not seek *mantiram* or *kani*. Her husband's brother's wife, who lived next door, once accused her of stealing a gold chain after a *kani* examination. Ashamed and angered, Rangam left the village, and prayed to Muniappa (a local deity) that she be exonerated. She believed she had been singled out for blame because her husband was an alcoholic and she was poor. When she returned in the evening, she learnt that chain was found at home. Since this incident, Rangam's faith in such magical methods has gone. She called belief in magic as superstition. "There is no one to be jealous of me" she said, attributing it to her extreme poverty.

She was convinced that people used *kani* as an excuse to show their jealousy towards their own kin.

This is all a lie. It is a case of jealousy *(vayiru ericcal)*. If you are doing well, those who envy you speak like that. Honest people don't talk like that. If one can kill people by doing *mantiram*, the world would not be there. That is all empty talk. People believe it.... I have studied till sixth standard.... Ten years ago, this happened. I have still not forgotten. I still have that resolve (*vairākiyam*).

Rangam's comments highlight the skepticism many women attach to such practices. They have seen many such 'magical investigations' turn out to be untrue. People, whether or not they perform the ritual, use it as an excuse to accuse a neighbour or relative of witchcraft, jealousy, or theft. Not all women buy into the theory that such investigations will uncover hidden truths. Like the Guruji of Jharsetli that Kakar talked about, they also believe that people are not sitting around waiting to commit sorcery on others (Kakar, 2002: 257). These practices are more widespread in the villages than in the city.

Some people claimed that being poor protected them from harm because poverty did not invite jealousy. As Murugesan's comment in the beginning of this article shows, he was a part of increasing group of young, educated men (and women) who strongly disapproved of *kani*. He would not "touch" his father's traditional occupation of making leather from animal skin, and preferred working in a factory instead. He worried about the impact of September 11, 2001 on his job. Murugesan worked in a shoe factory that exported its products to Italy. The company's orders were cancelled and he was told it was because of U.S. response after 9/11. Drinking garden lizard's blood as cure did not make sense to him.

Like Murugesan, Jamuna of Yelagiri was also unimpressed with *kani* sessions. She had lived in the industrial town of Hosur for a few years, and constantly expressed herself to be more travelled and knowledgeable than her friends in Yelagiri. She was unhappy to return to Yelagiri, but had to do so because of economic compulsions. For the past one year, Jamuna was not keeping well.[21] Her family thought she may have been possessed by a spirit and took her to a *mantirikarar.* Jamuna told me that she had been treated by a local folk healer near Ponneri (a bigger village) for spirit possession. Almost laughing, she narrated the experience.

I went because I was told I was caught by a ghost. They hit me with a whip! It (the ghost) will go only if it is there. Nothing 'caught' me. I had no faith. Only expenses remain. Eight hundred rupees. I told (them) I will not give money since there was no ghost!"

Whyte talks of a client in Uganda who refused to pay a diviner because "he did not believe her assessment of the cause of his misfortune" (Whyte, 1982: 2058). For some, it was not so much disbelief as distaste. Both Vasantha and her sister-in-law in Yelagiri, were critical of the magicians who give consultation for *kani*. "The more we see, the more bad things will happen", Vasantha's sister-in-law said. Vasantha claimed that magicians always say that someone has cast a spell if asked for cause of illness. "I do not believe them at all... If we give them ten rupees, they will say 'it is *seyvinai*", she said.

Casting Illness

I now describe the only meeting I had with a magical healer, Karuppan in Yelagiri. I was led to him by Prema. She was initially reluctant and asked me several times why I wanted to meet a magician (*mantirakarar*). No one wanted to accompany me. Finally, one day, we took an auto and went to the person's house on top of a small mound, right on the main road. Opposite his hut were lush green fields, which I came to know later were owned by him. Three women and one man were already in a meeting with Karuppan.

His consultation area was a small hut with a thatch roof. Dried shrubs were lying on a wooden landing. Karuppan's own house, another hut, was by the side of this hut. Karuppan was a tall, slim, dark man, fifty years old. His eyes were big, red and powerful. His speech and mannerisms were equally dramatic. Heavy smoking rendered his lips grey. He was in white shirt and *khaki* shorts. A multi-coloured scarf *(tuntu)* hung around his shoulders. His personal wealth was for all to see. He had a huge gold chain on his neck, two gold rings on his left hand and one on the right. He had some powders and black *mai* (pigment applied to the eyes) next to him.

Karuppan said he learnt magic *(mantiram)* from practitioners from Kerala and has practicing from the age of seventeen. He claimed to have clients from Pune and Delhi. His monthly income in 2002 was around two to three thousand rupees. Karuppan claimed to cure vaginal discharge (*ve<u>l</u>lai patuta<u>l</u>*), pain in the limbs (*kai, kāl vali*), *seyvinai*, diabetes (*cakkara viyāti)*, high blood pressure, infertility and mental illness. He went to a place called "Sanjeevi herb hill" to collect herbs. He listed the herbs he would collect at sunrise, at sunset, and some at midnight. "You should turn left and then collect with a right hand." He also removed the black thread around his hip and clothes and performed a *pūjā*. He usually went to collect herbs and prepared medicine during an auspicious time on new moon day.

Karuppan made his own *kulacam* (charms). He claimed not to do *kani*. Karuppan argued that he could cure sexually transmitted diseases such as AIDS. Yelagiri has recently seen a spurt of cases of AIDS, brought in by "people from below", from places like Madras. Small onions soaked overnight in buttermilk was a cure for STD. For epilepsy, Karuppan gave a medicine for three days, and put patients on a strict diet of pepper *racam* (watery soup) and to avoid oil and rice. In order to stay healthy, Karuppan did not drink coffee or tea. He had only *kanci*.

Like many others in Yelagiri and Tirupattur, Karuppan found allopathic medical system lacking in many ways. "A *siddha vaitiyar* will scold the patient. In a hospital no one will ask questions." Scolding a patient showed a kind of care and interest a healer had, which he and many women in Yelagiri believed, was lacking in biomedical practitioners. Karuppan positioned himself as a practitioner of *Siddha* medicine while the people of Yelagiri saw him as a magician. In his view, his rude behaviour was, therefore, justified. His duty was not only to cure the afflicted person of physical suffering, but also to act as a disciplinarian and point out the faults in their way of living. Most of his clients "come after they have tried English medicine. They tell me that themselves. I then ask them to stop taking English medicine." Karuppan did not treat his wife or his three children (two daughters and one son). His treatment would not work on them. When I finally got some time to talk to him, he asked me not to tape his conversations. Fake sorcerers and magicians were a real problem, Karuppan felt. He particularly did not like men who misbehaved with other women or female clients.

The cook in the guest house where I stayed did not think much of Karuppan. She said, "He takes money claiming to tie some *kulacam*...five hundred to thousand rupees. That is a lot." Her complaint about Karuppan was similar to women complaining about the increase in consultation fee among biomedical doctors. Karuppan seemed to agree; he claimed he had *kulacam* in different price ranges; five hundred, thousand or four thousand rupees. But Karuppan worried whether his practice would survive after his lifetime. His son expressed no interest in learning *mantiram*. Like healers elsewhere in India, Karuppan claimed to provide cure for many of women's health problems, such as infertility, dysmennorhea and vaginal discharge.

Conclusion

Women partake in the state's health care apparatus not because they have been told that it is good, but because they see it as essential for their ownselves. Their anger is not so much that there are no facilities available. Except for Yelagiri in 2002, the other places were reasonably connected with the state apparatus. Women in the villages of Tirupattur have to travel between six to ten kilometres before they can access a Government facility. For their counterparts in Chennai, distance is not a problem. The issue is of affordability, in a city that is becoming more expensive everyday but where their salaries as 'servants' has not necessarily increased.

For women, therefore, finding various methods to take care of their health becomes important. In Chennai, women spoke very little of magic and rituals. They talked more about the role played (or not played) by alcoholic husbands. In Tirupatur and Yelagiri, however, sorcery accusations formed a significant part of their discourse about health. In the same breath, most of them expressed their doubts in the efficacy of sorcery examinations.

My conclusion that women in Tamil Nadu do not regard sorcery as all that important stems from another evidence. While Nabokov says the lack of literature on sorcery in Tamil Nadu is due to the fact that people either hated it or feared it (2000), the women I met for the most part were quite nonchalant. To my question about what they would do if they were ill, they would say in the same breath "we will go to the doctor. We will do *kani*." Those who consulted a sorcerer did not hesitate to say so. I did not get a sense of "feelings of disbelief, fear and abhorrence" about *kani* sessions (Nabokov, 2000a). As long as it offered them an explanation they already suspected, or something they could not get from consulting other health care practitioners, women seemed not to mind consulting *mantirakarar* for *kani*. Whyte suggests something similar when she points out the crucial role a client plays in a divination wherein the result must be acceptable to the client (Whyte, 1982: 2058). It could explain why *kani* sessions were more prevalent in rural areas where women thought they could be involved in treating illness, as opposed to biomedical examinations, where they are just told what to do. They feel a lack of agency when interacting with biomedical specialists while sorcery allows them more involvement in health care decision-making.

There was general agreement that a person casting a spell on them cannot be prevented. What could be done was to identify who cast it and caused the illness, and find ways to remove the spell. Women were active agents in this process. I am not arguing here that because women took decisions to consult sorcerers, that it is good for their health. On the contrary, my meeting with a sorcerer in Yelagiri and one old Muslim magician in Tirupattur (who was almost blind) left me feeling quite concerned. While the sorcerer exuded over confidence, the Muslim cleric merely did his job of tying amulets because people asked for it. He was not too confident of it himself.

My argument is that for some women, the effect of sorcery was very real, felt in their body or mind but with real social causes. Some women I met did not agree completely with the power of sorcery.[22] They were very critical of the *pūcari*, *mantirakārar* or *vaitiyar*, the men involved in predicting and removing sorcery spells. They were also not sure if that was the only way to approach the problem. Rather than consult a sorcerer at the end of "hierarchy of resort" (Romanuci-Ross, 1977), I found most women to be simultaneously engaged in consultation with various systems of medicine at the same time.

When an illness does not respond to any treatment, women tend to blame it on *seyvinai*. I found this opinion more acute among women in Yelagiri. They felt that jealousy had the potency to create severe misfortune. Neighbours and relatives were accused as participants. But the social structure of the place is such that most of the neighbours were kin. There were strict sanctions against marrying out of the community. Most marriages tended to be within the hills, with women moving from one hamlet to another. So, women felt they were surrounded by relatives who could create harm if provoked. In approaching a sorcerer to check whether their suspicions were correct, or to even remove a spell, women were only exercising their agency. They wanted to know what was wrong with them, why it had happened, who had caused the affliction, and what could be done to alleviate their suffering.

Notes

1. Crea's *Contemporary Tamil Dictionary,* 2004: 471.
2. In the areas where I did fieldwork, a sorcerer/magician is also a "healer" to whom people go to obtain a cure. A magician or sorcerer is called a *mantirakarar*, and the word *mantiram* can also mean 'magic' or spell in Tamil.
3. Yela-giri meaning the 'mountain of cardamom'.
4. For a detailed history see Danielle Edwards, 1999.
5. There were no Urdu medium schools in Tirupattur in 2002.
6. *Dosam* can mean 'sin' or 'fault'. It refers to adverse influence believed to be caused by planetary movement. See Fuller, 2004: 241.
7. This is where Nabokov did research. Perhaps Prema went to a *cami.*
8. A sorcerer. Unlike her, though, I did meet one *mantirakārar.*
9. For a detailed discussion on sorcery rituals, see Nabokov's monograph (2000). In her article in the same year (2000a), see the footnotes.
10. Nabokov translates *seyvinai* as a metalinguistic phrase which means 'making a verb active' (*see* Notes to Article 4, Nabokov, 2000:193) or an 'activating process' to describe the point when a sorcerer infuses life into the image he makes for counter-sorcery (2000:57). I find this translation very inadequate to explain what people meant by the term. They saw it as an act by itself.
11. A command; can also mean 'removal' as in removing evil eye, pollution (*tītu).*
12. *Kuri*—Reading signs or fortune (*Crea Dictionary*, 2004:339).
13. Kakar (2002: 172) offers a more textual explanation of a *mantra* as well as its use in *tantrism.* He defines a *mantra* as a "sequence of sound units with a characteristic pronunciation and intonation".
14. For a detailed discussion on sorcery, magic, and witchcraft in India, see Fuller, 2004, article on misfortune.
15. The closest word to this in the dictionary is *koluvu*—to entangle or catch.
16. An exorcist/healer. Nabokov calls them "independent religious entrepreneurs" who received the ability to interpret signs through visions and visits from goddesses (2000a).
17. Nabokov finds resonance in Sax (1985) analysis of *pal* or fruit.
18. A corruption of *irukkaravanga*—the haves as opposed to *lladhavanga,* the have-nots. *Iruppu*—to have, in this case, wealth.
19. Belief in evil eye is present across many cultures (for examples in Egypt, *see* Inhorn, 1994).

20. The verb *varugai* means 'coming'. A disease or ailment 'comes'. And it comes to a 'body', not a person.
21. Saraswathi, the CRHSE coordinator told me that Jamuna's poor health was due to the number of abortions she underwent. Jamuna refuted this claim to me.
22. Nabokov says men are the usual targets of sorcery spells (2000: 49). But I found women saying they were also vulnerable to sorcery spells.

References

Ahearn, Laura M. (2001). Language and agency. *Annual Review of Anthropology*, 30:109-137.

Cre-A. 2004. *Contemporary Tamil Dictionary*. Chennai: Cre-A.

Edwards, Danielle. (1999). Unpublished report submitted to CRHSE.

Fuller, C.J. 2004 [1992]. *The Camphor Flame: Popular Hinduism and Society in India*. Princeton: Princeton University Press.

Gold, Ann Grodzins and Bhoju Ram Gujar. (2002). *In the Time of Trees and Sorrows: Nature, Power and Memory in Rajasthan*. Duke University Press.

Hancock, Mary. (1999). *Womanhood in the Making: Domestic Ritual and Public Culture in Urban South India*. Colorado: Westview Press.

Inhorn, Marcia. (1994). *Quest for Conception: Gender, Infertility and Egyptian Medical Systems*. Philadelphia: University of Pennsylvania Press.

Janzen, John M. (1978). *The Quest for Therapy in Lower Zaire*. Berkeley: University of California Press.

Kakar, Sudhir (2002). *Shamans, Mystics, and Doctors: A Psychological Inquiry into India and its Healing Traditions*. Oxford: Oxford University Press.

Kapadia, Karin. (1995). *Siva and her Sisters: Gender, Caste and Class in Rural South India*. Boulder: Westview Press.

Lambek, Michael. (1993). *Knowledge and Practice in Mayotte: Local Discourses of Islam, Sorcery, and Spirit Possession*. Toronto: University of Toronto Press.

Nabokov, Isabelle. (2000). *Religion Against the Self: An Ethnography of Tamil Rituals*. Oxford: Oxford University Press.

_______. (2000a). Deadly power: A funeral to counter sorcery in South India. *American Ethnologist*, 27(1):147-168.

Nichter, Mark and Carolyn Nordstrom. (1989). A question of medicine answering: health commodification and the social relations of healing in Sri Lanka. *Culture, Medicine and Psychiatry*, 13(4): 367-390.

Romanuci-Ross, L. (1977). The Hierarchy of Resort in Curative Practices: The Admiralty Islands Melanesia. *In Culture, Disease and Healing: Studies in Medical Anthropology*. David Landy. ed. New York: MacMillan.

Sax, William S. (1991). *Mountain Goddess: Gender and Politics in a Himalayan Pilgrimage*. New York: Oxford University Press.

Trawick, Margaret. (1992). *Notes on Love in a Tamil Family*. Berkeley: University of California Press.

Unnithan-Kumar, Maya. (2003). Spirits of the womb: Migration, reproductive choice and healing in Rajasthan. *Contributions to Indian Sociology,* 37(1 and 2): 163-188.

Van Hollen, Cecilia. (2003). *Birth on the Threshold: Childbirth and Modernity in South India.* Berkeley: University of California Press.

Whyte, Susan Reynolds. (1982). Penicillin, Battery Acid and Sacrifice. *Social Science and Medicine,* 16(23): 2055-2064.

INDIAN MEDICAL SYSTEMS

4

"God's Hospitals" with "No Superstition!" On the Place of Healing Shrines in Contemporary India

Shubha Ranganathan

Indigenous Healing in India: Pluralisms and Marginalities

The last few decades have seen a proliferation of scholarship on the varieties of medical systems in India, particularly following the publication of Leslie's (1976) seminal volume *Asian Medical Systems*. With respect to India, the co-existence of myriad and variegated forms of healing has long been recognized by anthropologists and historians of medicine.[1] Much of the literature on medical pluralism in India has focused on the parallel existence of two broad categories: biomedicine or Western medicine on the one hand, also referred to as 'cosmopolitan medicine' (Dunn, 1976) or 'modern medicine'; and 'Indian medicine' or 'indigenous medicine' on the other hand.

Two related trends can be discerned in the discourse on indigenous medicine. Firstly, the scholarship on Indian medicine has concentrated on the elite 'high' traditions, leaving out other traditions such as non-Sanskritic and folk medical traditions, Unani, Siddha, and religious healing (Attewell, 2007). Practices of 'faith healing' or 'folk healing,' including visiting indigenous shamans or shrines reputed to heal afflictions, are also usually left out of the discourse on Indian medicine, even though they are resorted to in large numbers in India, particularly among sufferers of mental illness (*see*, e.g. Addlakha, 2008; Dwyer, 2003; Sébastia, 2007, 2009).

Secondly, indigenous medicine is largely conceptualized in terms of its relation to biomedicine: it is constructed either as the *opposite* of biomedicine, or as another *kind* of medicine. At the same time, it is increasingly recognized that these binaries—local and western, indigenous and biomedical, traditional and modern—are no longer tenable (Attewell, 2007; Pati and Harrison, 2001). Contemporary Indian medical traditions like Ayurveda and Unani have been transformed into "modern traditions" (Bode, 2008: 3), drawing on images from Indian civilization and culture, as well as modern science and technology. Having acquired means for procuring and maintaining credibility and legitimacy, through recognized courses, universities, and degrees, they have succeeded in projecting themselves as both professional and traditional. On the other hand, the 'folk' traditions, including unregulated and unlicensed 'faith healers', largely do not fall within these institutionalized spaces and are deemed 'illegitimate' and 'unscientific' by the state, reflecting the politics of healing (Ram, 2010).

These observations indicate the complexities in the dialectic between the indigenous and the biomedical. Drawing on an ethnographic study of persons staying in the Mahanubhav temples for healing of spirit affliction, the chapter explores the transactions and negotiations between multiple contesting discourses in healing. Although conventional wisdom and academic discourse would draw up a differentiation between 'modern' and 'traditional' healing, or between 'biomedical treatment' and 'indigenous healing', patients themselves do not follow the same lines of distinction. This chapter highlights these complexities and complications by looking at how healing temples position themselves *vis-à-vis* biomedicine. At a time when the integration of indigenous healing shrines in mainstream health service delivery systems is being vigorously debated and pursued, these findings provide a critical perspective on discourses of 'collaboration' and 'integration'.

The Mahanubhav Healing Shrines in Maharashtra

The Mahanubhav sect is one of the many 'Little Traditions' of religion comprising folk movements, cults, and sects in Maharashtra (Kosambi, 2000). The thirteenth century saw the rise of various devotional sects as part of the *bhakti* movement that worked to challenge the orthodox Brahmanical religion (Feldhaus and Zelliot, 1984). Founded by Chakradhar (approximately A.D. 1194-1274), during the rule of the Yadava kings, the Mahanubhavs have a monotheistic belief in one God incarnated in five *avatars*, the Panchakrishna or the "five Krishnas" (Raeside, 1976).[2]

The Mahanubhav sect has a long tradition of providing succour to people suffering from various kinds of afflictions, particularly spirit-related afflictions (Skultans, 1991; Zelliot, 1988). The local term for spirit-related affliction is *baher cha dukkha*, namely, affliction that is caused by *baher cha* forces.[3] These spirit-related afflictions are understood as part of one's *dukkha*, a term with many layers of meanings. Most generally, *dukkha* means 'suffering'. However, it can also mean 'illness', 'pain', 'unhappiness', or 'distress'. Thus, spirit possession is understood as a particular kind of affliction caused by cosmic forces that are not of this world (hence 'outside'). Afflicted persons—who are termed 'patients'[4]—stay in the temple for a specified ritual period and participate in worship activities and rituals. The most important ritual is the *āruti* which is believed to induce trance in afflicted persons, thereby drawing out the ghost from the person.

The Temple Discourses of Healing

Healing Temples as 'God's Hospitals'

How do the Mahanubhav temples position themselves *vis-à-vis* biomedicine? When talking about the healing temples, patients and monks drew from both 'religious' and 'scientific', 'modernist' discourses of healing. Thus, they described the temple as a holy site that heals people through the power ("*shakthi*") of the place. D.T. Baba and S.R. Baba described how the temple at Sukene was constructed on the site (*sthaan*) where one of the five avatars rested during his travels. S.S. Baba said that the Mahanubhava temple at Phaltan was the birth place of another *avatar* and, therefore, had God's power (*shakthi*) concentrated in it.

At the same time, patients and monks also described temple healing in 'modern' and 'scientific' language. For instance, they often described the temple as a "hospital", using the English word. Thus, Satyabhama described the temple as "basically a temple for ill and afflicted people", particularly those affected by spirit-related problems. Her mother described the temple as "God's hospital", using the Marathi word *davākhānā*.[5] While elaborating on the amount of expenditure incurred on Satyabhama's treatment and her frequent stays in the temple, she said: "We spent about a hundred thousand rupees on her treatment." When I asked her if she had spent that amount of money on hospital treatment she retorted vehemently: "Not *those* [allopathic] hospitals—*this* hospital! *God's* hospital!" She then explained that they often referred to the temple as *devāchādava-khānā*: "God's hospital". Similarly, Mainabai explained: "This [temple] is nothing but a hospital! We all call this a hospital, God's hospital."

Patients also drew comparisons between the use of medicinal substances in allopathic treatment, and the rituals of *smarana* and *sevā* in the healing temple. Pramila explained:

When you go to a doctor, how do you get well? You have to take medicines, right? In the same way, here, you have to do *sevā* and *smarana* to get well.

Similarly, Satyabhama compared the rituals of the temple to medical treatment:

We get well here because of God. He makes us well. Just like when you go to a hospital, you get well by taking medicines, in the same way when you come here and do *smarana*, *paaraayana* [prayer readings], and *sevā*, you get well.

One of the monks described the *sevā* in the temple as analogous to medicine.

People get well through doing *sevā*. They get the fruit of their *sevā*. Just like a doctor gives medicines which have the power to cure, the *sevā* cures the person.

Another monk compared the deity in the temple to "a doctor who understands the *dukkha* and removes it". Every illness had its own specified period, he said, which one has to endure.

One has to endure the illness till it lasts. Just like doctors carry out tests and then give the prescription that one has to follow for ten or fifteen days, in the same way, one has to endure the illness for the period that it lasts.

In one Mahanubhav temple, there are even formal procedures for the 'admission' of patients into the temple. Every potential patient is first 'interviewed' by the monks and the head of the temple trust to determine that she satisfies the criteria to be 'admitted' into the temple. Only those who suffered from 'unidentified' symptoms and had been found to be free from HIV/AIDS and cancer were 'admitted', as one of the monks explained:

We do not accept those patients who are very sick and for whom there is no cure. We only accept those patients who do not have any identified physical illness but are still ill. Those patients with doubtful symptoms, who have been having serious physical symptoms since a long time, have to show a certificate from a doctor testifying that they are free from HIV/AIDS, cancer and other such serious illnesses.

The 'admission procedures', 'intake interviews', and 'selection criteria' illustrate the extent to which the temples have become medicalised into treatment centres whose primary function is to cure people from illnesses. The fact that patients with 'incurable' illnesses are denied admission into the temple also suggests the concern of the temple management with the 'curing rate' of the temple. These narratives clearly illustrate that the Mahanubhav temples are regarded as not just sacred spaces, but also as curing institutions analogous to modern hospitals.

However, apart from medicalization, what is also important here is the characterization of the shrine as a different *kind* of hospital/clinic for a different *kind* of illness—the *baher cha* illness. Thus, ghost affliction ('*baher cha dukkha*') is understood as a particular kind of affliction that differs from medical illnesses. While ghost illness is caused by unknown cosmic forces that are not of this world (hence 'outside'), medical illnessis caused by known natural forces. Biomedicine is seen as dealing with the 'medical' aspects of the problem, while the temple deals with the possessing ghost. As a monk explained:

Doctors don't really give medicines for the illness as such. They give medicines for appetite and sleep. They deal with patients as 'mentally affected' and give them medicines to calm them down. For the *illness*, patients can only get well at the temple.

Another monk reiterated:

Doctors can treat medical illnesses; temples heal ghost illnesses. Doctors can treat the illness if it is a medical illness. But when they cannot even diagnose the illness, when they carry out tests and discover new symptoms each time, then they realize that it's a *baher cha* illness or an illness caused by *karni* [sorcery]. These people would only get well through worshipping God.

Yet, the monks were not averse to patients receiving both medical treatment for the symptoms and temple healing to remove the possessing ghost. In some Mahanubhav temples, allopathic doctors made visits to the temples on specific days of the week, offering medical consultations. In fact, such arrangements worked to prove the 'modern' and 'rationalist' temper of the shrines.

Healing Temples as 'Modern' and 'Rationalist'

The monks in the temples also emphasised the 'scientific' nature of the healing in the temples. Thus, D.T. Baba spoke of the power of the temple "vibrations" (using the English word) to heal ill people since it was "touched" by God who visited that spot.

Just as a dog locates a thief through the trace of smell that he has left, God left his trace through his touch when he came here. When one puts one's head on the *otta*[6], that touch comes alive.... Since he visited this place, his touch remains here and through his power, suffering is removed.

Similarly, A.J. Baba described temple healing as providing "energy plus" to patients by making available a peaceful temple environment and routine for them. On coming to the temple, people's energy is renewed, he explained. Mahendra Swami explained how the "peaceful environment" of the temple helped patients who needed a change.

D.T. Baba explained how the temple practices of circumambulation (*pradakshina*) and prostration before the deity (*dandavata*) functioned as physical exercise for patients:

From a psychological perspective, one gets exercise. That is why prostrationis done. Just like the *suryanamaskara*, it provides exercise for all the important eight joints of the body. Circumambulation too works as an exercise.... Thus, all the activities of the temple routine are based on a scientific perspective.

The above narratives illustrate the use of the language of modern science and rationality to portray temple healing as 'scientific' and 'logical' rather than magical and supernatural. The use of the terms "vibrations" and "energy" from alternative medicine suggests an attempt to construct temple healing as something that is logical, scientific, and explicable by the laws of nature as opposed to something that is supernatural, magical, and unfathomable. In line with this, the monks in the temple at Phaltan also repeatedly asserted that there were no 'superstitious' practices in the temple. For instance, S.S. Baba spontaneously brought up the topic of superstition, saying:

In the past, about 25 years ago, there used to be numerous superstitious practices in the temple. However, subsequently, we abolished all these rituals. Now, there is no superstition in the temple... Now, there are more of those patients who have true faith and less of those who have blind faith (*andhashraddha*).

By admitting to the existence of 'superstitious' practices and "blind faith" in the past that had subsequently been abolished, S.S. Baba's claim of the temple being presently free from superstition becomes more credible. To support this claim, he also pointed out that he often advised patients to seek medical treatment in addition to temple healing. In fact, the statements, "we have no superstition here" and "we advocate both medical treatment and temple healing" were often heard from the monks in the temple complex of Phaltan, as were discussions about 'blind faith', 'imaginary witchcraft'. Their discussions of witchcraft (*karni*) were complex—while they held that witchcraft often did cause people to get possessed, they also added that in many cases, witchcraft was not 'really' involved but was 'imagined' by participants. Thus, S.S. Baba complained about the problems that occur when people harbourdoubts and suspicions about others having performed black magic against them:

Most problems are caused because people do not understand and do not have faith. Because people doubt others. Doubting is the biggest cause of family problems—when people begin to doubt other family members.

Clearly, the monks' views about *karni* could not be reduced to simple 'beliefs' in possession and witchcraft. Rather, they revealed a complex mixture of skepticism and belief. These narratives bring out the fluidity in the temple discourses of healing. Although conventional wisdom and academic discourse would draw up a differentiation between 'modern' and 'traditional' healing, or between 'biomedical treatment' and 'indigenous healing', patients and monks do not follow the same lines of distinction. In fact, the temple discourses of healing make space for the biomedical, even while possession is framed as a non-medical *baher cha* illness.

The narratives of the monks and patients resist the urge to frame temple healing as *either* 'traditional' *or* 'modern'. Rather, they move between *both* of these categories, drawing from so-called 'traditional' discourses, as when describing the temple as a holy place, as well as drawing from 'scientific' discourses, as when describing temple healing in the language of "vibrations", "energy", and "exercise". Thus, the spaces of the Mahanubhav healing temples are characterised by constant negotiations between the 'traditional' and the 'modern', the biomedical and the indigenous. Such cross-overs and engagements between the 'traditional' and the 'modern' have also been found by Csordas (2004) in his studies on Navajo healing and Halliburton's (2005) study of spirit possession in Kerala. For instance, Halliburton found that in Kerala people incorporated 'modern' idioms from psychology and psychiatry into their 'traditional' discourse of possession. Thus, one person explained "depression" as what one felt when one was possessed by a spirit. Similarly, Dein, Alexander and Napier's (2008) study among East London Bangladeshis found that local healers (*imams*) used medical and psychological idioms in their discourses of religious healing. On the one hand, they spoke about 'depression' as a biomedical diagnosis, which requires psychiatric intervention. At the same time, they opined that when 'depression' did not respond to such biomedical treatment, it might indicate that it was actually a case of *jinn* possession which would require exorcism. These findings illustrate that the binary categories of 'traditional' and 'modern', 'global' and 'local', 'expert' and 'lay', 'scientific' and 'magical' suggest a dichotomy that exists more in discourse than in practice.

Re-thinking Healing: From **Medical Systems** *to* **Medical Practices**

Much of the conceptualization of indigenous healing follows from the notion of the existence of alternate 'medical systems'. Following

Dunn's (1976) categorization of medical systems into 'local medical systems' (including 'primitive' or 'folk medicine'), 'regional medical systems' (e.g. Ayurveda and Unani), and 'cosmopolitan medicine' (biomedicine), scholars have identified medical systems as watertight compartments (despite the fact that Dunn pointed out that local systems are always in contact with other systems). The literature on medical pluralism reflects the same notion of medical systems: there are references to cross-fertilization and cross-prescribing[7]; it is acknowledged that 'traditional systems' are increasingly becoming modernized and commercialized; and it is recognized that patients adopt a pragmatic approach in their use of pluralistic therapies. Yet, the literature on medical pluralism maintains the existence of independent, autonomous healing systems.

The use of the term 'system' carries certain implications. As Attewell (2007) has pointed out, it connotes a coherent, homogenous body of knowledge and practice, although, in actual practice, there is much more heterogeneity and variation than allowed for in the term 'system'. This chapter has shown how, even within indigenous discourses of possession and healing, there is room for biomedicine to complement indigenous healing. Patients and monks do not have ready-made beliefs about the causes of illnesses but deploy various kinds of languages and make use of various types of therapies (Das and Das, 2007).

I suggest, therefore, that instead of speaking of *medical systems*, which implies universal, static, and systematized knowledge systems, it might be more useful to focus on *medical practices*, which are dynamic and diverse. The focus in the latter shifts to what these practices do. An emphasis on medical practices rather than systems also draws attention to the agency of the afflicted. At a time when the integration of indigenous healing shrines in mainstream health service delivery systems is being vigorously debated and pursued, these findings provide a critical perspective on the place of healing shrines.

Conclusion: The Place of Healing Shrines in Contemporary India

I have tried to give demonstrate the complex ways by which the patients and monks frame temple healing as simultaneously spiritual and scientific. At the same time, the monks' narratives about 'scientific healing' also have to be understood in relation to two broader socio-political trends in the state of Maharashtra. Firstly, the rationalist anti-superstition movement in Maharashtra has been engaged in a drive to 'expose' and illegalize the practices of 'charlatans', 'quacks', and 'unscientific' monks through lectures and demonstrations. While they have succeeded in getting many godmen and *tantriks* exposed and arrested, healing centres have also been the target of their rationalist and reformist activities and have faced threats to closure.

Secondly, healing shrines have come under the radar of both public and Government scrutiny particularly following the Erwadi incident on 6th August, 2001 when a fire in a private home attached to a *dargah* in the town of Erwadi, Ramanathapuram district (Tamil Nadu, India) caught fire and 27 mentally ill inmates, chained to their beds, perished. The incident sparked widespread public outrage and heated debates about legal and human rights issues related to mentally disabled persons from various quarters—the media, mental health and human rights activists, legal experts, mental health professionals, non-Governmental organizations, and the general public. The Supreme Court of India issued *suo motu* notices to the State and Central Governments, asking them to submit reports on all unregistered bodies for mentally disabled persons. Numerous private mental asylums were closed and inmates transferred to mental hospitals. The Supreme Court's action spurred increased vigilance over indigenous healing centres all over the country—in a process that Davar and Lohokare (2009) referred to as "witch hunting" (p. 61). The aim of this monitoring was to either close down the healing centres and pressurize people to take recourse to mental hospitals, or make it mandatory for healing centres to obtain a licence and comply with the directives of the Mental Health Act. Clearly, healing shrines are regarded either as superstitious and regressive spaces, or as potential mental health institutions. It is clear that the monks' attempts to legitimize temple healing as modern and scientific is at least in part a response to these developments.

At the same time, the drive to transform healing shrines into modern scientific institutions has the danger of resulting in considerable homogenization and commercialization of these spaces. Such developments are seen in the 'high' Indian medical traditions of Ayurveda and Unani, which have certified themselves as professional and modern, with their institutions, degrees, and technologies (Bode, 2008). Indigenous healing shrines are still relatively shielded from market forces. However, with government requirements of licensing, with the push to become incorporated in the mental health sector, healing shrines are likely to align themselves according to government requirements and specifications. This means one would expect increasing commercialization and marketization of shrines as 'healing spaces'. Paradoxically, such streamlining might in fact reduce the healing power of these shrines. Perhaps the most powerful aspect of healing shrines is their dynamic and fluid quality, which is capitalized by patients in a variety of ways. The temple discourses of healing that alternate between the biomedical and the indigenous element of healing shrines illustrates this complexity and dynamism, which is perhaps at the heart of the healing dimensions of these spaces.

Notes

1. Different phrases have been used to speak about the existence of plural medical traditions in India. While Khare (1996) speaks of a "heterogenous cultural model" of practiced medicine, Sujatha (2007) refers to the "pluralism of genres".
2. The Mahanubhava sect practices in the worship of five incarnations (*avatars*) of Parmeshwar (God)—Krishna, Dattatreya, Govind Prabhu, Chang Dev Rao (Chakrabani Prabhu), and Chakradhar. The last *Avatar*, Chakradhar, is considered to be the founder of the Mahanubhav sect. According to Raeside's (1976) account, Chakradhar, known as Haripaldev, was the son of Vishaldev, a Gujarati Brahmin minister from Bharuch. Haripaldev died at an early age but his body was reanimated by the soul of Chang Dev Raul, the third *avatara* (incarnation) of Parameshwar. He later became the disciple of Gundam Raul (Govinda Prabhu), the fourth incarnation of God. The early Mahanubhav texts describe the next twelve years of his life as a phase of seclusion ('*ekaanku*'), during which he travelled in Andhra Pradesh and Maharashtra. This was followed by a phase of pilgrimage, during which he travelled and preached his doctrine, acquiring many disciples. Minute details are given about his travels, including the names of all the villages where he stopped, the number of days he stayed in any one place, and so on. Chakradhar's open opposition to the Brahmin orthodoxy earned him the hatred of the Brahman ministers of the king, Ramdevraja Yadava. He was eventually arrested and beheaded by them. His death is estimated to have

occurred in A.D. 1274. After Chakradhar's death, the followers gathered around Gundam Raul, till his death. When he died, the leadership of the sect was taken over by an ardent devotee of Chakradhar, Nagdev. After Nagdev's death, the sect became a scriptural tradition, with devotees basically following the sacred texts rather than any person or *guru*.

3. '*Baher cha*' (literally, 'of/from the outside') refers to 'outside' forces related to the supernatural or spirit realm. *Baher cha* afflictions are those caused by supernatural factors such as ghosts and not by natural forces.
4. In the Mahanubhav temples, the term 'patient' is used by healers, monks, and the afflicted to refer to afflicted persons staying in the temples for 'treatment', as distinguished from those who make a day trip to the temple for worship. By using a term that draws from the biomedical model, I do not intend to pathologize possession or to draw attention to the afflicted status of persons experiencing possession. While I am aware of the need to problematize the use of this term, that issue is beyond the scope of this paper. I use this term in keeping with its usage in the local context of the temples.
5. *Davākhānā* could be translated as clinic, medical dispensary, or hospital. I prefer the meaning of hospital here as in this context patients are referring to the temple not simply as a dispensary of medicines but as a place that one goes to when one is sick; therefore, 'hospital' would be more appropriate.
6. The *otta* is characteristic of all Mahanubhav temples. It is a platform placed in the *sanctum sanctorum* of the templeand worshipped. Typically, it is covered with an ornate cloth and stone idols of Krishna and the other incarnations of God are placed on it and worshipped.
7. Bode (2008) refers to allopathic doctors prescribing Ayurvedic tonics such as Septilin and Ayurvedic doctors prescribing antibiotics.

References

Addlakha, R. (2008). *Deconstructing Mental Illness: An Ethnography of Psychiatry, Women and the Family*. New Delhi: Zubaan.

Attewell, G. (2007). *Refiguring Unanitibb: Plural Healing in late Colonial India*. Hyderabad: Orient Longman.

Biehl, J., Good, B., and Kleinman, A. (Eds.). (2007). *Subjectivity: Ethnographic Investigations*. Berkeley: University of California Press.

Bode, M. (2008). *Taking Traditional Knowledge to the Market: The Modern Image of the Ayurvedic and Unani Industry 1980-2000*. Hyderabad: Orient Longman.

Csordas, T.J. (2004). Healing and the human condition: Scenes from the present moment in Navajoland. *Culture, Medicine and Psychiatry*, 28, 1-4.

Das, V. and Das, K.R. (2007). How the body speaks: Illness and the lifeworld among the urban poor. In J. Biehl, B. Good, and A. Kleinman (Eds.).

Subjectivity: Ethnographic Investigations (pp. 66-97). Berkeley: University of California Press.

Davar, B. and Lohokare, M. (2009). Recovering from Psychological Traumas: The place of Dargahs in Maharashtra. *Economic and Political Weekly*, 44 (16), 60-67.

Dein, S., Alexander, M., and Napier, A.D. (2008). Jinn, psychiatry and contested notions of misfortune among East London Bangladeshis. *Transcultural Psychiatry,* 45(1), 31-55.

Doron, A. and Broom, A. (Eds.). (2010). *Health, Culture, and Religion in South Asia: Critical Perspectives*. Oxon: Routledge.

Dunn, F.L. (1976). Traditional Asian medicine and cosmopolitan medicine as adaptive systems. In C. Leslie (Ed.). *Asian Medical Systems: A Comparative Study* (pp. 133-158). Berkeley: University of California Press.

Dwyer, G. (2003). *The Divine and the Demonic: Supernatural Affliction and its Treatment in North India*. London. Routledge Curzon.

Feldhaus, A. and Zelliot, E. (1984). *The Deeds of God in Rddhipur*. Translated from the Marathi and annotated by Anne Feldhaus with introductory essays by Anne Feldhaus and Eleanor Zelliot. Oxford: Oxford University Press.

Halliburton, M. (2005). "Just some spirits": The erosion of spirit possession and the rise of "tension" in South India. *Medical Anthropology*, 24, 111-144.

Khare, S.R. (1996). Dava, daktar and dua: Anthropology of Practiced Medicine in India. *Social Science and Medicine*, 43 (5), 837-848.

Kosambi, M. (Ed.). (2000). *Intersections: Socio-cultural Trends in Maharashtra*. New Delhi: Orient Longman.

Kosambi, M. (2000). Introduction. In M. Kosambi (Ed.). *Intersections: Socio-Cultural Trends in Maharashtra* (pp. 1-12). New Delhi: Orient Longman.

Leslie, C. (1976). *Asian Medical Systems: A Comparative Study*. Berkeley: University of California Press.

Pati, B. and Harrison, M. (Eds.). (2001). *Health, Medicine, and Empire: Perspectives on Colonial India*. Hyderabad: Orient Longman.

Raeside, M.P. (1976). The Mahanubhavas. *Bulletin of the School of Oriental and African Studies*, 39 (3), 585-600.

Ram, K. (2010). Class and the clinic: The subject of medical pluralism and the transmission of inequality. In A. Doron and A. Broom. (Eds.). *Health, Culture, and Religion in South Asia: Critical Perspectives* (pp. 15-34). Oxon: Routledge.

Sébastia, B. (2007). A protective fortress: Psychic disorders and therapy at the Catholic shrine of Puliyampatti (South India). *Indian Anthropologist,* 37 (1), 67-92.

Sébastia, B. (2009). The last resort: Why patients with severe mental disorders go to therapeutic shrines in India. In B. Sébastia (Ed.). *Restoring Mental Health in India: Pluralistic Therapies and Concepts* (184-209). New Delhi: Oxford University Press.

Sībastia, B. (Ed.). (2009). *Restoring Mental Health in India: Pluralistic Therapies and Concepts*. New Delhi: Oxford University Press.

Skultans, V. (1991). Women and affliction in Maharashtra: A hydraulic model of health and illness. *Culture, Medicine, and Psychiatry,* 15, 321-359.

Sujatha, V. (2007). Pluralism in Indian medicine: Medical lore as a genre in medical knowledge. *Contributions to Indian Sociology (new series)* 41 (2), 169-202.

Zelliot, E. (1988). Introduction. In E. Zelliot and M. Berntsen (Eds.). *The Experience of Hinduism: Essays on Religion in Maharashtra* (pp. xv-xx). Albany: State University of New York Press.

Zelliot, E. and Berntsen, M. (Eds.). (1988). *The Experience of Hinduism: Essays on Religion in Maharashtra.* Albany: State University of New York Press.

5
Emergence of Ayurveda as a Classical Tradition

K. Girija

In this chapter I will look at the process through which a pure Ayurveda is historicized as the classical tradition[1] of Kerala at the cost of a variety of practices or Ayurvedas. Most of them were non-codified traditions and some of them were indeed codified textual traditions and as old as 'Ayurveda'. By the twentieth century, medical practice gained a respectful status as well as became an earning profession.[2] The negotiation and competition to control a commonly shared public space of medicine led to various public interventions. This includes capital investment in establishing educational institutions, producing medicine with shelf-life, printing and publishing books on medicine, forming associations of *vaidyas* (medical practitioners) and continuously debating the notions of health and body in the public sphere. Individual body becomes a social body and an object of knowledge around which a variety of debates begin to occur. These formations, along with print culture, changing economic relations, new associations and institutional frameworks emerged in the eighteenth and nineteenth century India acted as an umbrella space for the intermingling of a range of "subjects positioned unequally, in their renegotiation of knowledge and power" (Gyan, 1999). In these processes some practices attained the role of a professional classic tradition with various kinds of validations or accepted truth claims of colonial modernity[3] (Ayurveda). At the same time, they adhere to their own tenets. Some others got pushed to the margin as folk medical practices (*nattuvaidyam*). Even within Ayurveda, some practices did not get a prominent role though they were an integral part of that tradition and had been an important specialized and unique medical tradition of a particular region[4] for quite some time (*vishavaidyam*). Some other practice was not at all seen as a healing tradition even though its medicines and methods of treatment often overlapped with those of Ayurveda (*kalari*). It is often termed as sports medicine even when people largely depend upon this healing system for bone injuries and muscle injuries.[5] Some others were left as esoteric because of the secrecy in their practice and medicinal preparations (*Siddhavaidyam*[6], *Ottamulivaidyam*[7]).

I will unravel the process of rendering certain knowledge forms more visible and hence authentic at the cost of certain other knowledges. I will also point out a few continuities and ruptures in the reconfiguration of *nattuvaidyam*. Scholars have argued that the reconfiguration of Ayurveda has happened through the selection and rejection of modern elements (Panikkar, 2007; Sivaramakrishnan, 2001; Alavi, 2007). The selective choice of colonial modernity in its interaction with and administration of indigenous practice is equally relevant in rendering visibility and authenticity to certain practices. The process of acquiring authenticity and authority for one among many indigenous healing practices, as the classic tradition of India, hints at a powerful textual tradition's capacity in joining hands with similar kinds of classical practices in other regions. The process also renders invisibility to other age-old textual traditions such as *siddha vaidyam* by making them an esoteric practice or just a subset of Ayurveda. In this process what is erased or underplayed are the contributions and the role played by a range of indigenous practices or 'Ayurvedas' in rendering one among them as an authentic classic tradition. The diverse practices were not stagnant; they also reconfigured, renegotiated and asserted themselves. The Neo-literate *vaidyas* of these practices, especially those who got access to the secular modern educational space, played an important role in this process. Their renegotiation sometimes acted as a threatening and hence controlling force in the consolidation of an authentic tradition. The whole process cannot be seen as a unique feature of a particular region like Kerala. The authenticity and authority claim of a particular practice is strengthened through making alliance with similar practices in other regions and also through the contours of a nation's imagined territory.

What Constitutes Ayurveda?

Let us start from the most basic question. What constitutes Ayurveda? Is it *tridosha* principle[8] of body? Is it the *Samhita* texts (*Charaka Samhita* and *Sushruta Samhita)* which Ayurveda claimed as its source? Is it divinity of the age old texts and yet their contemporaneity? Is it Sanskrit language that was widely used for codifying medical practice? Is it patronage? Or is it something else? Let me examine now each and every elements employed for asserting the validity of Ayurveda as a classical tradition.

If it is *tridosha* principle that makes Ayurveda distinct from other practices, then almost all *nattuvaidyam—kalarivaidyam*, *visha-vaidyam*, *marmani vaidyam*, *siddha vaidyam*, *chintamani vaidyam*, *ottamulivaidyam* etc. to name a few is more or less based on this principle. So, it is not easy to say how a codified and textual Ayurveda became a distinct and authentic traditional medical practice of a region among all these practices. Ayurveda has very close interaction with all these traditions. What is Ayurveda itself is a contested issue, because all of these medicinal traditions are based on *tridosha siddhantham.* The plants and herbs, minerals and metals used in treatment are varied, based on their availability in each specific region. The combination of their usage also differs in each tradition. This is equally applicable to Ayurveda medicines too.[9] If that is the case then what is unique in Ayurveda about *tridosha* principle?

To consider the textual tradition of Ayurveda as its source, one has to take into account other textual traditions that co-exist with Ayurveda. Ayurveda practice is believed to be based on "the great three some" (*bṛhattrayi*), the *Charaka Samhita*, *Sushruta Samhita* and *Ashtanga Hridayam* (Wujastyk Dominik, 1998). All over India the first two *samhitas* are believed to be widely used by Ayurveda. Bit in South India *Sushruta Samhita* and *Charaka Samhita* were rarely used in the nineteenth century[10] (Raghavan, 2010). Especially in Kerala, Ayurveda practitioners did not use *samhita* texts for their practice. The accepted Sanskrit texts among Brahmin *vaidyas* were *Ashtanga Hridayam* and *Ashtanga Sarasamgraham* which were believed to be written after the *samhita* period.[11] However, the widely used texts across communities were *Sahasrayogam, Dharakalpam, Vaidyamanorama, Chikitsamanjari, Yogamritam, Sarvaroga-chikitsaratnam, Vaidyasarasamgraham* etc.[12] Written in Sanskrit, Malayalam, Manipravalam[13], Tamil or Arabi-Malayalam.[14] These were all written or interpreted by well-versed *nattu vaidya/Ayurveda* practitioners of Kerala (Unnikrishnan, 2011; Vinayachandran, 2011). Apart from these texts there were other textual traditions.

Siddhavaidyam has an age old textual tradition believed to be given by gods to *rishis* just like *samhitas* in Ayurveda. Agastyar *rishi* is believed to have brought the practice to earth and gave it to 84 *siddhars* (some believe this as 18 *siddhars*) who further taught it to their disciples.[15] *Siddhavaidyam* is believed to have originated in Dravidian tradition and it is largely seen in southern Kerala and Tamil Nadu (Banerjee, 2010). In contrast to *Siddhavaidyam's* Dravidian tradition, Ayurveda argued for and claimed an Aryan origin[16] (Varier, Krishna, 1906; Varier, 1980). The older texts that are available in *Siddhavaidyam* were mainly written in Sen-Tamil, though some of them were also in Sanskrit. Some of the important texts in *Siddhavaidyam* that describes medicinal compositions using metals and herbs are *Rasaratnayogam, Rasasamuchayam, Rasavaisheshikam, Vagbhatanidhanam, Rasahridaya, Rasaratnakara, Rasarnava* and *Rasaratnasamuccaya* (Unnikrishnan, 2011). The seemingly important difference between consolidated Ayurveda and *Siddhavaidyam* is that the former uses more plants, herbs and roots and the latter uses purified and processed minerals and metals more in its medicinal composition rather than plants and roots. In many occasions, in order to articulate itself as an important *vaidyam* the *Siddhavaidyas* claim that they are Ayurvedic practitioners. In studies on Ayurveda too *Siddhavaidyam* is treated as part of Ayurveda. If that is the case then how does *Siddhavaidyam* became only a subset of Ayurveda? And how is Ayurveda validated as the only age old textual tradition of a region?

There is a third claim about divinity and contemporaneity of the age old *samhitas*. This is an indication of a different relationship with a knowledge carrying text and notions of time (*kalam*). The text is seen as an open source for all who want to interpret it or use it. The late nineteenth and early twentieth centuries witness a large proliferation of printed texts, both in Sanskrit and in Malayalam on indigenous medicines. All over India texts were produced in a large scale by Indians and orientalists on *vaidyam* (Banerjee, 2010). In this re-production the available texts on *vaidyam* were seen as open sources for further interpretation and use. This is irrespective of their nature and the language in which they are codified since they were not author specific or period specific. Most of them were either interpretations of the existing old texts or interpretation of them by incorporating the experiences of *vaidyas* who had written them. The name of the writer as well as the time of writing was less important till early twentieth century. The writer or interpreter has a different relationship not only with the text, but also with the time of the text. For most of them the ancient quality or *aura* of a text symbolizes its authority and divinity rather than its outdated nature, which was the constant accusation raised by biomedicine practitioners and department officials. It symbolizes the deep-rooted nature of a text or a traditional practice. This is a journey from one time to another time without negating or erasing the old time with the existing present or a projected future. This is also a back and forth journey, but not a nostalgic one of upholding a glorious past in order to validate the present. The past itself is as important as the present. Without the past, the present has no value of its own. It is a relation with another time in order to connect with the present time or rather the emphasis is on the inter-connectedness. In this journey through time the author or interpreter see themselves as mere instruments in preserving the knowledge of a divine past. Varier sees this period as a time where making books was not seen as writing one's own ideas (Raghava, 2009), in spite of including the writer's view and experience in texts. In this view, the subject is configured as an instrument in producing change, rather than an active and conscious interventionist.

Alathur Manipravalam enna vaidyagrantham is a text belonging to medieval period and written in Manipravalam language.[17] Many verses from this text were reproduced in other texts on *vaidyam* i ncluding *Sukhasadagam* and *Yogamritam*, two oldest texts of the nineteenth century. Later twentieth century popular texts such as *Chikitsamanjari*, *Sahasrayogam* etc. also reproduced *slokas* from *Alathur Manipravalam*. The author of this text is unknown. Many times the authors were just the ones who edited and compiled a variety of literature taken from various sources across India. A *vishavaidyam* series had been published in *Dhanwantari* for four years continuously from its very inception (1903). This was written by Channazi Kumaran Moossad *vaidyar*, a well known *vishavaidya* of central Kerala. The series was posthumously published as a book in 1958 by P.K. Brothers, Calicut. The purpose was to use it as a text in teaching *vishavaidyam* at *Arya Vaidya Pathashala*. But the name of the author is given as P.V. Krishna Varier, the one who listened, noted down, edited and corrected the essays.[18] If this was the case in mid-twentieth century, it would be difficult to locate the authenticity and authority of older texts on the basis of authorship. In the re-production of available materials on *vaidyam* through print, the choice of the authors and interpreters were entirely selective and subjective. The effects of such selection could only be analysed through the existing texts and literature on *vaidyam*. So, the authority of divinity and contemporaneity used to validate Ayurveda is not convincing in the context of the multiplicity of texts used by diverse *vaidyas* in Kerala.

The fourth claim is about Sanskrit as an authentic language used in codifying *vaidyam*. Sheldon Pollock observes that European histories of Indian literature uphold histories of Sanskrit and its congeners, Pali and Prakrit. According to Pollock this is a fascination of the "Romantic Europe's preoccupation with origins and lines of descent" (Pollock, 2003). However, in Kerala books on *vaidyam* have not been written only in Sanskrit. Other vernaculars such as Malayalam, Manipravalam, Arabi-Malayalam and Tamil have equally been used for documenting *vaidyam* (The Usman Committee Report, 1923). A large number of Telugu and Kannada books are also seen in other parts of South India.[19] Moreover, in some languages the script used for writing texts on *vaidyam* is different from the script used for other purposes.[20] This indicates that languages had a special technique to document and preserve the knowledge of *vaidyam*. Some languages also show the tendency of becoming a monolingual universal apparatus that is capable of representing scientific knowledge, like Sanskrit and Persian. By nineteenth century, new languages evolved and replaced some of the old ones in documenting *vaidyam*. For instance, Urdu evolved as a Pidgin language from Persian and Arabic speaking esoteric practitioners of North India and is used in representing the new Unani in the nineteenth century (Alavi, 2007). Similarly, Hindi begins to emerge as the language of Hindu *vaidyas* in Punjab. In contrast to Hindi the Gurumukhi speaking *vaidyas* claim an indigenous Ayurveda that is preserved through their language (Sivaramakrishnan, 2006). A variety of languages emerged and begins to represent *vaidyam* from late eighteenth century onwards. The neat divide between reading, rote learning and writing also changed by this time. The scribes meant to do writing were extinct by late nineteenth century. The relation between script and speech and the different techniques within script also transformed within the advent of print culture.

So, the validation using *tridosha* principle, divinity, codified nature and language used for that codification does not bear sufficient truth value for Ayurveda to become the unique cultural practice of a region since these are equally claimable by other codified and non-codified traditions. Besides codification is also possible in an abstract level in memory which is precisely the basic nature of many non-textual practices. Classic Ayurveda itself has emerged out of the compulsion to speak in equal terms to modern medicine, a knowledge system that was morally and financially supported by the state and authenticated by science. The scholastic literary tradition was established as the authentic tradition through the association of its practitioners with rulers, regional *rajas* and landlords. In the seventeenth and eighteenth centuries many of the practitioners worked as *kottaram* (court) *vaidyas* of *rajas*. This continued in the colonial period too; their connections as translators, subordinate officials etc. and their correspondences with the colonial officers helped them to legitimize and establish their practice as an authentic tradition. They further ascertained the authenticity and authority of their medical practice by making connections with sacred texts (the *Vedas*) and *vaidyam* (*Charaka Samhita* and *Sushruta Samhita*). The oldness and divinity of the texts are used to highlight its stability and contemporary relevance. Thus, the *samhitas* symbolises an everlasting truth carrying capacity of selected practices. These attributes work as the norms of classical. Paradoxically, the same conceptions are played against indigenous medicine by many of the biomedicine practitioners and the state officials of British Malabar. They say, it is archaic and hence, stagnant and no valid research has happened to test either the validity of treatment or the composition of medicines used for treatment.[21] The same points of view and tools create different meanings in different epistemological frameworks to argue for and against a group of practices. The above said arguments are played out through print publications and in the newly formed association of *vaidyas* and *pathashalas* in claiming authenticity and authority for Ayurveda which I did not want to elaborate in this chapter.

The theorization of indigenous medical practices or rather indigenous knowledge has always been happening at the cost of their relation with modern medicine/knowledge and the state (Arnold, 2000; Harrison, 1994; Pati and Harrison, 2001; Langford, 2002). The tools used in this epistemological framework end up with the predictable questions of scientificity, rationality and multiple lacks in indigenous practices in relation with biomedicine. Raising these theoretical issues with regard to a collection of diverse practices is difficult within the universal epistemological paradigm, since universality[22] underplays diversities. So, these arguments end up in focusing on selective practices among a collection of practices. In the selection of particular practices, the choice had always been between either codified and partially codified practices or non-codified practices. The epistemological paradigm that upholds rationality and scientificity itself is premised on codified practices and their normative frames.[23] So, they easily communicate with another set of codified practices with a similar nature. The classical Ayurveda of upper caste practitioners had thus got a prioritized position among a variety of Ayurvedas. Modern epistemological space has initiated a selective choice in its interaction with indigenous practices by both promoting and demoting them in order to create a historic Ayurveda. Indigenous knowledge also reconfigures themselves through selective 'rejection and reform of the present' (Panikkar, 2007; Partha Chatterjee, 1997) and through 'in-house churning' (Seema Alavi, 2007; Sivaramakrishnan, 2001).

Notes

1. Ayurveda is described as a classical tradition by many scholars even when they agree upon the live interaction of Ayurveda with other popular medical practices. *See* Abraham, Leena and Sujatha, V. (2009), Banerjee, Madhulika (2010). Classical denotes that which stands the test of time with a universal appeal. Its influences spread across generations. It does not allow major

changes since it has its own perfection and beauty which is tested by time. It is old but does not become archaic because of its everlasting contemporaneity.

2. The *nattuvaidyas* including Ayurveda doctors who passed from professional Ayurveda colleges do not charge consultation fee even today. Instead they charge for the medicines prepared and sold by them and take a commission through that sale.
3. Colonial modernity means the rise of a number of key features and process in the course of seventeenth century. This includes the emergence of discourse on reason and rationality with the concomitant growth of science, the spread of literacy, industrial production with capital investments, the idea of increasing social mobility, the consolidation of nation-state, the secularization of society and the new texture of selfhood based on the liberal concepts of freedom, autonomy and individuality (Calhoun, Craig, 2002).
4. The first endogenous attempt to define Kerala as a unified geographical and political space came from Chattambi Swamikal in 1914 through his book, *Pracheena Malayalam* (Ancient Malayalam). All other definitions were based on exogenous parameters such as the presence of Portuguese in Kerala or Kerala as a residual part of a macro-unit, the South India (Raju, S., 1999).
5. Bone setting was never part of Ayurveda. Even today, none of the Ayurveda clinics provide treatment for bone-setting. But they provide post-operation care through oil massage and physiotherapy. *Kalarichikitsa* centres provide treatment for bone-fractures.
6. *Siddha* is one of the codified indigenous medical practices of south India. The textual corpus of *siddha* is mainly in Tamil. *Siddha* philosophy was initially critical of idol worship and temple systems. Later some *siddhars* merged with *Saiva bhakti* tradition. As in *vishavaidyam*, *siddhavaidyam* also used *mantram* and *tantram* in its practice along with medicines. In north India the *nathasiddhas* were like *tantrics* and they constituted a heterodox group more interested in iatrochemistry, a branch of chemistry and medicine rooted in alchemy.
7. *Ottamulis* are special medicines meant only for particular diseases such as jaundice, kidney stones, piles etc. The secret of these medical preparations are not available in any of the publicly circulated texts. This is treated as a secret knowledge of *vaidya* or his/her family who prepare those medicines.
8. There are three humors in the body, *vata, pitta, kapha* (which is often wrongly translated as wind, bile and phlegm. Dr.Valiathan translated these three humors as wind, fire and water.) They are aligned with opposite qualities such as hot-cold, wet-dry etc. and the equilibrium of these humors maintained health (Valiathan, 2003). The basic tenets of *nattuvaidyam* were more or less based on the same concepts of humors which relied on the fundamental macro and microcosmic connections between human beings and the cosmos in which they lived.

9. As stated in GO No. 475-476 dated 19.11.1917, Local and Muncipal Department (Medical), Government of Madras. "The Aryavaidyam or Indian system of medicine varies with the circumstances in different parts of India" (Tamil Nadu State Archive, TSA).
10. Thirumulpad notice that there is not even a single interpretation of *Charaka Samhita* from South India till late nineteenth century, 11-14.
11. Dhanwantari, 1916, *Chingam* (August), 14:1; Varier, 1980; Tirumulpad, 2010. *Ashtangahridayam* is believed to have belonged to a period around the second century before Christ (Sir Bhagvat Sinh Jee, 1896, *A Short History of Aryan Medical Science*).
12. Unnikrishnan, 2011, *Keralathile nattuvaidyam* (Traditional medical practice in Kerala); Varier, 1980, *Ayurveda charitram;* Varier, Raghava, 2009. *Alathur Manipravalam enna vaidyagrantham.*
13. Manipravalam is a mixture of Malayalam and Sanskrit.
14. The script is in Arabic and the language is Malayalam.
15. *Ibid.*
16. The history of *aryavaidyam* is based on *A Short History of Aryan Medical Science* written by Thakore Saheb of Gondal, Sir Bhagvat Sinh Jee in 1896, published by MacMillan Company, London. In this book the author has reproduced the story of *Vedas*. Brahma is believed to be the first god who composed Ayurveda consisting of one hundred chapters with one hundred *slokhas* in each chapter. The author reproduced the ideas of Max Muller and the concepts in *Manusmriti* in order to strengthen his *Aryavarta* story.
17. *Ibid.*, According to Varier this is a 600 years old book.
18. In the preface of the book Varier has mentioned that since Moossad did not know how to write essays, *Dhanwantari* appointed a person to note down what Moossad had to say on *vishavaidyam*. During the first six to eight months the appointed person had done this work. After that Varier himself had done the job of writing down Moossad's orally communicated knowledge on *vishavaidyam*.
19. *Ibid.*
20. I did not get any reference or evidence so far regarding this from any of the secondary literature. But, the Arabi-Malayalam material which I got from a *vishavaidya*, was given to two experts for translation. Both of them before reading the material, at a first glance itself told me the matter pertained to *vaidyam* because of its script. Shamshad Hussain, Asst. Professor, Malayalam Department, Sri Sankaracharya University Centre, Tirur and Noufal, Asst. Professor, Arabic Department, Farook College have read and translated the matter in Arabi-Malayalam. In the seventeenth century, Itty Achuthan, an Ezhava Vaidyan who had assisted Van Rheede in compiling *Hortus Malabaricas* has used *Kolezhuttu* Malayalam script (the script used by Brahmins) to write his declaration in the book. (Hortus Malabaricas, 1678-1693); Alathur *Manipravalam enna vaidya grantham,* an oldest text in *vaidyam* used old *arya* script (Varier, 2009), 10.

21. GO No. 475-476 dated 19.11.1917, *Indigenous Systems of Medicine*, Local and Municipal Department (Medical) 1917 (TSA).
22. Post-modern thinkers reject the universal nature of modern science and argue that it is inescapably rooted in the cultural singularities of the West. (*See* Bala, Arun, 2006).
23. Practices are codified in texts through observation and synthesis of these observations using abstraction, deduction, induction, analogy etc. in order to preserve them for a useful application in other similar situations in future. But this codified knowledge acts as a norm for regulating and modulating further practices once they get reified into the form of a prescribed or standard text. Nevertheless practices elude the strict boundaries of a prescribed text even when they follow certain elements of the text. They are always excessive of their modulating apparatus.

References

Abraham, Leena and V. Sujatha (Ed.) (2009). "Medicine state and society. Indigenous medicine and medical pluralism in India", Special section of the *Economic and Political Weekly*, Vol. XLIV (16) April 18-24, pp. 35-83.

Alavi, Seena. (2007). *Islam and Healing: Loss and Recovery of Indo-Muslim Medical Traditon*, 1600-1900, Delhi: Permanent Black.

Arnold, David. (2000). *The New Cambridge History of India: Science, Technology and Medicine in Colonial India*, Cambridge: Cambridge University Press.

Bala, Arun. (2006). *The Dialoge of the Civilizations in the Birth of Modern Medicine*, New York, MacMillan.

Banerjee, Madhulika. (2009). Power, Knowledge, Medicine: Ayurvedic pharmaceuticals at home and in the world: *New Perspectives in South Asian History*. Hyderabad: Orient Blackswan.

Bhagvat Sinh Jee, H.H. (1896). *A Short History of Aryan Medical Science*. London: MacMillan Company.

Gyan Prakash. (1999). *Another Reason: Science and the Imagination of Modern India*. Princeton, NJ: Princeton University Press.

Harrison, Mark. (1994). *Public Health in British India: Anglo-Indian Preventive Medicine 1859-1914*. Cambridge: Cambridge University Press.

Langford, Jean, M. (2002). *Fluent Bodies: Ayurvedic Remedies for Postcolonial Imbalance*. Durham, NC: Duke University Press.

Panikkar, K.N. (2007). Cultural Trends in Pre-colonial India: An Overview. In D. Raina and S. Habib (eds.) *Social History of Science in Colonial India, Oxford in India Readings*, New Delhi, Oxford University Press.

Partha Chatterjee. (1997). Our Modernity. *Issue 1 of SEPHIS-Codesria Lecture*, Council for the Development of Economic and Social Research in Africa. Indiana University, SEPHIS.

Pati, Biswamoy and Mark Harrison. (2001). *Health, Medicine and Empire: Perspectives on Colonial India.* Delhi: Orient Longman.

Paul, Benjamin D. (Ed.). (1955). *Health, Culture and Community: Case Studies of Public Reactions to Health Programmes.* New York: Russell Sage Foundation.

Pollock, S. (2003). *Literarary Cultures in History: Reconstructions from South Asia*, Delhi, Oxford University Press.

Raju, S. (1999). *Politics and Culture in Kerala: A Study of Travancore State*, Unpublished Ph.D. thesis, Centre for Historical Studies, SSS, JNU, New Delhi, 1-62.

Sivaramakrishnan, K. (2006). *Old Potions, New bottles: Recounting Indigenous Medicine in Colonial Punjab-1850-1945.* New Delhi: Orient Longman.

Valiathan, M.S. (2003). *The Legacy of Caraka.* New Delhi: Orient Blackswan.

HEALTH CARE DELIVERY

6

Is Diversity a Relation of Power?

A Study of Ayurveda, Unani and Allopathy in India

Priyam Sharma

In Indian society, the medical system comprises wide varieties of practices ranging from traditional healers, indigenous practitioners to that of modern biomedical providers. Different medical systems co-exist with each other despite each one having its individual, specific values, knowledge, rules, legitimacy, practicing techniques etc. that together contribute to the general understanding of bodily health and knowledge production. India is considered as one of the best examples of co-existence of different medical systems as various socio-economic and political groups embrace them with their own rationality for it.

Charles Leslie (1998:359) categorizes different kinds of medicinal systems. These are as follows:

(1) The Ayurvedic medicine of the Sanskrit classic text.
(2) Unani medicine of the classic Arabic text.
(3) The syncretic medicine of traditional culture, which evolved among learned practitioners from the thirteenth century to the nineteenth century.
(4) Professionalized Ayurvedic and Unani medicine which continued the syncretism of the past transforming learned traditional-cultural medicine by assimilating cosmopolitan medical knowledge and institutions.

(5) Cosmopolitan medicine is often called Allopathy to distinguish it from indigenous medicine and Homoeopathy. The term "indigenous" medicine is used in India to refer to the folk and learned dimensions of traditional-culture medicine, together with the classic texts.

(6) Folk medicine which includes midwives, bone-setters, supernatural curers of various types and other specialists, most of them are part-time practitioners.

(7) Popular-culture medicine that emerges with the institutions of mass society—industrial production of medicine, advertising, the school system. It continues the syncretism of traditional-culture medicine, modifying it with the concepts and practices of Western medicine. The popular-culture medicine utilizes patent medicines and drugs from modern medicine along with Ayurvedic, Unani and Homoeopathic medications.

(8) Homoeopathic medicine is a special form of popular-culture. It originated in Germany in the nineteenth century and is based on the concept of creating resistance to an illness by giving small doses of it.

(9) Learned magico-religious curing. All classes of people in India resort frequently to magical and religious therapy and practitioners range from illiterate villagers to sophisticated urban pundits.

These categories of different medicines provide pluralistic and diversified character of medical system in a society.

This chapter attempts to find explanations to some of the questions such as: Does co-existence of different medical system mean simply co-option? How does a particular medical system gains certain degree of authority to claim itself superior with respect to 'other' medical systems? And in this construction of the 'other', how other medical systems are affected by this power dynamics that operate in plural medical system? How do power relations influence this hiatus between the medical systems? The chapter also attempts to examine the changing inter-relationship among Allopathic and non-Allopathic systems of medicine, i.e. Ayurveda and Unani.

The reason for selecting these two systems of medicine is because of their historical antecedents. Both of them are ancient medical systems which constantly underwent change in theory and practice. Ayurvedic medical system is one of the ancient medical systems and is linked with the Hindu religious and social structure. It has adapted itself in various contexts with necessary modifications. Unani medical system is basically developed by ancient Greek medical practitioners. It was later borrowed and redeveloped by Arabs. It flourished in India since, the medieval period under the Mughal regime which also represents the great Islamic tradition in context of India. So, the idea here is to analyse two major medical systems from two different great traditions of India and to see how each system of knowledge fed into each other and how they responded to colonialism and modern medicine.

Diversity and Power Relations

Leslie (1998) argues that although cosmopolitan medical system exists in every country, most people continue to depend on the folk and traditional practitioners as well. Thus, there are other medical traditions that coexist in various ways with cosmopolitan medicine in India. Leslie and Young (1992) challenged the dominant popular belief that scientific bio-medicine or allopathy highly developed on the axis of modernization and Westernization. Also the idea that people once exposed to modernization and modern medicine would not depend on "traditional" medicine is refuted. Approaches that see the 'other' only in terms of, or opposed to the West, ignore the internal logic and nuances of 'other' knowledge (Sujatha, 2007). Scholars such as Charles Leslie argued that the medical systems of contemporary Asia are intellectually coherent. Each system of Ayurveda, Unani, and Chinese medicine consists of beliefs and practices having logic that is underpinned by networks of assumptions about therapeutics and so forth. Like medical systems elsewhere, the Asian systems are embedded in distinctive cultural premises and symbols. It is important to identify the cultural context in which the medical practices are taking place.

A diversified medical system tends to reflect hierarchical relations. Allopathic medicine enjoys a dominant status over the other medical systems due to its so called scientificity and rationality. Therefore, plural medical systems may be described as "dominative" ,i.e. one medical system generally enjoys a pre-eminent status over the other medical system (Baer, Singer, Susser, 2003). The central question around this diverse medical system is how 'power' and 'influence' is distributed in the process. Lines of conflict are multiple and shifting of power is a continuous process between competing groups. Scholars emphasized that power is not a physical entity that individuals or groups either have or do not have and it is also not devoid of social consciousness. It is an entity that flows from a variety of different sources. In case of power distribution among the various medical systems, it is the allopathic medicine that is considered to be more powerful, because they control various assets. These assets include the idea of rationality, reason and knowledge, rooted in scienticism, by virtue of which it ignores the 'other' medical systems as unscientific, irrational and unjust.

Young opines that those in dominant, powerful positions in the hierarchical structure which maintains the established order and ensure that power and privilege remain within the same social group (Haralambos, 1980:217). Madhulika Banerjee (2009) points out that Allopathic medicine lays down what is or not legitimate in the realm of public health. "Developments in scientific research are continuously guided by this and are legitimate until they fulfil criteria set by yardsticks of 'scientificity' set by biomedicine and its allied disciplines" (2009:10). This implies hierarchisation of knowledge systems that leads to power dynamics.

To understand the complexities involved in medical field and the ways through which different systems of medicines interact and construct unequal power relations between them requires systematic sociological study in placing these systems of medicine in the historical, cultural and social context in which they sustain. As the traditional practitioners continuously interact with socio-political, economic, legal and technological context, the diversity and richness of the traditional medicines increases substantially. Such context in which they operate is never static, but it is always at the state of flux. In a country like India, which is characterized by heterogeneity along with class and caste dynamics, rural and urban divisions, the understanding of interactions between the Allopathic and the

Ayurvedic, Unani medicine may constantly give rise to new questions about the dominant nature of Allopathy and also the power dynamics of the entire system.

Ayurveda

During British rule the Ayurvedic doctors and healers were most affected. Initially, the British were obliged to recognize the existence of older and culturally entrenched therapeutic beliefs and practices. They were often tolerant and even appreciative. This was partly because in their understanding of disease, eighteenth and nineteenth century Indian and European medicine shared much in common. Initially, the British appreciated that there was much they could learn from Ayurveda. The controversy between Orientalists and Anglicists in the early period of British rule affected attitudes towards the remnants of the Ayurvedic tradition (Brass, 1972). In 1822, the School of Native Doctors was established in Calcutta in which both Ayurvedic and Western medical subjects were taught. However, in 1835 the School was abolished and replaced by a modern medical college on the grounds that the basic principles of the two systems of medicine were incompatible and could not be combined (Brass, 1972). From this period onwards, the Western medical system became firmly established in British India.

Amidst the competing forces from the English medicine, one of the important achievements of Ayurvedic system during the nineteenth century according to Arnold (2000) was brought about by Bhau Daji. He dealt with the cure of leprosy and in the process he illustrated the mutual interaction of Ayurveda and other medical system like Allopathy. Daji combined the knowledge and techniques of the Western medical science with that of Ayurvedic medical system. Another example of interactions of two different medical systems was the interaction between Ayurveda and Unani. For example quinine had no traditional place in Ayurveda. Nevertheless, the efficacy of quinine in the treatment of malaria did gain recognition among the Ayurvedic practitioners in 1860s especially in dealing with Burdwan fever, the epidemic malaria then sweeping Bengal. Ayurveda had borrowed extensively from Unani, *sarsaparilla* root had been introduced from America to treat syphilis and several of the main ingredients used in Ayurvedic medicine in the 1890s were not native to India, but imported from the Middle East, Eat Africa, Central and South-east Asia (Arnold, 2000). Thus, we find that these medical systems did not operate in isolation and that they were constantly interacting and exchanging their knowledge in order to provide a better health care facility.

However, there was a sense of insecurity among the Ayurvedic practitioners on the possibility of marginalization due to the challenge caused by the Western medicine. The intellectuals during the eighteenth and nineteenth century were in a dilemma whether to discard the old and create a new cultural milieu or to preserve or retrieve the traditional cultural space, so that, the past is not swept off the ground. The efforts to deal with this dilemma led to the critical investigation of both present and past. This is the point when the protagonists of Ayurvedic medicine decided to take a critical stand and revitalize the Ayurvedic medical system.

The Ayurvedic revival assumed several forms. The location and translation of Ayurvedic texts from Sanskrit to English gave the movement textual authority and made its work accessible to greater audience. The printing infrastructure developed during the colonial period played a major role in spreading the Ayurvedic knowledge. By the end of the nineteenth century there were as many as fifty medical journals in the Indian languages. *Sanjeevini* in Bengali, *Raja Vaidya* in Marathi and *Dhanwantari* in Malayalam are some examples (Panikkar, 1995). From grassroots interactions with Western medicine, the traditional Indian medicine movement evolved into regional and all-India organizations. Ayurveda established strong local roots by setting up dispensaries. The indigenous revival was a war on two fronts—seeking to re-establish Ayurveda as the popular and culturally appropriate alternative to Allopathy, and also to supplant what was seen as ignorant and superstitious folk practices (Arnold, 2000). In Kerala, for example, *pathashalas* with the necessary infrastructure were created to bring into existence a group of well-versed in the discipline. Infrastructure was needed to professionalize the Ayurvedic practice to tackle the encroachment of Western medicine. The curriculum of the *pathashalas* was based on a combination of indigenous and Western knowledge. It also included subjects like physiology, chemistry based on the Western theory (Panikkar, 1995).

Another important step towards the revitalization of Ayurvedic medicine was the manufacturing and marketing of Ayurvedic medicine. It included the methods of standardization and commercialization of the Ayurvedic medicines. This standardization and commercialization was possible only if the Ayurvedic practitioners took initiatives and joined together to form manufacturing companies similar to that of Western medicines. With this view in mind there were several Ayurvedic companies that were established. In 1878 Chandra Kishore Sen in Bengal had opened a dispensary in Calcutta which took a large scale production form in 1898. In Kerala P.S. Varier established Arya Vaidyasala in 1902. The sales amounted to only Rs. 14,000 in the first four years, but increased to Rs. 1,70,000 in the subsequent four-year period. At one level these figures point towards the entrepreneurial success of these pioneers and at other level it also reflects the wide acceptance of Ayurvedic medicine among people. Though the reformation of Ayurveda was an important component in cultural awakening in colonial period, its methodology was a mix of both indigenous and Western sources. The pioneers of cultural awakening never hesitated to borrow things and ideas from the West. As Panikkar mentions, the reformation and revival of Ayurveda was something more than that of medicine. Rather it was clubbed with similar methods in other spheres like art, literature, dance, drama and other cultural mediums.

The apparent ability of the Western medical practitioners to deal with the local diseases encouraged Ayurvedic remedies. However, the situation got tensed with the passing of the Bombay Medical Registration Act of 1912 which gave recognition to practitioners of Western medicine, but excluded all others. The fear that all indigenous practitioners would be treated as 'quacks' was reinforced (Arnold, 2000). The practitioners of indigenous medicine were relegated to an inferior status as they were unrecognized by the state and therefore, deemed unqualified. The Act did not debar the practice of indigenous medicine, but it did not have the approval of the state (Panikkar, 1995). Indigenous practitioners wanted an equal share of state recognition and funding. The attitude of the state and its senior medical officers towards indigenous medicine remained largely one of hostility (Arnold, 2000). However, there are exceptions and one apparent exception in this case was Sir Pardy Lukis, Director General of IMS.

He recognized that since 90 per cent of the population lived in the countryside and had little access to Western medicine; it made sense to support indigenous medicine as far as possible so that the basic health needs could be met. In 1918 and 1920 the Indian National Congress passed resolution stating the 'undeniable claims to usefulness' of the Ayurvedic systems and established colleges and hospitals for instruction and treatment in accordance with the indigenous system (Arnold, 2000).

An interesting point to be noticed here would be the fact that in colonial period and before that, the fate of Ayurveda was much dependent on the issue of patronage. After independence the struggle of Ayurvedic medicine to find a prominent position had not decreased. Nehru had been quite influenced by the Western thoughts and values and argued that Allopathic medicine would be the best medical option for the Indians. Even the Bhore Committee Report recommended the extension of the Allopathic medicine throughout India. The Government of India only started acknowledging the importance of Ayurvedic medicines after identifying the revenue profits Ayurvedic medicines brought in. It was only with the Chopra Committee, Alma Ata declaration and the Chiang Mai Declaration, that the traditional medicines are being accepted as providing a holistic and inexpensive health care alternative. Ayurvedic system of medicine has passed through an active phase of revival and development. The Ayurvedic revival provides an example of the professionalization of an indigenous medical system which parallels the professionalization of modern medical system (Brass, 1972). The Ayurvedic movement is an attempt by an interest group to legitimize it, achieve recognition and respect in a modernizing society through the establishment of educational and research institutes, through the process of professionalization and Government patronage (Brass, 1972). There were the traditionalists who wanted the pure Ayurveda to be maintained and on the other hand there were the neo-traditionalists who wanted to incorporate modern features into Ayurvedic knowledge. Gandhi believed that Ayurveda needed to be reflexive while maintaining its distance away from biomedicine. However, it was the neo-traditionalists view that sustained providing it space in the market for the mass production of its medicine (Banerjee, 2004). It had now adopted itself to the laws of the global market. With the establishment of many autonomous institutions, Ayurveda is developing as a scientific discipline for the care of health and disease in the country. Ayurveda has conditioned itself from various religious sources like Buddhism and also from Unani. It has also adapted itself with respect to other medical systems including modern medicine. As we have seen, though adhering to its basic principles, Ayurveda has adapted in context of professionalization and standardization of Ayurvedic knowledge and medicine. The changes it went through by adopting concepts and methods from various sources clearly reflects the fact that Ayurvedic medical system is not static, but manifests in itself the features of multiplicity, adaptability, accessibility and effectiveness. The knowledge of Ayurveda has not only contributed to the enriching Ayurvedic practice, but also the general medical epistemology.

Unani

During the period of classical Islam (eighth to thirteenth century), an integrated Islamic world system flourished which covered all spheres of trade, politics, culture including medicine. India was a part of this trading and cultural ambit called Dar al-Islam. The knowledge of medicine was an immense interest to the Caliphs of the Islamic empires. Medical ideas were appropriated from the Graeco-Roman philosophical tradition represented by Hippocrates, Aristotle and Galen. Galen was influenced by the reasoning of Greek cosmology which treated the universe as a macrocosm reflected in the human microcosm. He thus believed that the human body had humours which needed to be kept in balance for the maintenance of good health. This is similar to the principle of Ayurveda that sees a link between the macrocosm and microcosm. The Umayyads (661-750) and the Abbasids (750-1258) showed immense interest in Greek medical literature. In fact it was during this period when the Greek medical texts were translated into Arabic and incorporated into the Arabic science. The famous medical texts of Ayurveda *Sushruta Samhita* and *Sameeka Samhita* were translated into Arabic during this period (Attewell, 2007). The Unani and Ayurvedic systems also adopted drugs from each other. There have also been cases of different medical traditions being incorporated into the Unani medicine. For example

Ibn Sina's exposition on pulse and use of mercury showed Chinese influence, use of calcined metals and minerals had its origin in therapeutic-alchemical *siddha* traditions (Attewell, 2007).

During Muhammad Tughlaq's rule an important text that was compiled was *Majumai-i-Zia-e*. The treatise was based on Unani and Ayurvedic medical works (Bala, 1982). Hakim Dia Muhammad, one of the other court physicians composed a text *Majmuah-i-Diyai*, which gives the names of drugs and diseases in Hindi (Attewell, 2007). During the reign of Firoz Tuglaq, the Muslim kings encouraged their court physicians to compose medical works and thus cultivate Unani medicine in India (Bala, 1982).

In the Mughal Empire, Persian replaced Arabic as the language of science and medicine. Persian language was considered the symbol of power and cultural aesthetics. Since, Unani medical texts were written in Persian, it acquired a distinct status and dignity. Unani medicine became the symbol of power and aristocracy. However, with the collapse of the Mughal Empire, there was devolution in the patronage of medicine. The language of Arabic came back to the sphere that controlled the spread of medical knowledge. This was because the orthodox and conservative practitioners of Unani wanted to control and store the medical knowledge away from the society at large. Arabic was used to restore the prestige of such families of practitioners who were worried about the spreading out of the medical knowledge by the increasing accessibility of Persian (Alavi, 2007). However, this Arabization also came with a price. Persian accommodated into itself both the Hindu and Muslim traditions that reflected the inclusive nature of Mughal period. As Unani withdrew into the Arabic fold, the religious divide became noticeable.

In the late eighteenth century the English East India Company inherited the fractured medical legacy of the Mughal period. The company allowed regional courts to patronize Persian medical literature. The Company also made Arabic translations of the European texts on anatomy. More importantly the company used Urdu and the printing press to popularize the new texts. Print system created a new sharing experience of medical knowledge. Materia medicas, pharmacopoeias, tracts on anatomy, medical dictionaries were all written in the Mughal Period also. But what were new in this period were the standardization of new knowledge and the introduction of medical knowledge in vernacular as the language of the new printed medical literatures.

The vernacular texts helped to create a new class of medically aware communities. Along with it, it made people aware of the potential of combining Unani medical knowledge with that of Western knowledge. The Company's intervention also shifted health to the wider public domain of social well-being and linked medical status to public service. Hakim Ajmal Khan one of the most important proponents of Unani grappled with the reorganization and reorientation of Unani and the plague crisis of Bombay in 1896 urged him towards the reform of Unani. He aimed to bring forth the knowledge about plague, its causes and prevention and to do so he had to modernize the text by writing in Urdu as it made more accessible to a layman (Attewell, 2007). In 1902 he started publishing a monthly journal which contained useful articles on Unani. Ajmal Khan was keen to borrow and internalize what was good and beneficial in other system. As Kumar (1997) says, his works were culture specific, but not culture blind. Ajmal Khan urged Unani to adopt Western knowledge where he considered Unani deficient, which included surgery, anatomy. Ajmal Khan was casting himself as the exponent of fundamental shift in the way Unani knowledge was to be approached. The presentation of knowledge was a key element in this vision. The texts were now written in plain Urdu with contents on easy reference (Attewell, 2007). He concentrated education incorporating different medical systems and in 1910 he organized an all India Ayurvedic and Tibbia conference which was an annual feature (Kumar, 1997). The All India Vedic and Unani Tibbi Conference (AIVUTC) played a major role in the reform of Unani. It was the first organization to lobby formally for the combined interests of Unani and Ayurveda. The Conference had three main objectives. Firstly, to further the institutionalization of Unani and Ayurveda, in separate or combined schools; secondly, to challenge the order of knowledge of indigenous medicine by breaking down traditional lines of transmission through families and encourage the horizontal dissemination of expertise among practitioners; and thirdly, and the most important, to provide a forum to lobby the Government for the support of indigenous medicine. The will to transform and project Unani and Ayurveda as modern bodies of knowledge and professions was at the core of these initiatives. The teaching institution represented one powerful mechanism in the modernization of the profession, providing new forms of knowledge transmission (Attewell, 2007).

The major blow to Unani and Ayurvedic systems came with the attempt of the British and Indian Allopathic doctors to secure Registration Acts, so that, no indigenous physician could be legally recognized (Metcalf, 1985). In 1912 the British Government passed the Registration Act which excluded the indigenous system from state patronage. Khan lobbied extensively against this act, but to no avail. Later in 1916 the matter was raised at the Central Legislative Council with the support of important national leaders. The Government responded diplomatically by employing a drug manufacture committee to enquire into the utility of the indigenous Unani medicine. It also agreed to open a few more Unani colleges.

After Independence, in 1946, the conference of Health Ministers opined that adequate provisions should be made at the Central and State provinces for research in Unani and Ayurveda. Following this institutions were established by the Government for the development of Unani, one of them being Central Council for Research in Indian Medicine and Homoeopathy (CCRIMH). In 1978 CCRIMH was split into four separate research councils, one each for Unani, Ayurveda and *Siddha*, Yoga and Naturopathy and Homoeopathy so as to develop these systems individually according to its philosophical foundations. Thus, CCRUM (Central Council for Research in Unani Medicine) came into existence the CCRUM had done some pioneering work in the area of drug standardization and had evolved standards for 277 single and 385 compound drugs. Unani medicines now export its products in the Middle East, Canada, USA, UK, Russia, and Singapore.

Allopathy

Each medical system develops and operates in its social context. And in doing so, it interacts with several other medical systems which developed in similar socio-historical context or in a different setting. But, the point here to be emphasized is that none of the medical systems operates in isolation and every medical system has a context in which it flourishes both in its knowledge and in its practices and this is also implied to Allopathic medicine.

Allopathic medicine itself went through a lot of approvals and disapprovals from its very beginning. Dissection which is an integral part of the allopathic system was initially forbidden by the Roman law. In Western Europe, with the collapse of Roman imperial authority, medicine became localized; folk medicine supplemented what remained of the medical knowledge of antiquity. With the Renaissance, came an increase in experimental investigation, principally in the field of dissection which advanced the knowledge of human anatomy. The Renaissance brought an increase of physiological research. Anatomist William Harvey described the circulatory system in the seventeenth century. In 1838 the cell theory was developed. This it can be said that modern medicine also went through certain shifts. Dissection which was disapproved in the medieval period got developed during the renaissance and with the advent of modern period.

The renaissance period gave a boost to the development of modern medicine. More scientific approach to medicine emerged and some doctors began to question the traditional ideas. One of the most important discoveries was the germ theory by Louis Pasteur, according to which microorganisms are the cause of many diseases. The discovery of microscopes by physicists, discovery of oxygen by chemists, the ultrasound technology, the discovery of X-Rays also fastened the process of understanding the cause of disease. Nuclear medicine was an important discovery in the field of medicine. It relies on the process of radioactive decay in the diagnosis and treatment of disease. The history of nuclear medicine is rich with contributions from scientists across different disciplines in physics, chemistry and engineering. There have been various medical instruments that were incorporated from the field of electronics. Modern medicine has also been refined on the basis of new subjects like biochemistry, biophysics. These examples reflect that modern medicine is also heterogeneous and has not developed completely on its own.

Western medicine does not only include scientific Allopathic medicine but also Homoeopathy which is a form of alternative medicine. Samuel Hahnemann, a German physician was the pioneer of Homoeopathy who found it in late eighteenth century. The lack of convincing scientific evidence to support Homoeopathy's evidence has caused it to be described as pseudoscience. However, Homoeopathy achieved its greatest popularity in the nineteenth century. One reason for the growing popularity of Homoeopathy was its apparent success in treating people suffering from infectious diseases, epidemics such as cholera. The death rates from cholera in Homoeopathic hospitals were much lower than that of Allopathy. This placed the Allopathic medical professions on the defensive. The last quarter of the century gave way to the germ theory. Both Homoeopaths and Allopaths came to use various forms of therapies and by 1912 some of the therapeutic practices of the two schools were virtually indistinguishable. This sharing of medical practice gave Allopathic medicine an opportunity to nihilate Homoeopathy, a process made possible by the continuing awareness of conventional doctors of developments within Homoeopathy. The Homoeopathic principles were translated into the views of the Allopaths. The Allopaths were able to incorporate Homoeopathy's two most distinctive concepts—the similar principle and the minimum doses—and explain them in their own allopathic terms (Jones, 2010). Though the Homoeopathic principles were criticized as unscientific by the Allopathic practitioners, still the major principles were incorporated within the Allopathic system.

The above related cases manifest the fact that the Allopathic medicine is not homogenous and are not unique. Homoeopathic medicine which also has its origin in the west is considered to be unscientific and alternative to the Allopathic medicine. An interesting point to note is that power and the dominance of the Allopathic medicine is not unique to the colonial countries, where it was imposed in opposition to the traditional medicine, but is also found in the West. In case of India, the standardization and the professionalization of Ayurvedic and Unani systems has to some extent have led to the marginalization of the other folk practices in medicine. It can be said that the power dynamics of medical pluralism depends on one's own cultural context.

Though the Allopathic practitioners opine that they are superior to that of alternative medical practitioners, there are empirical evidences that prove traditional medicines and allopathic medicines are quite similar on certain grounds. In fact Allopathic practitioners have used concepts that resemble fundamental ideas of alternative medicines. All medical systems are thus eclectic, heterogeneous. There is no system of medical knowledge that got produced without interaction with other systems of knowledge. Moreover, all the medical systems also are part of a larger social structure and therefore, it reflects the dominant ideas of time.

Conclusion

The notion of medical diversity and hierarchy are closely intertwined, which necessitate us to inquire the prevalent power relationship among various components of the pluralistic whole. The power relationship attempts to erase and marginalize the other. Therefore, one important task is to highlight these marginalized voices and to create adequate space for them to be heard. The case of medical diversity is somehow similar to that where the attempt is not only to see the various forms of medical practices prevalent in a regional context, but also to decipher the prevalent power relations between them and to disentangle the notion of 'other' and 'alternative' with the cognitive biasness that other and alternative is essentially irrational, unscientific and thus, ineffective. Therefore, the production of medical knowledge and its practitioners need to be understood in their specific context in which they are embedded.

References

Alavi, Seema. (2007). *Islam and Healing—Loss and Recovery of an Indo-Muslim Medical Tradition, 1600-1900.* Ranikhet: Permanent Black.

Arnold, David. (2000). *Science, Technology and Medicine in Colonial India.* Cambridge: Cambridge University Press.

Attewell, Guy. (2007). *Refiguring Unani Tibb: Plural Healing in Late Colonial India.* New Delhi: Orient Longman.

Baer, Hans A., Merill Singer and Ida Susser (Eds.). (2003). *Medical Anthropology and the World System.* Praeger Publishers.

Bala, Poonam. (1982). "The Ayurvedic System of Medicine: Its Fate in Medieval India", *Bulletin of the Indian Institute of History of Medicine,* (12): 22-27.

Banerjee, Madhulika. (2009). *Power, Knowledge, Medicine: Ayurvedic Pharmaceuticals at Home and in the World.* Hyderabd: Orient Black Swan.

Banerjee, Madhulika. (2004). Local Knowledge for World Market-Globalizing Ayurveda. *Economic and Political Weekly.* 39 (1): 89-93.

Brass, Paul. R. (1972). The Politics of Ayurvedic Education: A Case Study of Revivalism and Modernization in India in Susan H. Rudolph and Llyod I. Rudolph, *Education and Politics in India.* Delhi: Oxford University Press.

Haralambos, Michael. (1980). *Sociology Themes and Perspectives.* New Delhi: Oxford University Press.

Jones, Lyn Brierley. (2010). Boundaries or Bridges: What Should Homoeopathy's Relationship Be With Mainstream Medicine. *International Journal of High Dilution Research*, 9(32): 115-124.

Kumar, Deepak. (1997). "Medical Encounters in British India, 1820-1920", *Economic and Poltical Weekly,* 32(4): 166-170.

Leslie, Charles. (1998). *Asian Medical Systems—A Comparitive Study.* Delhi: Motilal Banarsidass Publishers Private Limited.

Leslie, Charles and Allan Young. 1992. *Paths to Asian Knowledge.* California Press.

Metcalf, Barbara D. (1985). "Nationalist Muslims in British India: The Case of Hakim Ajmal Khan, *Modern Asian Studies,* 19(1): 1-28. Cambridge University Press.

Panikkar, K.N. (1995). *Culture, Ideology, Hegemony: Intellectuals and Social Consciousness in Colonial India.* New Delhi: Tulika Publication.

Sujatha, V. (2007). Pluralism in Indian Medicine: Medical lore as a genre of medical knowledge. *Contributions to Indian Sociology.* Sage Publication.

Websites:

http://en.wikipedia.org/wiki/History_of_medicine
http://en.wikipedia.org/wiki/Physiology

7
The Role of State in Public Private Partnerships in Reproductive and Child Health Services

Jaya Goyal

This chapter focuses on understanding the role of Government in Public Private Partnerships (PPPs) in primary health services. It aims to understand PPPs in the most crucial part of health service delivery—reproductive and child health services which form crucial foundation pillars of a country's socio-economic development. The way actors in a partnership mainly the Government, private sector and NGOs interact with each other, has a bearing on the nature of services delivered and health outcomes for the population. The chapter uses case study method to understand three models or instruments of partnerships operational in primary health sector in Maharashtra. The study compares these PPP models of contracting, joint venture and a multi-stakeholder partnership on criteria like contractual design, leadership, financial management and monitoring all of which has a bearing on the success of the partnership. Findings point out to failures and success of PPPs, their reasons and implications for state to partner with non-state actors in health service delivery.

Introduction

In a striking contract to the Alma Ata Declaration of Health for All in 1978, where the role of state was central in providing healthcare, the idea of Universal Health Coverage (UHC) plan proposed by the

Government of India for the Twelfth Five Year Plan, is seen as retreating of the State's role to mere purchaser and manager of services while handing over the actual service delivery to the private sector (Dhar, 2012).

One of the strategies to achieve UHC is to "identify pathways for constructive participation of communities and the private-for-profit and not-for-profit sectors in the delivery of health care" as per the High Level Expert Group (HLEG) recommendations for the Twelfth Five Year Plan (The Planning Commission, 2011). PPPs in health forms an important recommendation of health systems development worldwide. In India too, PPPs in Health[1] are being considered as one of the key governance strategies for medical and health care delivery. Government of India and many State Governments have ventured out and experimented with various forms of PPPs over the last decade.

The idea of PPP is not new though. The non-state actors, mainly the NGOs have been collaborating with the State since 1950s mainly in malaria control and family planning programmes. In fact from the First Five Year Plan in 1951-56, the Government of India has entered into various collaborations and partnerships with both—for profit and with non-profit organizations. The question then arises on when, why and how a new terminology of PPPs emerged?

Baru and Nandy (2008) explains, "during the mid 1980s the idea of PPP was introduced into several disease control and reproductive and child health (RCH) programmes that received external funding, mainly from the World Bank which provided the rationale and guidelines for initiating and sustaining partnerships. The design of these partnerships was informed by the new public management (NPM) practices and techniques that emphasized a shift from the traditional administration to public management informed by notions of economic efficiency of markets. Gradually, WHO also endorsed the need for partnership between the state and market for financing, provisioning and research in health services."

Between the period of 2004 and 2006, Government's two apex policy-making agencies, the Planning Commission and the Ministry of Health and Family Welfare (MoHFW) prepared two documents to understand various policy implications of existing PPPs in social and development sector. Such a step was aimed at initiating a policy framework on the role of private sector in health, something which has not been spelt out explicitly in the Five Year Plan documents. This marked a major shift in the public policy from direct provisioning to indirect provisioning, at least on paper. Both documents recommended re-orienting the role of Centre and State Governments from direct delivery of services to service management and coordination in the wake of Liberlisation, Privatisation and Globalisation (LPG) trends. The Planning Commission's 'Report on PPP Sub-group' included the broad 'social sector' encompassing education, women and child development, culture, health, environment, urban development with emphasis on 'contracting' as the main instrument to enter into PPPs (The Planning Commission, 2004). It did stock-taking and reviewed emerging partnerships across various players in the health sector in India in year 2004. The MoHFW report elaborated extensively on the theme of PPPs in context to its programmes RCH-I and II. Both these reports sourced from Government, especially from Ministry of Health and Family Welfare were more like theoretical review on the concept of PPPs, their strengths, prerequisites and also various typologies or models of PPPs, but these were not illustrated with examples from the field.

At the same time, there was a surge of partnerships for primary health services especially host of RCH programmes like contracting in private doctors for emergency obstetric care, social marketing of contraceptives, institutional services like contracting-out of PHCs and urban healthcare centres. Thus, PPPs were being mainstreamed increasingly so in the primary health, with little evidence in Indian context on which kinds of instruments and arrangements worked and in which settings they did not. Although a concept in itself, PPP is actually a web of intricate relationships and processes between state and other multiple stakeholders making it exigent to evaluate. Analytical studies on PPPs using primary data in the Indian context are very few and hence there are serious gaps both at policy and at programmes in designing and implementing PPPs in health. Not many empirical assessments exist to guide Governments on how to best partner with the private players to achieve public health goals with equity, quality and effectiveness. In is in this context it is crucial to systematically understand recent experiences of state's role in entering into PPPs.

Present Study

In 2008, the author under the aegis of a Mumbai-based think tank called Observer Research Foundation undertook a study to review the PPPs in reproductive and child health services in India. The objective of the study was to identify PPP in primary health services, understand their typology or model and analyze them on institutional assessment criteria as suggested by the existing literature on PPPs. The purpose was to understand role of various stakeholders in the partnerships, their contribution, the conducive environment that led to the partnerships and finally to assess their limitations and advantages. The idea was to understand the determinants of successful PPPs and also factors leading to failures of PPPs to learn lessons and inform public policy on health.

Three cases of PPPs in reproductive and child health were selected after ensuring that there was a written understanding like a contract or a memorandum of understanding (MoU) with clear roles and obligations between the Government actor and the private player. These were—Project Dilaasa of Centre for Enquiry into Health and Allied Themes (CEHAT), a crisis centre in a municipal hospital for women victims of domestic violence; Bhavishya Alliance, a multi-stakeholder partnership for combating child malnutrition, the Mother NGO scheme for child health services under NRHM. In few other cases, a contract was present between the private provider and the Government, but this information was either unavailable or denied sharing, like in case of Federation of Obstratians and Gynaecologists Association of India (FOGSI), Maharashtra State AIDS Control Society (MSACS) and SEARCH, Gadchiroli. Other collaborations did not qualify in the study criteria as they were either corporate social responsibility (CSR) initiatives like L&T Hospital and Hindustan Liver Family Planning Promotion Trust (HLFPPT) or were NGO involvement in Government programmes like Janani Suraksha Yojana and Institute of Health Management Pachod (IHMP). All the three selected PPPs were based in Maharashtra. Maharashtra was purposefully selected as every Indian state has one of the constant contexts for all the case studies. Different states have varying nature of socio-economic and political context which could have interfered while accessing the PPP cases on various institutional factors.

The methodology involved in-depth case study analysis of the partnership. An interview schedule was developed for evaluating the case studies, using the evaluation criteria generated from the review of secondary literature. It constituted questions mainly open-ended in nature, on various aspects of the partnership categorised into four major themes—nature of the PPP; management of partnership; services delivered as per the partnership; and beneficiaries' perspectives about the services. The interview schedule was administered to two or more senior officials of the partnership, the government representative and the private partner.

Case 1: Dilaasa (By CEHAT) at K.B. Bhabha Municipal Hospital, Mumbai

Dilaasa was established as a first hospital-based crisis centre in India for women facing domestic violence in 2001. It is a joint initiative between CEHAT, an NGO working on health related research and advocacy in Mumbai and the Public Health Department of the BMC (Brihanmumbai Municipal Corporation). Dilaasa runs as a department ward in K.G. Bhabha Hospital which is one of 16 peripheral general hospitals of the BMC (Deosthali, *et al.*, 2005).

Before Dilaasa, women facing psycho-emotional abuse were completely ignored by the health system. On other hand, NGOs dealing with victims for psycho-social support had no linkages with the health system. Services to victims of domestic violence were hardly visible, *ad hoc*, unorganised and isolated from each other. Reason being that abuse like domestic violence takes place within the 'home' and considered a private matter and not a serious public health issue. There was complete absence of integrated services on physical and psychological post-violence trauma for victims of domestic violence in the public health domain.

Cases coming to Dilaasa are referrals from the outpatient or causality department of the hospital. Services at Dilaasa begin with rapport building session with the counsellor in a protective environment. Then a safety assessment of the women is ascertained whether she can return to her home with no risks of further violence. There is provision for temporary shelters like a 24 hour emergency shelter at the hospital in case of medical observations, injuries or one

Table 7.1: Roles and responsibilities of partners in Dilaasa

The Contract	*Roles*	*Responsibilities*
BMC (Bhabha Hospital, Bandra West)	Medical Superintendent of the Hospital provided leadership to Dilaasa and headed it.	Space—Rooms for counselling, legal aid and training.
	Dilaasa to be established as a department of the hospital—relational and functional space.	Temporary 24 hour Shelter for women victims.
	Dilaasa was completely owned by BMC, run in its name, all correspondence and liaison in its name.	Staff salaries—nurse, social worker, doctor, 12 trainers
	Joint decision making in consultation with CEHAT team.	Medical referral and support from other hospital departments.
CEHAT	Assisting BMC in setting up and running a crisis centre for women victims of domestic violence.	Provide trained full time staff for the project.
	Create environment and conditions based on mutual respect and care for women victims aimed at inter-departmental and NGO collaboration.	Technical assistance in setting up the crisis centre. Sensitization and training of the BMC hospital staff.
	To help BMC integrate the programme as a part of its service and replicate in other hospitals.	Secure funds for the project funds secured from Ford Foundation.

Source: Compiled from (Deosthali *et al.*, 2005).

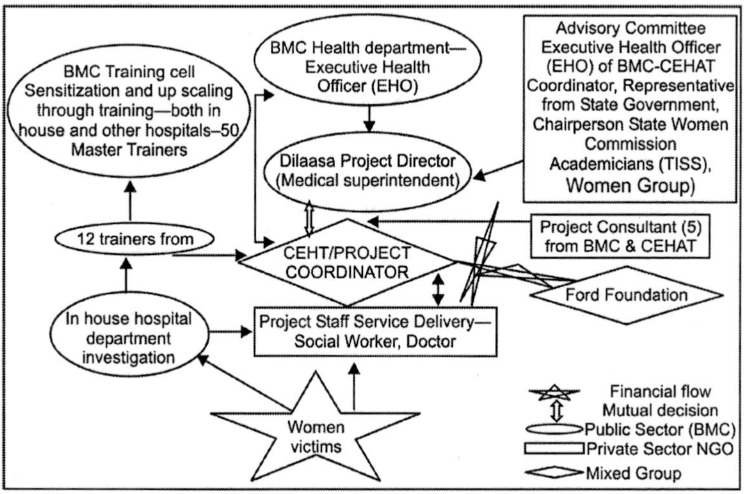

Source: Illustrations by author (Deosthali *et al.* 2005).

Fig. 7.1: Dilaasa Organisational Structure

night separation on grounds of safety. Many women are encouraged to file non-cognizable complaint or an FIR and given legal counselling. Follow-ups sessions also including joint meetings with the abusive members, were also organised to negotiate the interests of the women (*ibid.*). Since, the centre is based in a peripheral hospital, it caters to the surrounding populations of a Mumbai suburb—Bandra West. Roles and responsibilities of the BMC and CEHAT were delineated in the Memorandum of Understanding (MoU). Table 7.1 describes these roles and contribution of each of the partners.

Dilassa was conceptualized and implemented as a joint project, between equal partners with equal contribution of human resources, leadership and management, both from CEHAT and the hospital. This was its biggest strength. Figure 7.1 shows the structure of Dilaasa project. The leadership to Dilaasa was provided by the medical superintendent of Bhabha Hospital in capacity of Project Director while project coordination and implementation was done by CEHAT. All the decisions regarding the project like policy, programme activities and future direction are taken jointly by representatives of both CEHAT and Bhabha Hospital.

Case 2: Mother NGO Scheme

MNGO scheme was one of the largest Government sponsored programme of contracting private, not-for-profit sector, i.e. NGOs of varying capacities, to deliver maternal and child health services in un-served and under-served areas in the country. Department of Family Welfare, Ministry of Health and Family Welfare had introduced MNGO scheme in the Ninth Five Year Plan (1997-2002) as a strategy to implement its RCH programme. The National Budget Estimate for MNGO scheme during 2006-07 was ₹ 329.10 million which was 0.36 per cent of the budget earmarked for National Rural Health Mission (NRHM) in India (NGO Division, Government of India 2005).

The scheme involved large number of contracts between Government (at Central, State and District levels) and the NGOs of varying sizes and capacities across India. In fact MoUs are also signed between the Central Government and State Governments indicating their commitment to increase contribution to public health budget, preferably by 10 per cent each year; to increased devolution to Panchayati Raj Institutions and to develop performance benchmarks for release of funds (Ministry of Health and Family Welfare, 2005). The scheme follows almost a vertical structure involving NGOs, from advocacy, training right up to delivering services at PHC or sub-centre level.

Before MNGO scheme, most NGOs were working 'on' Government programmes independently rather than 'with' the Government. For instance, NGOs were contributing in RCH phase I programme limited to community mobilization or running of health centres. However, pinning accountability for the results was not possible and long term sustainability was weak. This had resulted in ineffectiveness of funds with no marked change in development outcomes. It was to address this challenge that GoI engaged NGOs through a formal and structured mechanism through the MNGO scheme.

The scheme innovatively took into account extreme diversification and variations in NGOs by classifying them in a hierarchy based on their size, capacity, nature of activities, credibility, past record etc. into—

- ***Regional Resource Centres***—These are large NGOs at state or national level involved in advocacy, capacity building and providing technical assistance.
- ***Mother NGOs***—They are large state level NGOs that have strong focus on health. Instead of implementing projects, they identify projects, monitor, evaluate and build capacities of smaller regional NGOs. The role of MNGOs is to fund and mentor the FNGOs, look after their capacity building and training needs.
- ***Field NGOs***—These are smaller NGOs that directly work with the communities on the demand side, baseline surveys, RCH orientation, creation of conducive working environment for ANMs, documentation etc.
- ***Service NGOs***—These are moderate to big sized NGOs working directly with the communities with adequate infrastructure and personnel capacities to provide clinical services (supply side) directly. They are to provide an

integrated package of clinical and non-clinical services directly to the community like safe delivery, neo-natal care, prevention of RTI/STI, treatment of diarrhoea and ARI, adolescent reproductive health, abortion and IUD services.

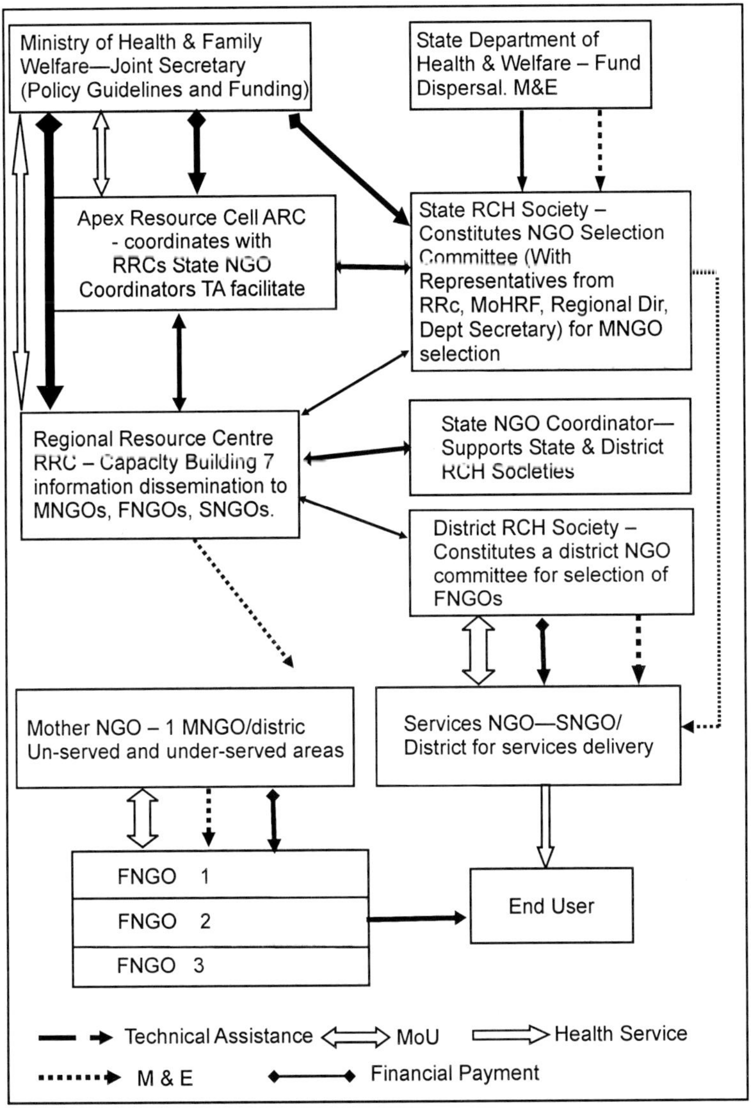

Fig. 7.2: Institutional Framework for MNGO Scheme

It was assumed that all kinds of NGOs would together complement the Government health delivery system for filling the gaps in RCH service delivery. Roles of participating NGOs are somewhat well defined but there is less clarity and diffusion of roles and responsibilities at various levels of Government from State RCH society, District RCH society, State NGO selection committees etc. (Bhat, *et al.*, 2007). In 2008, the MNGO programme was implemented in the country by 215 MNGOs in 324 districts with 800 FNGOs, 11 Regional Resource Centres (RRC) and 1 Apex Resource Cell (ARC) at the Central level (www.mohfw.nic.in).

Case 3: Bhavishya Alliance

Bhavishya Alliance was a multi-stakeholder partnership between Government, NGOs and corporates for combating child under-nutrition in India. Global Partnership for Child Nutrition (PCN), an international initiative brought together 3 international players to set-up Bhavishya Alliance as a registered non-profit trust in Mumbai (Bhavishya Alliance, 2007). They were the Unilever Group, Synergos Institute and UNICEF. At the first level, the partnership was formed between Bhavishya Alliance and Department of Women and Child Development, Government of Maharashtra through a MoU. The second level of partnerships was between multiple stakeholders in the Alliance, namely corporates, quasi-government and government organisations and NGOs. The alliance was based on the premise that under-nutrition is a complex issue requiring high level of synergies between significant sectors and major stakeholders. The focus of its intervention in Maharashtra was multi-dimensional including key areas like food and water, supporting infrastructure, capacity building, behaviour change and knowledge systems. The alliance began its programmes in 10 blocks of 5 rural districts of Maharashtra and in one urban slum in Mumbai in 2005. These were Thane and Mokhada blocks (Thane), Surgana and Peth blocks (Nashik), Dhargaon and Akkalkua blocks (Nandurbar), Dharni and Chikaldhara blocks (Amravati), Dhanora and Mulchera blocks (Gadchiroli) and L Ward (Mumbai).

With multiple stakeholders in a partnership in Bhavishya Alliance, there was a strong need to define the scope and intensity of involvement of the various stakeholders. During interviews with the BA representatives, they confirmed that role of each partner in that intervention was clearly spelt out. Each partner brought its own competency areas to contribute. Like infrastructure advocacy to the Government was taken by ICICI and HDFC with Tata Motors and ICDS representative as team members. HLL took behaviour change as their prerogative; core area of capacity building was given to ICICI Ventures and TATAs on the knowledge systems part of it. McDonalds was to fund a daycare programme where all anganwadi centres will

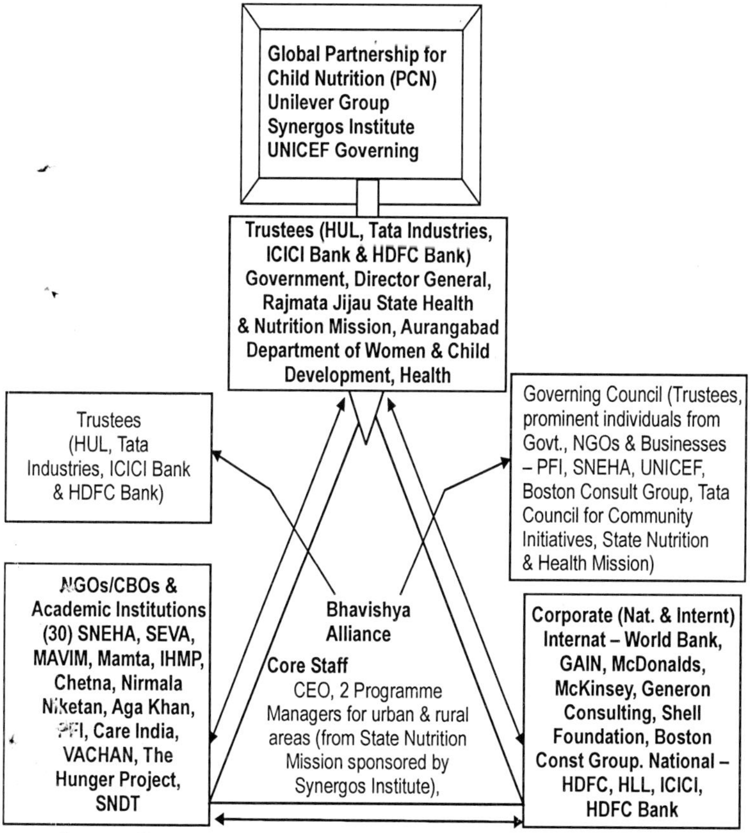

Source: Illustration by author Adapted from www.bhavishya.org.in

Fig. 7.3: The Organisational Chart for Bhavishya Alliance

have crèche facilities and would remain open up to 8 hours in a day. ICDS Commissionerate as Government partner in this initiative would train its entire staff and Nirmala Niketan, an academic institution would provide necessary technical and training inputs. The basic MoU template or generic contents were not shared.

Discussion and Findings

The assessment criteria for evaluation the PPP case studies used for the analysis is adapted and referred from criteria developed by Raman and Björkman (2000) and Bhat *et al.* (2007) in their independent studies. These studies cited determinants like leadership and ownership, contracting design, funding and risk sharing and monitoring as determinants to the success and sustainability of a PPP. Table 7.2 gives a brief comparison of the three cases. Since, Government is a key partner in these PPPs, the same criterion is useful to understand its role in partnering with the private actors for health services. Before discussing these three PPP cases on select criteria, it is imperative to know their current status as of now to know their sustainability and scalability after four years since this study.

Dilaasa services on extending support to women began in April 2005 at Bandra Bhabha Hospital, Mumbai. The contract was for a period of 3 years. Presently the services at Dilaasa are taken over by the municipal hospital. CEHAT phased out when its contract with BMC ended in 2007. With success of this PPP in one hospital, CEHAT took to mainstreaming Dilaasa in other municipal hospitals of the city. It initiated advocacy, training and capacity building of medical staff to set-up Dilaasa centre in municipal hospitals like Kurla Bhabha Hospital and M.T. Agarwal Hospital in partnership with the Health Department of the BMC and hospital leadership (Dilaasa and Pehel, 2005). Dilaasa is currently functional in two municipal hospitals of Mumbai.

The partnership between Bhavishya Alliance and Maharashtra State Government was struck in 2005. The assumption of partnership was that the Government would strengthen its programmes through managerial and technical interventions from corporate sector and NGOs without committing huge finances, while the corporate sector were partnering out of their obligation and responsibility to contribute

Table 7.2: Description of PPP cases on select criteria

Study Components	*Dilaasa, CEHAT*	*Mother NGO Scheme*	*Bhavishya Alliance*
Nature of the PPP	Joint Venture NGO-Mumbai Municipal Corporation Partnership on domestic violence	Contracting out model Maharashtra State Government and NGOs for RCH services	Multi-stakeholder partnership between Corporates, NGOs and Maharashtra Government for combating child malnutrition.
Participating entities in the PPP	1. Public Health Department of the BMC, Bhabha Hospital 2. CEHAT, an NGO	1. Ministry of Health Family Welfare, MoHFW, District RCH Society 2. NGOs acting as Regional Resource Centres (RRCs), Mother NGOs, Field NGOs, Service NGOs	1. Dept. of WCD, Dept. of Health, GoM, State Nutrition Mission. 2. Hindustan Unilever, HDFC, ICICI, McKinsey, McDonalds, Taj Group of Hotels, Nike Foundation, TCS. 3. Sneha, Institute of Health Management Pachod (IHMP), Seva, Chetna 4. Synergos, UNICEF 5. Nirmala Niketan, Inst of Hotel Management, Aurangabad
Objectives	Institutionalise domestic violence as a critical public health concern by establishing one-stop crisis-centre in public hospitals for women facing violence in homes and families.	Increase access and coverage of government reproductive and child health services in under-served and un-served area through various NGOs.	Strengthen government programmes by empowering the partners with necessary knowledge and skills to address the complexities of child malnutrition, through developing affordable and sustainable solutions.
Who initiate the partnership	CEHAT initiated the partnership with the Health Dept. of the BMC taking cues from Malayasian experience.	Union Ministry of Health as a centrally sponsored scheme. In Maharashtra –DoWCD, State RCH Society and District RCH Society.	Consortium of international private parties –Synergos Institute USA, Uniliver Group and UNICEF.
Funding arrangement	There is no funding from the BMC but indirect inputs are provided for infrastructure, staff and medical assistance. Project funded by Ford Foundation.	Grant-in-aid from GoI to State RCH society to MNGOs	Corporate partner contribute their expertise in developing specific initiatives like management systems, IT support or technical support, trainings etc.

towards the cause of under nutrition (Bhavishya Alliance, 2007). In 2008 when this study concluded, most partnerships in Bhavishya Alliance were formed, but the operations on ground had not begun. As per the current status, the initiative has ceased its operations since 2010. There are no apparent reasons visible in the public domain for its failure and the initiative's website is also not functional.

Progress on Mother NGO scheme is not promising. Agreements between the State RCH Society and NGOs began operationalising in 2005. Duration of the contract is short term, for 3 years from August 2005, extendable up to 5 years on its performance. As per officials from Maharashtra State RRC which is FPAI, till 2007 the scheme was still in the process of training and finalizing MNGOs, FNGOs and SNGOs. As against a high rhetoric of covering all districts in Maharashtra, currently there are only 5 MNGOs working in 6 districts working with 18 other FNGOs and 6 SNGOs under the RCH-II programme. The analysis proceeding would throw determinants and reasons for the successes and failures of these three cases.

Contractual Framework

Both Dilaasa and Bhavishya Alliance model of PPP is of hybrid in nature and they do not fall into any of the available models of PPPs. As per the contracting design, PPP models of the 3 case studies can be illustrated below in Figure 7.4. Dilaasa and Bhavishya Alliance resemble a joint venture type of a PPP. Joint Venture is a partnership where two or more partners commit certain share of resources (not necessarily financial), to establish a new organization or a programme. In Dilaasa, while the Government provided infrastructure and personnel support, CEHAT provided technical and training support. The main strength of such a PPP is that it is jointly owned by the partners who contribute equally; share equal risks thus, are equally committed to ensure its success and sustainability. Secondly although Dilaasa is a PPP, the services are still provided by the Government which is its main responsibility, and not by CEHAT, NGO. In Bhavishya Alliance also, the main partners jointly established it as an NGO and then roped in the Government agency as an equal partner.

The Mother NGO scheme on the other hand is an example of contracting-out model of PPP. Here the Government is paying a fee

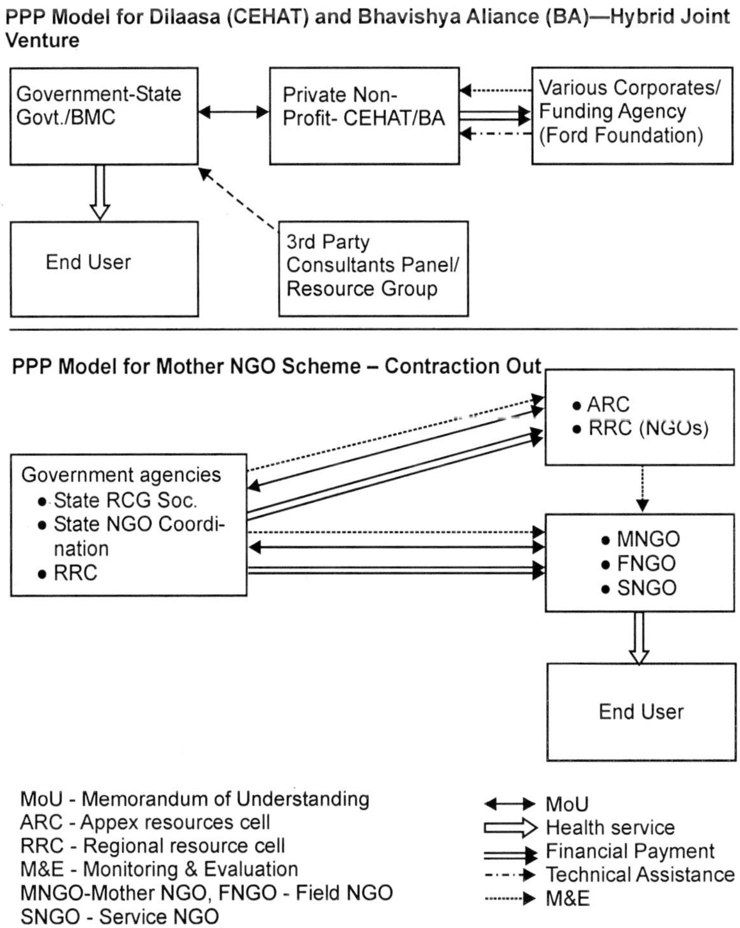

Fig. 7.4: PPP Models of above three case studies

to the NGOs to build capacities of functionaries and communities, and deliver services with or without Government infrastructure. A detailed MoU is signed between the Mother NGO and the District RCH Society. However, most of the contents of MoU are focused on exercising 'control' over the NGO, while the specification on service delivery is extremely brief and general. The contract mentions delineation of roles for NGOs for the actual delivery of services as per the GoI 'guidelines' which states need to follow. There is little scope for innovation or one could say more room for manipulation, both of which could result in ineffective delivery of services.

Contract is heavily biased in favour of the Government, as if prepared without any consultation with NGO partners. There is over-emphasis of rigid reporting and monitoring systems to multiple agencies at various levels thus diffusing their accountability. Such a type of contracting arrangement mires the Government into keeping a close eye on NGOs, rather than capitalise on strengths and experience of NGOs to strengthen its own service delivery systems. PPP in Mother NGO scheme is not based on mutual understanding and trust between partners and may not be sustainable for long term.

In only Dilassa model of PPP, did the actual provision of services remained in the hands of the state. For Bhavishya Alliance, the action plans were mainly on paper and services had not begun in 2008 during this report writing. And for MNGO scheme, reproductive and child health services will be delivered by Service NGOs in un-served and under-served areas and not by the Government.

Type of PPP model has a bearing on access, quality and costs of public health services. In India the state largely enters into a contract in or contract out PPP in health services. Examples include Seva Rural Gujarat, Urban Slum Healthcare project, Adilabad of Andhra Pradesh, Arpana Swasthya Kendra Delhi, Karuna Trust Bangalore, Chiranjeevi Yojana Gujarat, Mobile Health Service Sunderbans etc. Contracting is aimed at improving service access in geographically underserved areas, to improve quality of services and also to reduce the expenditures on the service by the poor. International experience indicates that contracting is effective only when used to deliver services in predominately poor areas and not for general population. For instance, contracting was successful in Bangladesh Urban slums project where there were high concentrations of poor residents. However, there are conflicting findings on contracting mechanisms like Cambodia's experience of contracting NGOs to provide primary health care to general population in nine rural districts between 1999 and 2001 was largely successful (Brad Schwartz and Bhushan, 2004).

Most of the PPP models fall under either demand side or supply side strategies. Demand side strategies include vouchers and insurance mechanisms like community health insurance, social health insurance and micro-credit. Remaining PPPs are all supply based strategies including contracting, social marketing, and social franchising. Studies strongly suggest that most PPPs in India are exclusively 'supply' oriented initiatives which eventually may not be effective in realizing the objectives of improved access, affordability, quality and equity in health services (Institute for Health Sector Development, 2004).

Experiences from other countries suggest that promising results are achieved when there is a combination of supply and demand side interventions like vouchers, insurance and risk pooling mechanisms, either within the same PPP or in more than one PPP for a particular health intervention (*ibid.*). For instance Janani in Bihar and Jharkand offers RCH services in partnership with its State Department of Health and Family Welfare through PPP models like franchising, social marketing, contract in, contract out and subsidies. The demand is generated through providing subsidies and access to services is increased by the remaining strategies.

Leadership and Ownership

Studies indicate that programmes where State Governments initiate a PPP or are involved from inception stage have more chances of success and are sustainable than a centrally sponsored PPP arrangement. It is so because of a strong sense of ownership resulting in pursuing the programme like case of Yeshaswani scheme in Karantaka, Urban Health Posts in Andhra Pradesh and Chiranjeevi scheme in Gujarat. These were directly implemented by the State Governments. It is unlikely that a centrally administered uniform model would succeed in diverse health settings in our country (WHO, 2001). The case in point is the MNGO scheme. Being a centrally sponsored scheme, the State Governments view it as being forced, with the only role of utilizing Central grants. Also with the scheme being decentralized, there was a leadership crisis at various levels—ARC at national level; state RCH society and RRCs; district RCH society and finally at MNGO level. This created a serious vacuum in leadership and procedural delays. ARC is responsible for technical inputs, training and overall coordination among RRCs in coordination with the State Governments. However, ARC was ineffective in uniting all its NGOs for shared unity of purpose, commitment or partnership orientation towards the cause. On the contrary, most NGOs were seen as competing with one another for maximum funding than for sharing knowledge or problem solving. Secondly, the relationship between NGOs and Government authorities resembled a buyer-contractor relation rather than that of equal partners. This adversely affected the ownership and commitment of various NGOs, which formed the very backbone of the scheme.

Dynamism and responsiveness of the medical superintendent of the municipal hospital, who led Dilaasa as a Programme Director, was crucial element in its success. It led to high ownership from the hospital on the whole. The leadership of the hospital's superintendent was instrumental in establishing Dilaasa as one of the wards of the hospital. Line of authority and accountability were clear as staff at Dilaasa including CEHAT project coordinator reported directly to the superintendent.

In Bhavishya Alliance, its governing council was the supreme decision making body that provided leadership and guidance to the programme. It comprised senior leaders from all major partners in the Alliance including the State's Rajmata Jijau Mother and Child Health and Nutrition Mission, Hindustan Unilever, ICICI Bank, Tata Industries, Boston Consulting Group, Population Foundation of India, SNEHA, Tata Council for Community Initiatives, HDFC and UNICEF. At the next level, there was a core team headed by a CEO and programme officers deputed from State Nutrition Mission, UNICEF and HUL. The leadership got diffused in many powerful players as they were jointly leading the initiative. The CEO responsible was a managerial post and hired for the job. The position was not mandated to provide the leadership to the alliance. Also with multiple type of State agencies involved like the Department of Women and Child, the ICDS Commissionerate, Rajmata State Nutrition Mission etc., there was no clear leader or leaders who represented the state as a whole and took decisions on behalf of all.

Financial Management and Risk Sharing

There is limited evidence on the financial management of PPPs, but existing research show that irregularities in flow of funds have been cited as one of the major weaknesses of PPPs, where it involves exchange of funds from the Government to the private player. Usually, the funds are routed from Central department to State departments, then to commissionerates or directorates at state level, to district or *zilla parishads* and finally to the agency. Many times the delays are also from the end of NGOs as they are not able to submit utilization certifications on time. Either ways, funding from Government has always been associated with inadequacy, delays, inflexibility and subjected to burdensome scrutiny and oversight (Annigeri *et al.*, 2004). However, one exception has been the Chiranjeevi Yojana in Gujarat where the private gynaecologists receive an advanced amount from the Government to perform institutional deliveries free of cost to BPL women.

It is evident that Government indulges in partial treatment and is biased towards the private for-profit sector in disbursing funds. It meant that while private for-profit agencies get their full reimbursements, NGOs are usually not given full budgetary support but only for sustenance purposes (Raman and Björkman, 2000). For instance, Karuna Trust Bangalore gets maximum up to 90 per cent grants for management of a PHC as remaining 10 per cent funds, is supposed to be raised from other sources. Contrary to this case, a Government-owned and corporate-managed, Rajiv Gandhi Hospital in Raichur Karnataka gets full reimbursement of all its expenses plus a service fee. Government's assumption that NGOs would raise the remaining funds from other sources during the course of PPP, seldom materializes. Thus, NGOs continue to sustain in low budgets in a PPP, which has adverse implications on the quality of services provided by them.

Dilaasa PPP involved no funding from the BMC. BMC provided indirect inputs through infrastructure (space in the hospital), staff and medical assistance for the centre. The initiative was sustaining through funds from Ford Foundation to CEHAT. In Bhavishya Alliance too there is no exchange of funds between Government and alliance or between Government and partnering NGOs. However, role and responsibility of the State Government varied from contract to contract. For instance depending upon the core competency of the corporate partner, they contributed their expertise in activities like developing management systems, IT support or technical support, trainings for the Government.

Corporate partner funded only in select initiatives like ICICI sponsored training of Government Health Department and ICDS staff at National Institute of Nutrition at Amravati; Taj Group of Hotels funded training rural youth in hospitality management and nutrition; refurbishment of health posts; setting up of nutritional rehabilitation centres; production and distribution of fortified and complementary weaning foods etc. The Government was to use management competencies of the corporate sector in strengthening its systems. While interviewing senior project staff, it was reiterated that the Maharashtra Government's involvement could be described as 'opening its windows for the winds of change of come in' without substantial investment of funds.

Because of no funding commitments both from the NGO or the Government, the only motivation that was binding the partners together was to exert on the issue at hand. In MNGO scheme, GoI released Rs. 16 lakh per MNGO as grant-in-aid to State RCH Society, which then releases it to district RCH society, in 3 yearly installments after appropriate evaluations. MNGOs can retain only 20 per cent of the amount for its operations and distribute remaining to its 2 or more FNGOs working in its district. It has been reported that this funding to NGOs is delayed as like in many other Government programmes. In addition, the budget does not provide for adequate resources to hire qualified personnel in NGOs, in which case NGOs dump additional load on the existing staff. NGOs find it difficult to sustain their activities from limited funding from the Government. The trend has adverse implications on the performance and sustainability of the Mother NGO scheme.

Most PPPs in India involved government to reimburse expenses or provide grant-in-aid to the NGOs (Raman and Björkman, 2000). Most of the time, this fund disbursal was mired in red tapism, thus, adversely affecting the partnership. On risk sharing, there is higher risk on the government especially when it funds PPPs because it is ultimately responsible for the services and if private provider falters, the responsibility will be entirely on the government. The MNGO model of PPP holds this observation true. Government invested financial resources to contract out service delivery to NGOs, without considering the risks associated with under-performance or variations in quality or access of services by NGOs. NGOs too are uncovered on risks if payments are delayed or not made. There is also no mention of any incentives for NGOs who perform exceptionally well or penalties for those who would not conform to service delivery outcomes.

Monitoring

Like any public programmes PPPs too need timely monitoring and evaluations more so when both public and private partners are involved, for various objectives—like for quality management, assessing service delivery outcomes to ascertain effectiveness, efficacy, equity and ease of access.

In Dilaasa, the monitoring of services is done by CEHAT through case presentations of women victims in weekly meetings. Here the social worker of the hospital presents few cases in presence of a panel of consultants (5 consultants jointly inducted by BMC and CEHAT). Such reporting helps the programme team gets a feedback to enhance their skills and gain more knowledge to deal cases in a better way. CEHAT brings these consultations out as reports however records of the cases are kept confidential. Bhavishya Alliance had a similar way to receive feedback of its programmes. It had an Internal Resource Group (IRG) of 5 members, mainly activists and experts. IRG assesses progress of the Alliance' projects in the field and bring forth the community concerns to the attention of the Governing Council on a monthly basis. Monitoring in both Dilaasa and Bhavishya Alliance was not in hands of the government, but done by third party that was a group of external experts or a funding agency.

However, in MNGO scheme, various state agencies were monitoring the scheme. A system of periodic reporting and monitoring resulted in many kinds of records and registers to be maintained by all the NGOs. These records were record of baseline data, indicators under each objective and activity, inventory records, financial records and staffing records. In addition, the MNGO was monitored at various levels of government like the State RCH society, State NGO coordinator, district RCH society and to RRCs.

Multiple government agencies involved in monitoring makes the exercise complex, repetitive and cumbersome. It also diffuses and confuses accountability of various partners as MNGOs are reporting to practically all levels of government agencies—State

RCH society, District RCH society, RRCs and State NGO coordinator. It can be extremely de-motivating and frustrating for NGOs to comply with such stringent norms of monitoring and at the same time be expected to deliver quality services, train and monitor smaller NGOs and above all, sustain scheme operations by raising external funds. With such high demand of monitoring on the shoulders of the Government agencies, it can hardly contribute in improving services at grassroots by way of support and constructive critique of its NGO partners. Evaluation reports about the current status and performance of the scheme across India, since 2005 were not available with ARC, Delhi. This is so when there was an extensive monitoring and information system (MIS) for the scheme created in partnership with National Informatics Centre (NIC), GoI.

Although the responsibilities of NGOs are clearly stated in the MoU, the government hardly conducts monitoring reviews in intervals to monitor the quality of services for mid-term corrections. Studies indicate that NGOs find it tough to conform to stringent bureaucratic procedures and documentation for reporting, monitoring and evaluation of services under the partnership arrangement (Bhat *et al.,* 2007). Most NGOs lack capacities, resources and are short of trained manpower, to comply with the requirements. Studies have also indicated that state and district health officials take no active role in monitoring the scheme. Thus, despite government investing considerable resources in M & E, it ultimately remains ineffective.

Conclusions

There are three main lessons emerging from each of the cases evaluated in the study. Dilaasa succeeds as a joint venture type of a partnership because of number of evident reasons. Firstly, the partnership was initiated by CEHAT, an NGO that acted upon complete dearth of services for a hospital based crisis centre for women victims of domestic violence. This conclusion falls in line with similar observations made by other studies that partnerships initiated by NGOs were more stable and effective than those started by the government. Secondly, CEHAT envisioned establishing Dilaasa not as its own unit running in a municipal hospital, but as a ward of the hospital itself. This ensured ownership by the state along with sustainability and scalability of the initiative. Finally, since Dilaasa was not funded by the State, but by a third party agency, quality monitoring was effectively achieved.

Bhavishya Alliance was a multi-stakeholder type of a PPP where the role of the state was more of a passive recipient of what the private sector was giving. Since there was no commitment of finances on the part of the government, state representatives were only one among many partners to set the agenda. In addition, the failure of the partnership can be attributed to two faulty assumptions on issue of child malnutrition. The first assumption stems from the neo-liberal framework followed by international donor agencies, that nutrition being a multi-sectoral problem requires managerial, technical and governance inputs from a cross-section of actors. The second assumption was that state services are poor because of lack of resources and hence there is a need augment and synergize with diverse resources in the private sector. Many social sciences studies have provided evidence that malnutrition is socio-political issue that cannot be tackled alone with managerial strategies. Also the problem of the state is not lack of finances but effective utilization of funds for equitable outcomes.

The Mother NGO partnership like many other contracting PPPs was hard to sustain as they are literally driven by written word. Such partnerships are not dynamic enough to resolve issues through mutual understanding and trust. Also in such a contracting-out PPP, the service delivery shifts (completely or partly) from the hands of the Government to the private player. Studies have pointed out that contract out partnerships demands elaborate monitoring on part of the Government, for which it has a poor track record of monitoring its own services (Harding and Preker, 2001). Also most PPPs in India are supply based strategies like contracting or social marketing which again face risk of sustainability owing to overlooking demand and sources of funding (Institute for Health Sector Development, 2004). For instance, if an NGO/corporate has taken up running of a PHC, a patient may still choose not to come to the PHC and instead go to a rural quack. Mere provision or ease of access of a service cannot always ensure desirable demand for it.

Instead of contracting health services to private actors and create parallel systems, government can involve private players to strengthen its own service delivery systems through other PPPs like social marketing, hospital autonomy, joint ventures, performance management where the onus of delivering services still rests with the government and it is directly accountable to people. PPPs initiated by the government usually lack leadership. Government must in consultation with partners, identify leaders who could act as a champion facilitator in directing the partnership, coordinate with all stakeholders and ensure its effectiveness. This leader could be an individual, groups of individuals, a committee/board with representation from all partners.

Health is a state subject, but at the same time being highly privatized, most states lack policies to interact with private health sector and also to engage them in any partnership. Private providers are extremely heterogeneous and diverse while government lacks an effective regulatory mechanism to register them. Policy makers seem to be excited about the idea that great changes in public health can be brought about without substantial increase in public fund allocation, through the magic *mantra* of public private partnership. But there are a number of policy lessons to be learnt from handful of PPPs already implemented. Locally applicable models of partnership are more likely to be successful. It is quite unlikely that a centrally administered model would work in diverse health settings in the country.

Acknowledgements

I would like the Observer Research Foundation for supporting this study and Prof. Surinder Jasawl, Dean, Research and Development TISS for her guidance and support. My special thanks to the representatives of the organizations interviewed in the study for their cooperation. They were Ms. Rashmi Thakkar an Ms Sangita Rege of CEHAT, Mr. Umakant Mangire, State NGO Coordinator and Ms. Nazneen Gidwani of FPAI, Dr. Isha Bhagwat and Ms Purnima Upadhyay of Bhavishya Alliance.

Note

1. There is no one agreed upon definition of a PPP. PPP is one where there is

a written understanding through an agreement or a Memorandum of Understanding (MoU) about the terms of reference, risks, investments, roles and responsibilities of the participating parities. This is the definition which has been considered for the study (Goyal, 2008).

References

Ahmedabad: Indian Institute of Management. Available at: https://205.186.138.171/assets/snippets/workingpaperpdf/2007-01-05_rbhat.pdf [Accessed December 27, 2012].

Annigeri, V.B. *et al.*, 2004. *An Assessment.* Available at: http://pdf.usaid.gov/pdf_docs/PNADC694.pdf [Accessed December 30, 2012].

Bhat, R., Maheshwari, S. and Saha, S., (2007). *Contracting-out of Reproductive and Child Health (RCH) Services through Mother NGO Scheme in India: Experiences and Implications.*

Bhavishya Alliance, (2007). *The Role of Multi-Stakeholders in Bhavishya Alliance on Corporate Engagement: A Journey of Thought to Action.*

Brad Schwartz, J. and Bhushan, I., (2004). Improving immunization equity through a public-private partnership in Cambodia. *Bulletin of the World Health Organization*, 82(9), pp. 661-667.

Deosthali, P., Maghnani, P. and Malik, S., 2005. *Establishing Dilaasa: Documenting the Challenges*, Center for Enquiry into Health and Allied Themes (CEHAT).

Dhar, A., (2012). Activists up in arms against new proposal on health care. *The Hindu.* Available at: http://www.thehindu.com/health/article3742403.ece [Accessed December 25, 2012].

Dilaasa and Pehel, (2005). *Mainstreaming Gender Concerns within the Public Health System*, Mumbai: CEHAT.

Goyal, J., (2008). *Public Private Partnerships in health: Opportunity for Reform or Privatisation.* An Investigtion of Reproductive and Child Health Services in India.

Harding, A. and Preker, A., (2001). *Private participation in health services handbook.* Human Development Network, The World Bank: New York, available at: http://siteresources. worldbank. org/INTINDONESIA/Resources/Human/PHS-Harding-01. pdf.

Institute for Health Sector Development, (2004). *Private Sector Participation in Health*, London: KFw Bankengruppe.

Jaya Goyal. *TISS.* Draft paper for HCU conference dated December 31, 2012. Only for internal circulation, not to be quoted. Page 16.

Ministry of Health and Family Welfare, (2005). *National Rural Health Mission Document.* Chapter 8 Partnership with Non Government Organisations, New Delhi: Government of India.

MoHFW, Government of India, *NRHM*. Available at: http://www.mohfw.nic.in/NRHM.htm [Accessed December 31, 2012].

NGO Division, Department of Family Welfare (DoFW), Ministry of Health and Family Welfare (MoHFW), Government of India, (2005). *Guidelines for DoFW supported NGO schemes.*

Raman, A.V. and Björkman, J.W., (2000). Public/Private Partnership in Health Care Services in India. *Health Administrator*, 21, pp. 1-2.

The Planning Commission, (2004). *The Report on the PPP Sub-group on Social Sector: Public Private Partnerships*, Government of India, New Delhi.

WHO, (2001). *Public Private Partnership for Tuberculosis Control: A Report of a Regional Meeting.*

EXPLANATORY MODELS AND HEALTH BEHAVIOUR

8
Community Participation in HIV/AIDS Healthcare Delivery

Reddy, K.S. and *Sahay, S.*

The concept of community participation continues to capture the attention of international health policy makers and analysts since a quarter of a century after it was formally introduced at the Alma Ata Declaration in 1978. The genesis of the idea and its conceptual development are primarily attributed to large multinational organizations particularly the World Health Organization (Zakus and Lysack, 1998). Since, then community participation in healthcare systems has become a growing theme in healthcare reforms in many societies (Youde, 2009). Community participation in health is a complex entity that has been extensively examined by a number of authors and continues to be of great interest even today (Rifkins, 1990).

Community participation refers to the active engagement of the populace in discussing their health concerns and ideas for improved healthcare delivery. However, there has been much speculation concerning the importance of community participation and whether countries have the structures and resources to successfully seek and incorporate the views and opinions of the populace in the design and implementation of health projects and programmes. Several studies have been conducted for assessing the community participation in healthcare, understanding barriers causing conflict and stimulants leading to co-operation between healthcare delivery providers and the community (Asthana and Oostvogels, 1996; Gruber and Caffery,

2005). Constraints, barriers and disputes may lead to conflicts while social values, social capital and awareness level lead to cooperation or sometimes it may occur in sequence. The factors being influencers for non-participation of people in the programme or acceptance of health care services are delineated through HIV/AIDS healthcare delivery.

HIV/AIDS is a serious health concern as it claims millions of lives and infecting 34 million people, worst affecting economic structure across nations (UNAIDS, 2012). Though there are very restricted modes of transmission of HIV, intensified human behaviour on these modes is cause of concern for the spread of HIV/AIDS. Several attempts have been made to control the spread of epidemic. It includes intervention, treatment, counselling, collaborations at all levels. Actively engaging communities in effective partnerships is considered critical for HIV prevention and treatment (Sahay, 2011). The programme managers have also realized the importance of community participation in healthcare service delivery for prevention and treatment of high risk population.

Although, new infections are declining, preventing the mortality of people with HIV/AIDS remains the primary focus of health care systems in different societies. If we are to understand the complex relationships that form the cluster of phenomena we call the AIDS epidemic, the disciplinary lines imagined between scientific paradigms and the clinical focus on the individual body on one hand, and the social sciences and humanities disciplines on the other must be breached (Marshall, 2005). Science can be seen as a social product and is inseparable from culture (Fleck, 1979) and hence the biomedical model alone will not be useful in fight against impediment of HIV/AIDS healthcare (Chattopadhyay and McKaig, 2004) and emphasis should be on socio-political and medical factors (Campbell, 2003).

Factors affecting Community Participation in HIV/AIDS Health Care Delivery (HHCD)

Foster (1969), an applied anthropologist has enlisted the factors that act as the barriers to change for innovations, social factors, cultural factors and psychological factors. Moreover, Foster noted that the factors which act as the barriers to change can act as stimulants to change as well. Range of factors that can explain barriers and stimulants to healthcare are social, cultural, economic, political, ethnic, gender and environmental factors and they are as important as the biological factors when attempting to find solutions or devising strategies to combat disease (Kalipeni *et al.*, 2007). Strategy for any intervention is that it should not only address surface cause, but also the root cause (Scheper-Hughes, 1994). Hence, it is necessary to understand such factors. There are different factors that lead to conflicts and cooperation in AIDS healthcare. These factors can be grouped into the categories discussed below. Purpose of this categorisation is not to give classificatory scheme, but to have a general idea about impact of these factors on HIV/AIDS healthcare.

Demographic Factors

Population is an important factor as economy in development of any nation it may be production, education or health. Developing countries with low economic resources and high population face many problems such as severe epidemic due to the lack of proper education and economic constrains. High population and increased rate of prevalence creates additional burden on existing healthcare facilities. Even though prevalence rates are low, the large populations of many Asian nations mean that large numbers of people have HIV infection (UNAIDS, 2006). Most infections occur around corridors or areas of development and industrialization where mobile populations, migrant workers, and commercial sex workers are key factors in transmission (USAID, 2011). In India, two-thirds of reported HIV infections are concentrated in mainly industrialized areas of six of the country's 28 states. HIV/AIDS has been termed as 'migrating pandemic' as developing countries are affected by new pattern of global migration of human labour for development (Erni, 1994). For example, in Zambia, modernization and migration among fishing community and alongside commercial sex work might be responsible for rapid spread of HIV and producing epidemic and cultural alternatives may increase the probability in involving sex work. In South Africa pandemic of HIV/AIDS occurs around migrant workers in construction industries.

Gender Issues

The literature on equity in health care delivery usually considers the sex variable as a component of need. Variations between men and women in health care use are deemed as exogenous, that is, resulting from different biological risk or unavoidable differences in attitudes towards health. Hence, sex and socio-economic status are assumed to be independent, which is hardly the case. Consequently, equity indices fail to fully capture socio-economic inequity, as it is partially controlled through the sex variable. In addition, gender inequity on the supply-side, due to prejudices or discriminations, is neglected. Studies show that a better understanding of equity in healthcare delivery requires the use of a larger array of socio-economic variables, and that the gender issue should not be neglected. Indeed, non-negligible differences appear across specific groups, which should help shaping health policies towards the most vulnerable populations (Perelman, 2007).

The balance of power in intimate heterosexual relationships is influenced by the gender role norms and beliefs of both partners. Men who subscribe to traditional gender roles are likely to exert control over the sexual relationship and to decide when, where and how sex occurs. Enforcing condom use is dependent on power dynamics within relationships that undermine women's choices and agency (Thege, 2009) and that place women at risk of HIV infection Thus, a woman's request to use condoms represents a challenge to prevailing traditional beliefs about gender roles, raising questions regarding the male's level of control over the sexual relationship as well as regarding the level of intimacy, trust, and commitment in the relationship (El Bassel, 2005). This is especially poignant given that women, particularly younger women, are most vulnerable to HIV and other types of sexually transmitted infections (STIs) (Chersich and Rees, 2008).

Cultural Factors

Cultural and community factors can have both positive as well as negative effect on prevention intervention programmes. These play important role in behavioural change as they help individual to assess risk and take a decision. In Swaziland, the culture of polygamy and differential definitions of adultery for men and women may act as barrier to learned behaviour for interventions (Wellings, 2012). Religious and moral beliefs may fuel the risk of stigma and scapegoating revolves around HIV infected people and it is more in case of homosexual people living with HIV/AIDS (PLHIVs) as culturally, homosexuality is reported to be considered as immoral and unnatural. Perception of West German's towards disease is failure of individual which may lead to non-acceptance by Insurance Companies for insurance of such people (Poore, 1998). In India, system of Devdasis and traditional entertaining occupation includes sexual activities among *Nat* communities (O'Neil *et al.*, 2004).

Todorova *et al.* (2006) delineated three points at which cultural differences may act as barriers in encounters between health professionals and clients: (1) Differences in definition and evaluation of symptoms; (2) Differential ordering of problems and priorities; and (3) Differential vulnerabilities to ego assault in the professional-client encounter. One way to promote beneficial health-related behaviours and health by social participation and empowerment would be to reform structural conditions such as the psychosocial work environment and work organization of important and substantial segments of the population (Lindstrom, 1994). Organisations have been shown to select structured organisational styles that are perceived to have an internal consistency to their situational environment, size and other concerns (Cummings and Worley, 1997). The settings approach to health promotion design and planning provides a good framework for exploring the state of health services in South African correctional facility (Poland *et al.*, 2001).

Economic Factors

Systematic disparities in rates of HIV incidence by socio-economic status were assessed among men attending three sexually transmitted disease (STD) clinics in Pune, India, to identify key policy intervention points to increase health equity. It was shown that by enhancing access to treatment and interventions among disadvantaged men, the disparity in rates of HIV incidence could be lessened considerably (Shepherd *et al.*, 2003). PLHA lead marginal lifestyles, use illicit drugs, and have lower socio-economic status, forming a group that professionals thought at risk of non-adherence (Chesney *et al.*, 2000). HIV infected individual is dependent on his/her social and economic situation, dealing with variable desires, feelings, affectivity and fears in their interactions with significant others (Schiltz and Sandfort, 2000). Studies in Africa reported that there is exchange of sex by young women for money or gifts in addition to other socio-cultural factors (Luke, 2005; Matasha *et al.*, 1998; Meekers and Calves, 1997; Nyanzi *et al.*, 2001; Nzyuko *et al.*, 1997). It is noted that at any given place and time commercial sex work is function of socio-economic factors and do not have any ethnic or cultural basis (Chattopadhyay and Rosemary, 2004), but no matter socio-cultural factors influence it. Hence, abstinence, being faithful, and condom use (ABC) strategy needs to be complemented by community-based economic ventures that promote economic security to reduce circular migration and keep families intact (Kalipeni *et al.*, 2006).

Biological and Psychological Factors

Most people are fearful of side effects prior to undergoing the regimen of drugs and many people who are on ART reported adverse events on starting therapy in different countries including India. While antiretroviral drugs are highly effective in slowing HIV disease progression, they can cause side-effects in some individuals, some of which can be life-threatening. Side-effects include severe skin reactions, hepatitis, anaemia and cardiovascular diseases. Some chronic side effects can be debilitating (e.g. chronic gastrointestinal intolerance) or cause long-term changes in body appearance like lipodystrophy and lipoatrophy etc. (Troll, 2011). The morbidity itself can cause stigma.

One major barrier to HIV prevention efforts is the social stigma associated with HIV/AIDS (Duncan *et al.*, 2005). It is defined as a powerful negative social label, stemming from a discrediting attribute of the individual, which radically changes their social identity (Goffman, 1963). It is observed that stigma of HIV cuts across society among all elements both vertically and horizontally (Parker and Aggleton, 2003), although there are several strategies to reduce the stigma among healthcare provider and community. Extent of stigma is more in case of women as positive women are more harshly judged and treated badly than men for almost same behaviour due to differentiation in gender roles and hence societal expectations and values (Gruber and Caffery, 2005).

Condom use though considered as most effective preventive method, social stigma associated with condom use is significant barrier as it points toward culturally prevented behaviour. In addition most serious observation is that people living with HIV-AIDS intentionally try to infect others due to denial, avoidance and anger about their status in society (Kerrigan, 2006). Psycho-social factor is one of the factors restricting the delivery of Highly Active Anti Retroviral Therapy (HAART). Research exploring linkages between stigma and HIV services uptake or the effect of HIV care and treatment programmes on stigma levels are largely missing and need to be prioritized (Bharat, 2011).

Marginalized sections which are labelled as 'isolates' are prone to fatalism and consider their body as porous thing and un-protective and such attitudes may fuel risk-taking behaviour. HIV negative individuals may become complacent due perception that HIV is now less serious issue because of the availability of HAART among HIV negative individuals (Kerrigan *et al.*, 2006). Stigma in rural India is still not well studied.

Political and Organisational Factors

Sexual act have socio-political meaning and vary with culture. Level and course of participation may shift along the continuum as participants negotiate the dynamics associated with power, conflict, and control (Cornwall and Jewkes, 1995; Wallerstein, 1999). This dynamics of power may be in healthcare delivery system or within community. The community, when considered as a real partner rather than a mere recipient of the results of its work, can be seen as an organisation with its own culture and structure (Berkeley and Springett, 2006). It is observed that in case of PLHA, member of household involved in long term political activities face less stigma than other household members. Hence, it is necessary to understand organisational set-up of a community under consideration. Also leadership plays important role at multiple levels and is political in nature and is influenced by wider context of national and global politics (Van der Vliet, 2004) hence political commitment is necessary for success of AIDS prevention campaign. War and political instability, Migration and violence against women have an impact on HIV prevention (Seidel, 1993; Farmer and Walton, 2000).

Discussion

The factors described above are interlinked and are complementary to each other and therefore, should be considered in holistic way. However, this effect will not be sustainable in absence of larger developmental measures aimed at commercial sex workers (CSWs) that requires modification of economic, political, and cultural values of the society. Barriers can occur with amalgamation of all these factors and to address issues it requires considering political and organisational, cultural, economic psycho-social and gender issues together (Parker, 1996; Adrian, 2006). Politico-economic policies and programmes have greater impact on prevention and treatment activities (Stevens, 1998; Clarke, 2006).

Experiences from a UK Department for International Development (DFID) funded project in Nigeria suggest that greater attention must be given to the impacts and effects of HIV/AIDS on communities, and the ways in which conflict can develop, emerge and sustain, resulting in severe breakdown of social cohesion and reduction of HIV/AIDS activities (Gruber and Caffery, 2005). In such cases, community mobilisation is the core strategy through success against HIV has been built. Fostering such mobilisation requires eliminating stigma, developing partnerships between Social and Government actors, and systematically involving communities and individuals infected and affected by HIV/AIDS (UNAIDS, 2002).

Community mobilisation and participation in healthcare delivery can be achieved by empowerment. Empowerment is a construct that links individual strengths and competencies, natural helping systems, and proactive behaviours to social policy and social change (Rappaport, 1984). Theoretically, the construct connects mental health to mutual help and the struggle to create a responsive community. It explores in term of wellness *versus* illness, competence *versus* deficits, and strength *versus* weakness. Werner (1997) stated that, "empowerment is the process by which disadvantaged people work together to take control of the factors that determine their health and their lives."

Empowerment of vulnerable section is necessary to avoid further transmission of HIV. In absence of any curative medicine prevention is given more importance and interventions are given more importance. Information, education and communication (IEC) is considered as most important strategy in awareness and abstinence, being faithful and condom use (ABC) to fight HIV/AIDS. But there are many socio-cultural factors which act as impediments to change behaviour and adopt safe practices. There are many strategies to deal with such obstacles and lead people and communities for their empowerment. To deal with non-participation of community in healthcare delivery; consultation, collaboration, and dynamic interaction between communities and researchers are seen as key interventions. Community engagement model for HIV prevention research at National AIDS Research Institute bring grassroots level community as peers who interact with researchers as partners in research (Sahay and Mehendale, 2011). It is viewed, global experiences about any programme suggests that critical attention must be to the impacts and effects of HIV/AIDS on communities, and the ways in which conflict can develop, emerge and be sustained.

Conclusions

Community participation needs to be given preference in healthcare delivery due to its effectiveness in creating awareness among people, reducing stigma and ability to address infrastructural constraints. As and when community participation is given importance, there is a need for understanding the process of healthcare delivery in the community which includes both the process of conflicts as well as cooperation, because this can be an empowerment issue which may help the people. Community participation is not an instrumental means but a dynamic process, which passes through different stages of cooperation and conflicts. These stages are shaped not by a single factor, but as a cumulative result of interaction between several factors.

Acknowledgements

Authors acknowledge the support of Indian Council of Medical Research for providing research fellowship for doctoral research and thank Dr. R.S. Paranjape, Director, NARI, Pune, for his guidance. Authors also acknowledge Dipak Wani and Kalyan Reddy for their suggestions in drafting this paper.

References

Adrian, M. (2006). 'Addiction and Sexually Transmitted Disease (STD), Human Immunodeficiency Virus, (HIV), and Acquired Immune Deficiency Syndrome (AIDS): Their Mutual Interactions', *Substance Use & Misuse*, 41:10, 1337–1348.

Asthana, S., and Oostvogel, R. (1996). Community Participation in HIV Prevention: Problem and Prospects for Community-based Strategies among Female Sex Workers in Madras, *Social Science and Medicine,* 43, 133-148.

Berkeley, D., and Springett, J. (2006). From Rhetoric to Reality: Barriers faced by Health for All Initiatives. *Social Science and Medicine,* 63, 179-188.

Bharat, S. (2011). A systematic review of HIV/AIDS-related stigma and discrimination in India: Current Understanding and Future Needs. *Journal of Social Aspects of HIV/AIDS*, Vol. 8, No. 3.

Campbell, C. (2003). *'Letting them die' Why HIV/AIDS programmes fail.* Oxford: James Currey.

Chattopadhyay, A., and McKaig, R.M. (2004). Development of poor commercial sex workers in India as an essential step in HIV/AIDS prevention. *AIDS Patient Care and STDs*, 18(3), 159-168.

Chattopadhyay, A., and Rosemary, G.M. (2004). Social development of commercial sex workers in India: An essential step in HIV/AIDS prevention. *AIDS Patient care and STD*, Vol 18, No. 3.

Chersich, M.F., and Rees, V.H. (2008). Vulnerability of women in southern Africa to infection with HIV: Biological determinants and priority health sector interventions. *AIDS*, 22 (suppl 4), S1-S14.

Chesney, M.A., Morin, M., and Sherr, L. (2000). "Adherence to HIV combination therapy". *Social Science and Medicine,* 50, 1599-1605.

Clarke, J.N. (2006). "Homophobia out of the closet in the media portrayal of HIV/AIDS 1991, 1996 and 2001: Celebrity, heterosexism and the silent victims". *Critical Public Health*, 16:4, 317-330.

Cornwall, A., and Jewkes, R. (1995). "What is participatory research?" *Social Science and Medicine,* 41, 1667-1676.

Cummings, T.G., and Worley, C.G. (1997). *Organisational Development and Change.* Cincinati, OH: South Western College Publishing.

Duncan, C., Harrison, M.G., Toldson, I.A., Malaka D., and Sithole, S. (2005). "Social Stigma, HIV/AIDS Knowledge, and Sexual Risk: A Cross-Cultural

Analysis". *Journal of Applied Biobehavioural Research*, 2005, 10, 1, pp. 1-26.

El Bassel, N., Gilber, T N., Wu, E., Go, H., and Hill, J. (2005). "HIV and intimate partner violence among methadone-maintained women in New York City". *Social Science and Medicine,* Volume 61, Issue 1, pp. 171-183.

Erni, J.N. (1994). *Unstable Frontiers: Technomedicine and the Cultural Politics of "Curing" AIDS*, Minneapolis: University of Minnesota Press.

Farmer, P.E., and Walton, D.A. (2000). Condoms, coups, and the ideology of prevention: facing failure in rural Haiti. In: Keenan J., (ed.) Catholic ethicists in HIV/AIDS prevention. Maryknoll, NY: Orbis Books, 108-19.

Fleck, L. (1979). *Genesis and development of a scientific fact*, In Trenn, T.J. and F. Brandley (Eds.), Chicago: The University of Chicago Press.

Foster, G.M. (1969). *Applied Anthropology*. Boston: Little, Brown, and Company.

Goffman, E. (1963). *Stigma: Notes on the Management of Spoiled Identity*. Garden City, NY: Anchor Books.

Gruber, J., and Caffrey, M. (2005). HIV/AIDS and community conflict in Nigeria: implications and challenges. *Social Science and Medicine*, 60, 1209-1218.

Kalipeni, E., Oppong, J., and Zarai, A. (2007), "HIV/AIDS, Gender, Agency and Empowerment Issues in Africa". *Social Science and Medicine,* Vol. 64, No. 5, pp. 1015-1018.

Kerrigan, D., Bastos, F.I., Malta, M , Carneiro-da-Cunha, C., Pilotto, J.H., and Strathdee, S.A. (2006). "The Search for Social Validation and The Sexual Behaviour of People Living with HIV in Rio de Janeiro, Brazil: Understanding the Role of Treatment Optimism in Context." *Social Science and Medicine,* Volume 62, 2386-2396.

Lindström, K. (1994). "Psychosocial criteria for good work organization". *Scand J Work Environ Health,* 20, 123-133.

Luke, N. (2005). "Investigating exchange in sexual relationships in sub-Saharan Africa using survey data", In Jejeebhoy, S.J., Shah, I. and Thapa, S. (Eds.), *Sex without consent: Young people in developing countries*. London: Zed Books.

Marshall, W.E. (2005). "Aids, race and the limits of science". *Social Science and Medicine,* 60(11), 2515-25.

Matasha, E., Ntembelea, T., Mayaud, P., Saidi, W., Todd, J., Mujaya, B., and Tendo-Wambua L. (1998), "Sexual and reproductive health among primary and secondary school pupils in Mwanza, Tanzania: Need for intervention". *AIDS Care*, 10(5), 571-582.

Meekers, D., and Calves, A.E. (1997). "Main" girlfriends, girlfriends, marriage and money: The social context of HIV risk behaviour in Sub-Saharan Africa. *Health Transition Review*, 7 (suppl.), 361-375.

Nyanzi, S., Pool, R., and Kinsman, J. (2001). The negotiation of sexual relationships among school pupils in south-western Uganda, *AIDS Care*, 13(1), 83-98.

Nzyuko, S., Lurie, P., McFarland, W., Leyden, W., Nyamwaya, D., and Mandel, J.S. (1997). "Adolescent sexual behaviour along the Trans-Africa Highway in Kenya." *AIDS*, 11(1), S21-6.

O'Neil, J., Orchard, T., Swarankar, R.C., Blanchard, J.F., Gurav, K., and Moses, S. (2004). "Dhandha, dharma and disease: traditional sex work and HIV/AIDS in rural India". *Social Science and Medicine, 2004*; 59: 851-60.

Parker, R. and Aggleton, P. (2003). HIV and AIDS-related stigma and discrimination: A conceptual framework and implications for action. *Social Science and Medicine*, 57, 13-24.

Parker, R. (1996). "Empowerment, community mobilization and social change in the face of HIV/AIDS". *AIDS*, 10 (suppl. 3): S27-S31.

Perelman, J., Mateus, C., and Fernandes, A.A. (2007). Inequity in Health Care Delivery: A Gender Perspective. iHEA 6th World Congress: *Explorations in Health Economics Paper*. Available at SSRN: *http://ssrn.com/abstract=994065*

Poland, B.D., Green, L.W., and Rootman, I. (2001). *Settings for health promotion: Linking theory and practice.* California: Sage Publications.

Poore, C. (1998). *"But Roosevelt Could Walk": Envisioning Disability in Germany and the United States.* Vol. XXXVII, No. 2, Ann Arbor, MI: M Publishing, University of Michigan Library.

Rappaport, J. (1987), "Terms of empowerment/exemplars of prevention: toward a theory for community psychology." *American Journal of Community Psychology*, 15, 121-148.

Rifkin, S. (1990). *Community participation in MCH/FP programmes: An analysis based on case study materials.* Geneva: World Health Organization, 1990.

Sahay, S., and Mehendale, S. (2011). "Engaging community to support HIV prevention research". *Eastern Journal of Medicine,* 16, 168-177.

Scheper-Hughes, N. (1994). "AIDS and the social body." *Social Science and Medicine.* 39, 991-1003.

Schiltz, M.A., and Sandfort, G.M. (2000). "HIV-positive people, risk and sexual behaviour". *Social Science and Medicine*, 50, 1571-1588.

Seidel, G. (1993). "The competing discourses of HIV/AIDS in Sub-Saharan Africa: Discourses of rights and empowerment *vs.* discourses of control and exclusion". *Social Science and Medicine,* 36, 175-194.

Shephered, M.E., Gangakhedkar, R.R., Sahay, S., Reynolds, S.J., Ghate, M.V., Rishbud, A.R., Paranjape, R.S., Bollinger, R.C., Mehendale, S.M. (2003). "Incident HIV Infection among Men Attending STD Clinics in Pune, India: Pathways to Disparity and Interventions to Enhance Equity." *J Health Popul Nutr,* 21(3): 251-63.

Stevens, P., and Hall, J. (1998). "Participatory action research for sustaining individual and community change: a model of HIV prevention education." *AIDS Education and Prevention*, 10 (5): 387-402.

Thege, B. (2009). "Rural black women's agency within intimate partnerships amid the South African HIV epidemic". *African Journal of AIDS Research,* 8(4):455-464.

Todorova, I.L.G., Baban, A., Balabanova, D., Panayotova, Y., and Bradley, J. (2006). "Providers' constructions of the role of women in cervical cancer screening in Bulgaria and Romania". *Social Science and Medicine,* 63, 776-787.

UNAIDS. (2002). "Report on the global HIV/AIDS epidemic." *Geneva: Joint United Nations' Programme on HIV/AIDS (UNAIDS).* Accessed on 17 April 2013.

UNAIDS. (2006). "Report on the global HIV/AIDS epidemic." *Geneva: Joint United Nations' Programme on HIV/AIDS (UNAIDS).* Accessed on 17 April 2013.

UNAIDS. (2012). "Report on the global HIV/AIDS epidemic." *Geneva: Joint United Nations' Programme on HIV/AIDS (UNAIDS).* Accessed on 17 April 2013.

USAID. (2011). HIV/AIDS Health Profiles. *http://www.usaid.gov/our_work/global_health/aids* Accessed on 17 April 2013.

Van der Vliet, V. (2004). *South Africa divided against AIDS: a crisis in leadership,* In Kauffman, K.D. and Lindauer, D.L. (eds.) *AIDS and South Africa: The Social Expression of a Pandemic,* New York: Palgrave MacMillan, pp. 48-96.

Wallerstein, N. (1999). Power between evaluator and community: Research relationships within New Mexico's healthier communities, *Social Science and Medicine,* 49, 39-53.

Wellings, K. (2012). "Sexual health: theoretical Perspectives." McGraw-Hill International. Open University Press. Berkshire. UK. Accessed on 17 April 2013.

Werner, D., Sanders, D., Weston, J., Babb, S., Rodriguez, B. (1997). "Questioning the Solution: the politics of primary health care and child survival with an in-depth critique of oral rehydration therapy." *Health Rights,* 1997. 964 Hamilton Ave. Palo Alto CA 94301.

Youde, J. (2009). "Government AIDS Policies and Public Opinion in Africa." *Politikon: South African Journal of Political Studies,* 36(2), 219-235. Doi: 10.1080/02589340903240161

Zakus, J.D., and Lysack, C.L. (1998). "Revisiting community participation." *Health Policy Plan,* 13: 1-12.

9

Public Health and People's Perception

A Study of Controlling Maternal Anaemia Among the Urban Poor in Tamil Nadu (India)

S. Sumathi

Public health has been defined as the health outcome of a group of individuals, including the distribution of such outcomes within the community. It is an approach to health that aims to improve the health of an entire population (Singh, P., 2012). As result, health and disease in India are matters of continuous external scrutiny. New Delhi is the site of the World Health Organization's (WHO) Southeast Asian Regional Office, and there are intense collaborations between the Indian Government and the International health bureaucracies of WHO, UNICEF, FAO, and other UN agencies and European, Japanese, and American health organizations. Indeed, some writers detect intrusion on India's sovereignty by multilateral and foreign aid organizations that try to direct the country's health priorities (Banerji, 1985, 1996; Patel, 1996; Bagla, 1997). With the result, many International projects were initiated and funds utilized at different levels.

Whether suspicious or gratitude is more justified, it is the case that major programmes to address population control, mother and child health... Frequently funded by outside the country, and population that elide national autonomy (Siddiqi, 1995). In these processes, India's alternative perspective offered richly varied knowledge complement to public health. An important theme in population health is the importance of social determinants of health and relatively minor impact that medicine and health can have on improving health overall. There is a very robust correlation between socio-economic status and health... Disease is not confined only to lower socio-economic groups but there is a continuous gradient from top to bottom of the socio-economic ladder (Singh, P. Indera, 2012).

In the UK, health promotion specialists are also increasingly aware that health-related behaviours are shaped and constrained by a range of social and community contexts and that the ways that individuals relate to wider social networks and communities have important effects on health and well-being. The Government Green Paper *Our Healthier Nation: A Contract for Health* (Department of Health, 1998a, b), for example, highlights a range of complex factors affecting health and emphasizes 'social environments':

> Neighbourhoods where people know each other and trust each other and where they have a say in the way the community is run can be a powerful support in coping with the day-to-day stresses of life, which affect health. And having a stake in the local community gives people self-respect and makes them feel better. [Para. 2.16]

Some of the most interesting public health studies have thus tried to grasp the lived complexity of the interplay among systematic and irregular, professional and popular, exotic and domestic practices from the patient's and as well as healer's perspective under variety of ritual, ideological, institutional and regional conditions (Banerjee and Banerjee, 1995; Burghart, 1988, 1996; Daniel, 1984; Kakar, 1982; Lambert, 1992; Longford, 1995; Marglin, 1987; Rhodes, 1984). Thus, health and illness are manifested at cultural level and created an impact on the community through systematic knowledge transmission. Keeping these basic theoretical premises the social/cultural factors, specifically the perception about anaemia has taken for analysis in this chapter.

Some Theoretical Inputs

Several studies carried out during the last 50 years have shown a high prevalence of maternal anaemia (WHO, 1982; 1992a; 1992b).

The causes and consequences of maternal anaemia are manifold (ICMR, 1989; Prema, 1981; Usha *et al.* 1995). Nutritional deficiencies such as iron, folic acid, and Vitamin B12 deficiency are the main causes of anaemia (Allen and Ahluwalia, 1997; Ramachanderan, 1984; Nair, 1999). Poor socio-economic conditions, poverty, illiteracy, contaminated environment and cultural beliefs are some contributing factors of anaemia.

A person's beliefs about his or her perceived susceptibility to a condition or disease figure prominently in models of health behaviour such as the Health Belief (Janz N.K. Beaker; 1984, Rosenstock, I.M., 1974), the Theory of Reasoned Action (Ajzen, I. Fishbeing, M., 1980), Subjective Expected Utility Theory (Edward, W., 1954; Sutton, S.R., 1982), and Protection Motivation Theory (Rogers, R.W., 1975, 1983). These models assume that perceived susceptibility (also referred to as vulnerability or risk) is essential in motivating behaviour. The Maternal anaemia seen as a medical or technical problem and narrow technical solutions sought without understanding the essential causal factors such as perception of the community about anaemia.

Simonds and Katz Rothman (1992) suggested, "Pregnancy, induced and spontaneous abortion (miscarriage), stillbirth and infant death all take their marriage from the lives of those who experience them and the social worlds in which they occur." Cecil, R. (1996) comparative studies into pregnancy loss in a number of different cultures and different historical periods have revealed an array of attitudes, beliefs, and practices. She further argues (1997) the increasing medicalisation of pregnancy...as resulted in a shift of responsibility for the care and support of women from the informal sphere of family, friend and neighbours to the formal sphere of medical and nursing professions. The operational research project professional, policy makers, and health professional need to be responsive to these aspects and understand the people's perception to provide public health services.

In this chapter, an attempt was made to understand the causal factors and the ability of large multi-disciplinary teams to come to grips with the ground-realities. The most focused aspect was **people's perception about certain 'diseases'** and its impact on health behaviour. The intricacies of the project process presented here will be useful in planning and implementing future projects of managing specific health problems. My chapter has been divided into two parts; the first one gives comprehensive details about the process of the project and the next part deals with the issues related to people's perception using content analysis. The main argument presenting in this chapter was that people had their own perception about certain health problem and may not consider certain disease as 'disease' as epidemiologist prescribed.

Project Background

'Development' is a broad term encompassing modernizing projects intended to mobilize resources, increase productive activity, and alleviate collective needs, but the last fifty years of intense development have led to unforeseen results, some of which are hazardous to public health and welfare (Greenough, 2003). As a result, many operational research projects were launched at the UN level to understand the existing ground realities. An operation research project was planned by UNICEF, Chennai to address the maternal anaemia, the disease, by empowering women of the local community to determine whether the implementation of a suitable development programme can reduce maternal anaemia.

An Operation Research (OR) is an analytical method of problem solving and decision-making that is useful in the management of organizations. In operation research, problems are broken down into basic components and then solved in defined steps by mathematical analysis. This project has proposed to compare the existing government health delivery system with an **alternative approach**. In an alternate approach, the local community members, particularly women's groups, get into the process of empowerment, to assess and analyze the problem of maternal anaemia and decide on interventions and methods of implementation in partnership with the local field functionaries.

UNICEF (Chennai office) took the initiative and brought together the experts from several fields—epidemiology, urban studies, economics, and anthropology—to discuss and formulate the project. UNICEF (Chennai office) introduced the framework paper, which formed the basis for the project.

1. The major and primary objectives of this project was to reduce the rate of anaemia especially among the pregnant women of the urban poor.
2. In order to achieve the primary objective a single research question was formulated which the present project envisaged to answer at the end. It was:
   Can empowerment of local communities improve implementation of identified set of interventions that will result in a demonstrable reduction in maternal anaemia?

Study Area and Project Phase

The study was conducted in the UBSP (Urban Basic Infrastructure for the Poor) and non-UBSP areas of Dindigul and Tirupur towns of Tamil Nadu. The whole project was planned to be conducted in three main phases: (a) Base Line Survey, (b) Intervention phase, and (c) Evaluation. The Epidemiologist and the Anthropologist conducted Base Line Survey (BLS) with different objectives. Epidemiologist to collect data on the levels of anaemia in the beginning and compare with the levels of anaemia after intervention with the same samples. The Anthropologist collects both quantitative household data and qualitative data on awareness, food habits, and traditional practices of treatment pertaining to anaemia among the communities of the two towns. The Anthropologist also assigned to process document the whole project.

The whole intervention was planned to be carried out in a participatory and learning mode. In this phase the local community, governmental agencies and the project personnel were supposed to work together as equal partners. The impact of interventions was planned to be measured by gathering data on the proportion of women in the age group of 15-45 years with Haemoglobin (Hb) levels < 11 gm/dl in the first three months (Baseline) and comparing it with similar data generated in the last three months (Evaluation) in Dindigul and Tirupur districts. A similar study on the same communities/ samples in the last three months of the project was planned to be conducted to evaluate whether there is any change in the broad parameters because of interventions. The original period to complete the project was 24 months of which three months were for BLS, 18 months was for the intervention phase, and three months was for evaluation. The methodologies to be followed by the disciplines were well determined by the Project experts.

Methodology

Keeping in view the primary objective and the research question, the methodology was determined. The study included all women in the age group of 15 and 45 years. The Anthropologist used four major techniques for data collection. They are Focus Group Discussions, in-depth interviews, Case Study and Household Schedule. Focus group discussions (FGDs) had drawn from five different categories among Post-pubertal girls, Married women with children, Married women without children, Post-menopausal women, and Married men. FGDs conducted among four different communities, namely *Pallar, Chakkilier, Paramalai Kallar,* and *Muslims* and verbal informed consent was obtained. These discussions addressed themes related to people's perceptions of anaemia, including identification and classification of anaemia, factors perceived to affect mother's health or type; and its impact on the newborn. In-depth interviews and FGDs were tape recorded, transcribed, and manually coded by the Anthropologist through several rounds of iterative discussion. Key terms were listed and their meanings discussed and defined. Findings were translated into English and arrived at final interpretations.

The data generated through this survey was analyzed in terms of the four areas, *viz.* UBSP-intervention, UBSP-control, non-UBSP intervention, and non-UBSP control areas. It was found that there was no significant difference between the four areas. Whereas the differences in terms of communities, cutting across the four areas, have been significant. Hence, the analysis was continued in terms of the major communities.

Local Terminology and Traditional Classification of 'sogai'

We followed the transcript-based analysis. Each of the transcripts prepared by reconciling the tape-recorded conversation, the notes taken during the Focus Group and non-verbal observation during the Focus Group interviews, which were recollected through memory.

The analysis includes identifying recurrent words, phrase, ideas, and located the context of recurrence systematically. Finally, the results correlated with the study objectives and findings were drawn. The partial results were presented here to substantiate the argument, which posed here for the present chapter.

The group/communities well aware of the term ***'sogai'*** and their understanding spontaneously could relate it with equivalent English term **'anaemia'**. They strongly believe that it could affect mothers, children, and men also. The major factor responsible for it was poor food consumption due to poverty. The communities consider it as a **'normal phenomenon and so natural'** especially **during pregnancy.** These perceptions repeatedly reflected through verbal and non-verbal mode by all the communities. *Sogai* during pregnancy considered as so common as they consume **abnormal food** like sand, chalk, charcoal, ash, bricks etc. They classify sogai/anaemia as *vella sogai* (white coloured), *Manja sogai* (yellow coloured), *Neer sogai* (water accumulation in the knee), and *Mann sogai* (sand *sogai*). They also ultimately relate anaemia with jaundice and locally call it as '*kamalai*'.

The four major communities among the urban poor in Dindigul and Thirupur are the Chakkiliyar (SC), Parayar (SC), Paramalai Kallar (OBC), and Muslims. The knowledge and awareness of anaemia derived through focus groups varied according to the age and experience. However, community-wise, the four major communities feel that maternal anaemia is a normal condition, which does not need any specific medical attention. The women groups use different linguistic terminology, which perhaps reflects their awareness of the problems of anaemia. Each community segregates the food items into "hot and cold", "normal and abnormal" and "good and bad" in different trimester periods during pregnancy. Greens and vegetables considered as good food to reduce anaemia. The household survey shows that majority of the households depend on public hand pump for their source of drinking water and public toilets for their personal use. The household food expenditure shows that the majority of them live in poor conditions. These results show that the awareness about *sogai* was very high among the communities.

Community-wise observation indicates that Chakkiliyar are the most affected group in respect of poverty and lack of other facilities compared to Parayar, Paramalai Kallar, and Muslim. Their perceptions of anaemia, however, have little variation while their food pattern, cultural practices, varies considerably. The members of the Kallar community marry at young age with the tradition called *sudandram* means the privilege of Mother's Brother to marry sister's daughter. Such practice resulted in many pregnancy wastage. Muslims consider non-vegetarian food is good while other communities feel that vegetarian food is good during pregnancy. Each community had their own traditional curative practices like soaking pealed banana in the earthen pot water over night and drinking in the morning, consuming fresh limejuice dipped with red iron rod, keeping the red iron rod on the main blood vessel nerve, eating *sathu mavu urundai* (cereal flour) and so on.

Discussion

The interviews and FGDs reported here shed light on local community perceptions of anaemia in Tamil Nadu, information that is of great importance for public health practitioners and policy makers. Lucas and Baird (2007) revealed the same results through their study as "Although programming often targets interventions to low birth weight of newborns and VLBW, the emergent theme of the interviews suggests that weight *per se* is not perceived to be a significant local determinant of newborn health or well-being, nor a trigger for care seeking. These findings are similar to those found in studies from the developed world" (Lucas, P.J., Roberts, H.M., Baird, J., Kleijnen, J., Law, C.M., 2007).

The community people consider the various observable characteristics of anaemia, and then categorize the affected people accordingly into types. Criteria for categorizing anaemia among the communities include their habits, growth, level of activity or vigour, frame and overall appearance. Overall health judged according to type; apparently, much like epidemiologist learn to recognize the affected by appearance. In developing a conceptual framework that addressed local understandings of the anaemia, it was decided that local knowledge should be included as a possible etiology of the types of *sogai* described, but did not justify an explanatory model in and of itself.

The term 'explanatory model' was originally conceived to describe individuals' understandings and decision responses to illness episodes (Kleinman, A.M., 1980). More recently, the term has been used interchangeably with 'cultural model' (Strauss, C., Quinn, N., 1997; Blum, L.S., Pelto, G.H., Pelto, P.J. 2004). Although individual explanatory models vary within a group, the construction of each individual model is influenced by environmental and social factors that are largely shared by group members. Thus, it is possible to build a group-wise model through cultural consensus, which was the main concern of the project. As explanatory models are constructed to explain, cope with and make decisions about illness episodes, Pelto and Pelto (1987), argue that the construction of local explanatory models reflect, and may be largely determined by the treatment or management options available to that community, extending the explanatory model to consider the wider ecological framework.

Although, that the project explanatory model of the epidemiologist positioned **maternal anaemia** as **'high risk'** and ultimately lead to death, if it was not taken care. It was emphasized in the entire core group meeting throughout the project. Whereas, on the other hand the local explanatory model, does not conceptualize the disease in the same way and perceive it **as a routine** phenomena in the process of pregnancy. There was some overlap between local categorization as *manja sogai*, with *kamalai* (Jaundice), and those who were indeed severely affected with anaemia. It was likely that the community's method of categorization does not target for extra care that appeared relatively healthy in their perception. As a result, many pregnant women were at high-risk in these communities and were overlooked.

Thus, it was found that the explanatory model of the local communities, especially about the type of *sogai* with traditional classification, might be largely influenced by the indigenous knowledge related to the local available health system and their culture as a whole. In the areas people faced with numerous barriers to accessing formal health care system. It was observed that the probability of seeking health care increased as the perception of risk increased, as the case in most communities. However, only the most severe cases that were ill for more than one month and unresponsive to home or traditional medicines were perceived to be at risk. This suggests that the community's system of risk classification, as compared with allopathic criteria, has a high threshold for what constitutes risk with the pregnant mothers.

The low sensitivity of the local explanatory model as a system of risk classification may be, in part, a conditioned response to the perceived inability of the formal health system to address the health needs of pregnant mothers who require care a hypothesis that requires further study in this community. As access to feasible solutions for a given illness episode increase, it is possible that local explanatory models will shift to reflect these changes. Similarly, a demand-side shift may occur in the local explanatory model as families become more aware of appropriate pregnant women care behaviours, signs of illness and care-seeking options. An understanding of the local explanatory model is essential for informing public health programmes, especially for framing public health concerns in locally relevant ways. In particular, programmes that rely on the identification of maternal anaemia as a criterion for prescribing care seeking outside the home or promoting additional care at home, must understand how *sogai*/ anaemia was conceptualized locally and its relevance in the local model. As such, the challenge for public health professionals now becomes one of promoting the seriousness of the disease and perceiving it as a disease become a frame or constitution, as an important determinant of public health in a locally relevant way.

Although skilled health professionals/epidemiologist recognized anaemia as an important determinant of pregnant women's health, it was found to be nearly irrelevant to members of all the community who relied instead on a set of observable criteria and judgement, based on their experience in assessing pregnant women' overall well-being. If additional care for and treatment of illness with anaemia are to be most effective, public health practitioners must reframe the disease anaemia in a locally relevant way. Referral criteria should take into account the capabilities of the health system to provide quality care for pregnant women at high risk of morbidity and mortality.

The Lessons We Learnt

In a multi-disciplinary research project a clear understanding on the methods and objectives—that is means and goals—by all the researchers is important. Terminological clarity and frequent discussions/exchange of notes between all the researchers is the minimal requirement if the overall goals are to be achieved. The term 'empowerment' referred in the project more as a scientific understanding of the disease rather than their perception about the health problem.

In a project with participatory learning mode as the methodology, all efforts should be made to create enabling conditions for all the stakeholders to participate—this includes all the researchers, agencies and the local communities. All the researchers/agencies involved in the project should be sensitized to the requirements of a participatory mode—i.e. accepting all the stakeholders as equal partners and giving due consideration to their cultural understanding. Their day-to-day life situation and perception about the issues are very important in achieving the universal generalizations.

References

Alen, Lindsay H. and Ahluvalia, N. (1997). *Improving Iron Status through diet: The application of knowledge concerning dietary Iron Bioavailability in human population* (Internet: OMNI_Project@jsi.com)

Ajzen, I., (1991). *The theory of planned behaviour. Organizational Behaviour and Human Decision Processes*, 50, pp. 179-211. Abstract-PsycINFO I $Order Document.

Ajzen, I. and Fishbein, M., (1980). *Understanding Attitudes and Predicting Social Behaviour*. Englewood Cliffs, NJ: Prentice-Hall.

Banerji, Debabar. (1985). *Health and Family Planning Services in India*. New Delhi: Lok Prakash.

_______(1996). "Political Economy of Public Health". In Das Gutpa *et al.,* Eds., *Health, Poverty and Development in India*. 295-314. Delhi: Oxford University Press.

Bagala, Pallava. (1997). "South Wants Place at Table in New Collaborative Effort." *Science*. 277 (26 September): 1918-19.

Blum, L.S., Pelto, G.H., Pelto, P.J. (2004). Coping with a nutrient deficiency: Cultural models of Vitamin A deficiency in Northern Niger. *Med. Anthropol.*, 2004; 23: 195-227.

Cecil, R. (1994), I Wouldn't Have Minded a Wee One Running About: Miscarriage and the Family, *Social Science and Medicine*, 38, 1415-22.

Cecil, R. (1996), in Edited Volume by Donnan and Graham McFarlane, *Culture and Policy in Northern Ireland, Anthropological Perspective in the Public Arena*, The Institute of Irish Studies, The Queen's University.

Edwards, W. (1954). The theory of decision making. *Psychological Bulletin*, 54, pp. 380-417. Abstract-PsycINFO I $Order Document.

Greenough, Paul (2003), The Social and Cultural Framework of Health and Disease in India, in edit. Vol. *Sociology and Social Anthropology* by Veena Das, New Delhi, Oxford University Press.

ICMR (1989). *Evaluation of the National Nutritional Anemia Prophylaxis Programme*, New Delhi: ICMR.

Janz, N.K. and Becker, M.H., (1984). The health belief model: a decade later. Health Education Quarterly, 11, pp. 1-47. Abstract-MEDLINE I Abstract-PsycINFO I $Order Document.

Lucas, P.J., Roberts, H.M., Baird, J., Kleijnen, J. and Law, C.M. "The importance of size and growth in infancy: integrated findings from systematic reviews of scientific evidence and lay perspectives", *Child: Care, Health and Development*, 33(5), (pp. 635-640), 2007. ISSN: 0305-1862.

Nair, Madhavan K. (1999). Iron Absorption and its implications in the control of iron deficiency anemia, *Nutrition News*, Vol. 20, No. 2.

Prema, K., Neelakumari, S., and Ramalakshmi, B.A. (1981). Anemia and Adverse Obstetric Outcome, *Nutrition Reports Interventions*, Vol. 23, No. 4, p. 637.

Patel, Tara. (1996a). 'Millennium Target Hinders Leprosy Fight'. *New Scientist*. 152 (19 October): 5.

_______, (1996b). 'Dengue Fever Outbreak Angers Indian Judges'. *New Scientist*. 152 (26 October):10.

_______, (1997). "Poisoned Water Sparks Cancer Fears". *New Scientist*. 154 (17 May):10.

Rajaratnam, Anel, Rajaratnam, Jolly, and Kamaladass, T. (1997). Maternal and child health practices and nutritional status of Malto Tribals in Bihar, *Man in India*, Vol. & No. 1, pp. 29-32.

Ramachanderan, Prima (1984). *Anemia in Pregnancy*, 21, p. 749.

Rogers, R.W., (1983). 'Cognitive and physiological processes in fear appeals and attitude Change: A revised theory of protection motivation'. In J.T. Cacioppo, R.E. Petty and D. Shapiro (Eds), (1983). *Social Psychophysiology: A Sourcebook* (pp. 153-176). New York: Guilford Press.

Simonds, W. and B. Katz Rothman, 1992. Centuries of Solace: Expression of Maternal Grief in Popular Literature, Philadelphia: Temple University Press.

Singh, P. Indera, (2012), in Edited Volume by Gopala Sarana and R.P. Srivastava, *Public Health, Genomics and Disease*, New Delhi, Rawat Publications.

Siddiqi, Javed. (1995). *World Health and World Politics: The World Health Organization and the UN System*. Columbus SC: University of South Carolina Press.

Strauss, C., Quinn, N. (1997), A. *Cognitive Theory of Cultural Meaning*. Cambridge University Press: Cambridge.

Usha, Krishnan, R. *et al.* (Eds.) (1995). *Anaemia—The weak get weaker, Safe Motherhood* (Issue II), Bangalore: Astra-IDPL Ltd.

WHO (1982). *The Prevalence of Nutritional Anemia in Women in Developing Countries: A Critical Review of Available Information.* Geneva: WHO.

_______ . (1992a). *National Strategies for overcoming Micronutrient Malnutrition.* Geneva: WHO (Document A45/17/1992).

_______. (1992b). *The Prevalence of Anemia in women: A Tabulation of Available Information (Maternal Health and Safe Motherhood Programme)* 2nd edition. Geneva: WHO.

10
Health Culture among Breast Cancer Patients

A.K. Sinha and *Reetinder Kaur*

The interplay between culture and health is truly complex and invites consideration of a kalaeidoscope of causes, experiences, expressions and treatments for a plethora of human ailments (Maclachan, 2006). Every community has a health culture of its own—its own conceptualisation of its health problems, its health practices and is corps of practitioners. As a component of each community's overall culture, the health culture shaped by the interplay of a number of social, political, cultural, and economic forces (Banerji, 1975). The various health institutions available and accessible, and the cultural perceptions, and cultural meanings of various health problems form an integrated whole: an interacting sub-cultural complex which has been called "health culture" (Banerji, 1982). This concept has made it possible to study diffusion of health culture, introduction of various health programmes from outside as purposive interventions with a view to bringing about a desired change in the health culture of a community. As it is a sub-culture, health culture is also affected by changes in the overall culture of a community, which are mediated by various ecological, social, demographic, economic and political forces (Banerji, 1982).

Cultural perceptions of health problems, their cultural meanings and the cultural response to these problems, both in terms of formation of various institutions to deal with various health problems and actual (health) behaviour of individuals or groups, form this sub-cultural complex. Because of its cultural connotations, health culture is subjected to change as a result of cultural innovations, cultural diffusions and purposive interventions from outsides to bring about a desired change in health culture. Health culture also undergoes change with change in the overall culture and change within it has repercussions on the overall culture. Further, as health problems of a population are usually a function of the latter's ecological background, cultural, economic and social setting, and the political structure, it is possible to link once again the entire spectrum of health culture to these issues because health problems form a key factor in the shaping of the health culture of a population (Banerji, 1982).

Contrary to popular usage, culture is not merely a set of social fictions. Rather, culture is the entire non-biologic inheritance of humans. Some aspects of culture can be linked with particular ethnic groups, although this cannot be taken to mean uniformity from person to person or it becomes mere stereotyping. Cultural domains can also be linked with other kinds of social groupings; for example "culture of medicine" refers to the knowledge and social processes of health professionals. Other aspects of culture are not limited to any particular group (Hufford, 1997).

Research Methodology

The present study is conducted among 100 Sikh breast cancer patients from three districts, namely Faridkot, Bathinda and Sri Muktsar Sahib of Malwa region of Punjab to understand the health culture among them. The respondents were first identified from Guru Gobind Singh Medical College, Faridkot using purposive sampling. This hospital was selected because this is the only Government hospital in the vicinity of the study area where all the facilities of cancer diagnosis and treatment are available. The reason for using purposive sampling was to get the sample according to the requirement of objectives of the study. Besides some caregivers, and doctors were also interviewed to strengthen the data. The main objective of the study is to understand health culture among breast cancer patients.

Analysis

Culture is not merely a complication or problem in medical care.

From surgical intervention, to family support, to chemotherapy, to religious ministry, culture is the source of all problem solutions. The recognition of medicine as culturally rooted, and of all communities as vast and rich reservoirs of varied resources for dealing with illness, is essential to effective medical care (Hufford, 1997). In the present study, the data are analysed thematically and divided into various themes such as knowledge regarding breast cancer, beliefs related to breast cancer and cultural construction of body and related concerns.

Knowledge Regarding Breast Cancer

For the analysis, this section is further sub-divided into two sections namely description and the terminology used for cancer and symptoms of breast cancer and reasons for downplaying symptoms.

Description and the Terminology used for Cancer

During the interviews, none of the respondents and their family members used the term 'cancer' as they believed that it is such a dreaded disease that using the term alone would cause cancer to them. They described cancer as a disease which spreads very fast as it develops its tentacles all over the vital organs of the human body and ultimately leads to death. The terms like *pinnā* (rounded mass), *gath/ gaṇḍ* (dense mass), *rasauli* (tumour) and ulcer were used to describe the disease. The respondents also described cancer as an incurable disease.

In the study, it was found that the names of cancer varied among the respondents. The widely prevalent names of cancer include *maṛī bīmārī* (bad disease), *chandari bīmārī* (dreaded disease), *bhairi bīmārī* (worst disease), *oprī bīmārī* (unknown disease), *jaṛ wālā phoṛa* (rooted sore), *māṛe karmā wālī bīmārī* (disease caused due to bad *karmā*) and *Bikaner wālī bīmārī* (disease treated at Bikaner).

Symptoms of Breast Cancer and Reasons for Downplaying Symptoms

Symptoms refer to subjective assessment of their condition based on their experience of some unwanted conditions. A doctor may derive important ideas from patient's expression of symptoms but primarily tend to rely on medical diagnostic procedures but the medical anthropologists views expression of symptoms as a social construction (Winkelman, 2009). In the study, women's stories were anchored in descriptions about their experience in becoming aware of overt changes in their breasts or perceptions that their breasts did not "feel right". A variety of changes were reported, including small lumps, pain, swelling in breast, unusual softness and small marks on their skin. Varying levels of pain intensity were described, including '*tīkhi piṛ*' (shooting pain), '*chubhan wālā dard'* (pinching pain) and pain like pinching of needle—*"aiven lagdā koi suyian chabho reha hove"* (It feels as if some one is pinching needles). Similarly, descriptions of breast lumps varied from *"Kuchh ajīb ja"* ('something odd)" to more detailed images of lumps with the use of terms like *"gaṭh"*, *"ganḍ?"* (dense mass). Not all of the women consistently linked their breast changes to breast cancer. For example, for some women, breast pain was attributed to muscle pain, whereas for others, it was viewed as an early sign of breast cancer. Similarly, although breast lumps, especially those without any pain, were viewed by some of the women as "milk lumps" or normal lumps, other women immediately associated a lump with breast cancer.

The breast changes were plausibly associated with other factors such as menstrual cycle phase, injury, or muscle strain. Some women considered these alternatives first and either sought ways to deal with the symptom or adopted a 'wait-and-see approach' (thinking the symptom could resolve itself). Some women seemed to conceal their concerns about the possibility of breast cancer to protect their family from worry.

The making of symptoms is a complex activity involving individual cognitive processes and negotiations with oneself, caregivers and the healthcare professionals. The construction of symptoms as possible signs of cancer was not always straightforward rather the respondents tried to downplay the symptoms. The social context played a very important role in naming and assigning meanings to the changes which the respondents recognised in their bodies. Some of the cases relating to downplaying symptoms and late diagnosis are as follows.

Case 1: A respondent (F/54 years) was diagnosed with breast cancer in an advanced stage told that she ignored the *tikhī pīṛ* (shooting pain) and *gaṭh* (lump) she experienced in her breast. She admitted thinking that it could be cancer but as a deeply religious woman she believed that cancer is caused due to bad *karmā* and she did not want to "believe it" and tried to "think it was something else". She appeared to draw on her strong belief as a devout Sikh as well as a good person that she would be protected from serious diseases, such as cancer, and downplayed the possibility of cancer.

In this case, the respondent tried not to believe that her symptoms are due to cancer as she believed that diseases like cancer are caused due to bad *karmā* and as said earlier being a deeply religious women, she downplayed the symptoms.

Case 2: A respondent (F/44 years) was undergoing symptomatic treatment at Postgraduate Institute of Medical Education and Research, Chandigarh. She shared that it was her efforts to protect her family from worry and maintain family honour that she downplayed her symptoms. When she told her husband and mother-in-law about the symptoms, it was already too late and she was diagnosed with advanced cancer later on.

It can be summarised from the case that life of a woman is deeply integrated into family spheres. Thus, women sometimes try to hide symptoms in order to save their family from *'chinta'* (worry).

Case 3: A respondent (M/56 years, husband of 52 years old advanced breast cancer patient) shared that it was seven years back, when his wife first noticed lump in her right breast. She shared this symptom with him and he immediately told her to visit a gynaecologist but she ignored. In the past seven years, she never complained about the lump or pain in the lump or whether it was increasing or decreasing. Suddenly in April 2011, she told only when she was not able to bear the lump in her right breast and the right arm. Her husband and her sons took her immediately to Guru Gobind Singh Medical College, Faridkot from where she was referred to PGIMER, Chandigarh for palliative care after confirmation of her advanced stage.

Sometimes the women are so much focused to fulfil their gender roles that they tend to ignore their health problems and advice of their 'significant others'. The above cited is such an example.

Case 4: A respondent (F/44 years) was undergoing active treatment at Bikaner. She shared her experience of noticing lump in her breast as: *"Mai kise nu dasayā nahī, apne āp nū bahūt majbūt kittā, aṇdro tan bahūt darī hoī si"* (I did not tell anyone, made myself strong, but I was scared from inside).

She hides the symptoms from her family till the time pain became unbearable for her. On asking about the reason why she did not share her symptoms with the family, she told that she is a woman, she has a whole family to take care of her and if she would discuss her small problems with the family, life would be difficult for them. She explained that her role as a woman is to provide them good life and not to make their life worse.

It was found that a number of respondents tried to be strong so as to save their families from unnecessary worry and hide their symptoms from them. Especially, for the women, families are centre of their lives and women's roles, and responsibilities revolve around their family. The female respondents agreed that the family unit not only provide a sense of identity but also social, economic and emotional support.

Regarding sources of information about this disease, researchers have also collected some cases.

Case 5: A respondent (F/36 years) was undergoing symptomatic treatment at PGIMER, Chandigarh. She told that one day her father-in-law was reading a Punjabi newspaper and told her about the increase in breast cancer cases in Bathinda region. Her mother-in-law who was sitting close told her that any lump painful or painless could be dangerous and may lead to breast cancer. Then, she discussed with them about hard mass in her left breast which she did not reveal earlier as she considered it to be normal. Her mother-in-law took her to a gynaecologist in Faridkot who referred her to PGIMER, Chandigarh for further examination. They went to Department of Medicine where the medical examination confirmed cancer. Then she was referred to Department of Radiotherapy. Her left breast was removed and after the surgery, radiotherapy was given. After the treatment, her condition improved, she visited many *desi* healers (quacks) in Bathinda. At the time of interview, she had metastasis in bones and she was undergoing chemotherapy again at PGIMER, Chandigarh.

The findings suggest that female cancer patients were concerned about their health, and their family members played an integral role in supporting prompt evaluation of cancer symptoms. The other source of information includes the mass media. In the above stated case, it is clear that mass media in the form of print media played an important role in cancer diagnosis.

Interestingly, as the respondents reflected on their symptom experiences, almost all mentioned the need for more information and open communication between the patients, caregivers and health care providers.

Beliefs Related to Breast Cancer

Cultural beliefs affect both the risk factors for cancer as well as meaning of disease by establishing norms of behaviour and providing guidance for its members to respond emotionally, cognitively and socially to this disease. These beliefs may also lay to delay in health-seeking behaviour and may prolong the interval between first appearance of symptoms and the first visit to the doctor (Kishore *et al.,* 2007). In the present study, it was found that there are a number of beliefs related to cancer. The term cancer was not used by the respondents rather they used variety of other terms for cancer. There are also a number of misconceptions such as belief that cancer is contagious and it is caused on account of an injury. The other misconceptions include the cancer fatalism and belief that cancer becomes incurable after surgery.

For better understanding, this section is also further sub-divided into four themes like cancer is caused due to *karmā* and *kismat,* cancer is a contagious disease, cancer fatalism, and cancer becomes incurable after surgery.

Cancer is Caused due to *Karmā* and *Kismat*

Within Sikhism, all living beings are described as being under the influence of three qualities of *māyā*, namely *rājas* (mode of passion), *tāmas* (mode of ignorance), and *sātav* (mode of goodness). It is due to the influence of three modes of the nature of *māyā*, *jivās* (individual beings) perform activities under the control and purview of the eternal time. These activities are called *karmā*. The underlying principle is that *karmā* is the law that brings back the results of actions to the person performing them. This is the *Gurbāni*'s (*Sri Guru Granth Sahib*) law of *karmā*. Like other Indians as well as oriental school of thoughts, the *Gurbāni* also accepts the doctrine of *karmā* and reincarnation as the facts of nature. Some of the narratives related to *karmā* as a cause of cancer are given below:

> "*Karmā karke hoyā, rabb hi thik karugā*"
> (It is caused due to *karmā*, only God will cure it).
> "*Karmā karke hundi hai eh bīmārī*"
> (This disease is caused due to *Karmā*).

Some of the cases related to *kismat* as a cause of cancer are discussed here.

Case 6: A respondent (F/62 years) attributed her disease to *kismat* and she told that after diagnosis with cancer, her faith in God has become more strong. She drew upon her religious beliefs and accepted the disease as *kismat*. She took comfort in the belief that God would protect her from the disease.

The narrative of *kismat* and a lesson from God appeared in some of the cases. In this narrative, the respondents asserted that cancer experience leads to the renewed and enhanced religious faith in God. The respondents drew strength from her religious belief that her *kismat* is in God's hands.

Case 7: A respondent (F/39 years) accepted her diagnosis with breast cancer as a part of her *kismat* and had faith that whatever would happen is in God's hands. With this belief, she underwent her treatment and considers her cancer experience as an important lesson from the God.

Case 8: A respondent (F/46 years) attributed her breast cancer to her *kismat* and explained that her fate is in God's hands. She further told that she reassured her husband that she would be fine as she accepted the disease as her fate and believes that she could cure herself through *sewā* (service of God). She narrated: "*Jo honā oh hoke rehnā*" (Whatever is going to happen is going to happen).

Further, she explained that in Sikhism, *pāth* (individual prayer), going to Gurdwara (Sikh temple) for communal prayer and *sewā* are very important. Through her devotion for God and *sewā*, she could attract God's grace and seek God's protection. It emerges from these cases that some respondents accepted cancer as their *kismat* and as a lesson from God. They also believed that their fate is in God's hands and through individual prayers, and service of God, the disease can be cured. Some of the verses from *Sri Guru Granth Sahib* in relation to *kismat* are given below:

> *Akhrā sir sanjog vakhān* II (SGGS, p. 4)
> (From the Word, comes destiny, written on one's forehead)
> *Visriā jinhā nām tinārā hāl kaun* II (SGGS, p. 397)
> (What shall be the fate of those who forget the *nām*).

Through a number of cases and narratives, the respondents attributed the cancer causation to their *kismat.*

Cancer is a Contagious Disease

Some of the cases relating to beliefs regarding spread of cancer are given here.

Case 9: A respondent (F/43 years) told that she contracted cancer from her mother-in-law as she considered cancer as a contagious disease which can be spread by sharing food, utensils, toilet, room and clothes. For her, coming in contact with a cancer patient and sharing of any of the above mentioned things leads to its spread.

Case 10: A respondent (F/40 years) told that after her diagnosis with cancer, she avoids eating among those who have a cancer patient in their family. She believes that she can again be affected with cancer by sharing food with other cancer patients.

In some cases, people distanced themselves from cancer patients in fear of contracting cancer from them. These cases not only relate to the belief that cancer is considered as a contagious disease but also to the fact that there is a widespread stigma associated with cancer.

Case 11: A respondent (F/55 years) narrated her experience of cancer as: "*Bāhar log kehnde sī ke ehdā kapṛā lailea tān sānu hoju bīmārī. Kamwālī ne vī aunā chaḍ dittā.*" (People used to say that if they would wear my clothes, they would also be afflicted by this disease. My servant also left working at my place due to fear of cancer contagion.)

She also believed that cancer is contagious and during her course of treatment she did not allow her children to come near her. During this time, she confined herself to a room and never cooked or shared food with anyone. It was her sister-in-law who supported her during this time and told her not to think about what people say and how they behave with her.

Due to fear that cancer spreads from one person to another led some of the cancer patients to worry about health of their family members. A case relating to this is given below.

Case 12: A respondent (F/38 years) was in advanced stage of cancer. She was undergoing her treatment at GGS Medical College, Faridkot. She shared that she did not allow her daughter to come close to her as she fear that she might be afflicted by the disease. On asking the reason, she replied that cancer is contagious. She narrated her fear as:

> "*Mainū darr lagdā, merī dhee nu nā hoje.*"
> (I fear that my daughter might get afflicted.)

The contagion appeared to be an important cause of cancer according to the respondents. The researchers were asked by a key respondent about the reason why they are working on such a disease and this would also lead them to affliction with cancer.

Cancer Fatalism

Cancer fatalism is the belief that death is inevitable when cancer is present. Fatalism is traditionally conceived as the perception that events and/or health issues are out of individual control. The fatalistic individual assumes that the outcome of the disease will be negative. It has been identified as a barrier in health-seeking behaviour of patients especially to participation in cancer screening, detection, and treatment. Fatalistic beliefs about cancer have been implicated in decision-making about cancer (Beekan *et al.,* 2011). A number of studies report that cancer fatalism leads to delay in cancer treatment (Conrad, 1996; Mayo *et al.,* 2001; Powe and Johnson, 1995; Phillips *et al.,* 1999). Cancer fatalism is a multi-dimensional construct which is guided by a number of factors such as awareness, perceptions and beliefs about the disease. According to Powe and Johnson (1995), cancer fatalism is a "categorical surrender of human being to the external forces of life which destroy human personality, potential, hope and even life itself."

Some of the important narratives described by the respondents in relation to cancer fatalism are:

> "*Es bīmārī da koi ilāj nahī*" (This disease is not curable).
> "*Mainū tān maut dī sajā hogi*" (I have got the death sentence).
> "*Cancer dā matlab maut haī*" (Cancer means death).

In a number of narratives, cancer has been described as a disease which means death. As a result of this belief, a number of cancer patients desired death. The desire for death among the cancer patients has been associated with depression, hopelessness, physical suffering, low social support, poor spiritual well-being, and low self-esteem in a number of studies of patients at the end-of-life. It may be affected by such factors as the fear of increasing dependency and the readiness for death (Rodin *et al.,* 2007). The five respondents in the present study repeatedly talked about their desire of death. Some of the narratives of the respondents are given below:

> "*Mainu jehar deke mār deo*" (Kill me by giving poison).
> "*Es bīmārī dā ilāj kraun nalo tān bandā mar hi jāve*"
> (It is better to die than to get oneself treated for this disease).

Cancer Becomes Incurable after Surgery

One of the major barriers to seeking health care services among breast cancer patients was the belief that cancerous growth increases after the surgery and after the surgery, cancerous cells grows much faster than before. So, the surgery as the treatment of cancer is not considered as an ideal option. This is a common belief in the area under study and similar belief is held by the *desi* healers (quacks) in the area who usually say:

"*Kainchī nahī lagī honī chāhidī*"
(No scissor should have been used).

Some of the important narratives in relation to this belief are:

"*Chīra nahī lagwānā chahidā es bīmārī chh*"
(No incision should be made in this disease).
"*Chīre to bād bachnā bahut mushkīl hai*"
(It is very difficult to survive after incision).

The doctors were also asked about the belief. They have another take on this belief. They explain that scapula is used to scrape the cancer cells during surgery and one scapula is used only once. If due to ignorance it is used for more than one time, it can also affect the normal cells and may aggravate the disease. So, they believe that surgery should take place in presence of an experienced surgeon.

Cultural Construction of Body and Related Concerns

Chemotherapy induced hair loss is one of the most distressing side-effect of treatment of cancer. Preparing patients for hair loss is a significant challenge for health care providers, and yet little is known about the process of preparing from the perspective of cancer patients themselves. Since preparation for hair loss has been identified as a key role for health care providers, understanding more about this crucial period may enhance ability to support cancer patients through this potentially difficult time.

In the study, an attempt has been made to understand the hair loss as a process which include preparing for hair loss, experiencing hair falling out, realising the altered sense of self and minimising effects. It was found that the breast cancer patients prepared themselves for hair loss by gathering information from three sources which include health care providers (doctors and nurses), other cancer patients undergoing treatment and information material in form of posters, pamphlets etc. It was observed that talking and discussing with fellow patients was the most important source of information seeking. This is known as social comparison. Social comparison helps to gain information about the treatment, side-effects, ways of coping etc.

During the experience of hair falling out, the respondents explained their experiences in context of gender and religious identities. They also felt that family members ignore them and they feel isolated and uncomfortable. As hair loss means a loss of religious identity apart from loss of gender identity, thus, body image concerns in relation to hair loss were more prominent. A number of verses from *Sri Guru Granth Sahib* (149, 344, 443, 941, 981) have also been discussed to support the narratives of respondents.

The respondents in the present study, especially the women considered hair as a symbol of womanhood, loss of which leads to the realisation that some important part of identity as a woman is lost. Thus, the efforts have been made by them to minimise their hair loss. This is in line with findings by Rosman (2004). The respondents in the present study told that they felt that changes to their appearance had rendered their diagnosis to be public knowledge, and even their attempts to camouflage their appearance had further led to their identity as cancer patients. In order to minimise the hair loss caused due to chemotherapy, the respondents tend to cover their heads with either turban or a *dupattā* respectively usually black in colour.

It is clear that the hair loss is an unavoidable side-effect of undergoing chemotherapy, and it is often experienced as distressing or traumatic. Research suggests that hair loss may also have a psycho-social impact on patients self-esteem, body image, and self-concept, but little is known about the category of patients that might be more vulnerable or resilient to these effects, and what factors might ameliorate this distress. One population of interest among researchers in relation to body image is the breast cancer population. Since breast cancer directly affects an individual's physical self, the disease may also affect body image. Breast cancer changes a woman's body in several ways including surgical scars and loss of a part of the body, tactile changes, sensory changes, swelling in their limbs and hair loss. There may also be changes in physical abilities, weight gain and/or swelling, fatigue, night sweats, early menopause and functionality of body parts (Price, 1993; Pelusi, 2006).

The diagnosis of breast cancer encompasses not only physical, but also social and psychological implications because of the importance of the breast in a woman's body image, sexuality and motherhood. Women may experience a range of concerns and fears including physical appearance and disfigurement, the uncertainty about recurrence and the fear of death (Mahapatro and Parkar, 2005). There is a cultural construction of woman's body and womanhood. Thus, understanding body in context of culture is very important.

In Punjab, the women wear *salwār kamīj* and the women residing in the villages usually cover their head with *dupattā* wrapping it around their upper body. This type of dressing saves them from being noticed but this does not mean that they do not have body image concerns. The case studies relating to body image concerns of respondents suffering from breast cancer are discussed here.

Case 13: A respondent (F/34 years) in a post-operative stage shared that her family is very supportive especially her husband but she feels as if she has lost an important part of her body. Moreover, the scars of surgery remind her of her loss (loss of her breast). She told that this loss is irreparable and she will have to live with this loss whole of her life. The female relatives who visit her ask questions such as:

> How much part of breast is removed?
> Is it possible to do something to hide the loss of breast in terms of surgery?
> How you cover the surgically removed portion?
> She explained that she finds it difficult to answer such kind of questions and she feels:
> "*Koi pardā nahi rehā*" (There is no privacy anymore).

She means that she has lost her privacy in family, among relatives and among health care providers. These difficulties make her to hide the breast with a *dupattā* spread all around for most of the time.

Case 14: A respondent (F/40 years) in a post-operative stage told that soon after her diagnosis with breast cancer, her husband and in-laws told her parents to take her to their place as they were not ready to support her treatment. Her husband told her that he is not ready to accept her with changes in her body post-surgery (removal of breast). Now, she was staying with her parents who are paying for her treatment and supporting her in every possible way.

Case 15: A respondent (F/46 years) told that her husband has become much more supportive towards her after surgery. It is interesting to note that this makes her feel that something is wrong with her and she is not the same person anymore. This feeling makes her think that as she has lost the most important characteristic of being a woman and that's why her husband has become indifferent towards her.

The breast cancer patients described the changes that they felt in their breasts in detail, but they also reported 'wait-and-see approach' that they initially followed which lead to delay in their diagnosis. The women considered loss of breast as loss of womanhood and an intrusion in privacy. In some cases, they also reported separation from their husbands as a result of bodily changes that followed cancer. Furthermore, the breast cancer patients also mentioned that people have become indifferent towards them after their cancer diagnosis. One important aspect that adds to the body image concerns among breast cancer patients is that their health care providers do not pay attention to social consequences of biological changes due to cancer. One important study conducted by Thomas-MacLean (2004) investigates the subjective experiences of women diagnosed with breast cancer in an attempt to understand the social context in which breast cancer occurs. Through exploring women's experiences of embodiment, this phenomenological study focused on the long-term changes to embodiment. The author further explained that embodiment is the idea that:

> ...we do not simply have bodies, but that we are our bodies. It has been suggested that the body has various dimensions, including one's physical being and the 'sociological body', which exists as "dialectic between the subject and society".

The above mentioned narratives can also be analysed in this context which distinguishes between a social body and a physical body. It was found that social body is very important for the cancer patients, but their socio-cultural perceptions are not fully understood by their doctors which leads to a number of body image concerns among them. These body image concerns of the respondents are not addressed.

Discussion

There are wide cultural variations in how diseases are understood and encompassed, and anthropological insights into these variations are useful in informing both the management and treatment of problem (Strang, 2009). The differences in description and terminology used for breast cancer were found. Some of the respondents shared the initial symptoms with their family members or 'significant others' but there were others who downplayed their symptoms. The reasons for downplaying symptoms include belief that cancer is caused due to *karmā* or *kismat*, gender roles, stigma associated with cancer, to save the family honour and the family members from worry. The other reasons include the belief that lumps especially in breast are common 'milk lumps' or due to menstrual cycle. The downplaying of the cancer symptoms leads to the late diagnosis and delay in the treatment. Here, open communication can play an important role as stated by some of respondents in whose cases the open discussion led to sharing of symptoms by the respondents which led to early diagnosis.

The common beliefs of respondents related to cancer can be summarised as:

- Cancer is caused due to past *karmā* and *kismat*.
- Cancer is a contagious disease and spreads from one person to another.
- Cancer is incurable and a fatal disease.
- Cancer grows faster after surgery or any attempt made to remove the cancerous mass. This makes it incurable.

As in Punjab, the women wear *salwār kamīj* and the women residing in the villages usually cover their head with *dupattā* wrapping it around their upper body. Thus, the body image concern in relation to breast cancer was not in relation to public appearance but a concern related to women themselves. The women told that the scars of surgery reminds them of their loss which they consider to be irreparable and moreover, the questions asked by other women from their family as well as social network makes them realise that they have lost their privacy. Sometimes, the women suffering from breast cancer takes the social support extended to them in a negative connotation and feels that there is something wrong with them.

Illness is a socially constructed phenomena based on the value of life and health. The specific nature of stigma associated with a serious illness may be dependent on whether the individual can be blamed or held responsible for its occurrence, whether the illness has potentially serious consequences for others, the illness, and/or whether it results in a decreased level of competence. Once a stigma becomes evident to others, persons become labelled as outsider, and expectations and assumptions are associated with the individual from which patterns of response from others emerge during interaction. As the person internalises the label, it becomes a part of his/her identity, and thereby, a part of the self that generates behaviour. In the present study, it was found that a stigma is associated with breast cancer because of following reasons:

Firstly, it is believed that cancer is caused due to *karmā* and the individuals are held responsible for the disease. This leads to labelling of the individuals with cancer as 'cancer patients' which leads to their seclusion as a result of related stigma. Stahly (1988) rightly said that the disease like cancer motivates the individuals around cancer patients to believe that 'they get what they deserve' and this belief helps them to save themselves from fear of getting the disease.

Secondly, the treatment of cancer leads to a number of bodily changes and disfigurement which leads to labelling of cancer patients, and they receive a new identity which is different from their previous gender and religious identity. In this case, stigma is both from outside as well as from the individual as he/she feels different, isolated and secluded from the rest.

Thirdly, it is believed that cancer is contagious and spreads from one person to others. The others around the cancer patients believe that cancer can also affect them. This creates a fear regarding cancer and people choose to stay away from those who suffer from cancer to save themselves from the disease.

Fourthly, it is believed that cancer will increase debilitation and lead to eventual death. This belief also leads to cancer related stigma. Sontag (1978) also pointed out that illnesses are stigmatising because they represent potential or existing physical limitations; they are associated with particular negative images and myths, and therefore, take a symbolic meaning. Thus, an attempt has been made to reconstruct the health culture among the breast cancer patients of Malwa region of Punjab.

References

Banerji, D. (1975). Social and cultural foundations of the health services systems of India. *Inquiry,* 12 (2): 70-85.

Banerji, Debabar. (1982). *Poverty, Class and Health Culture in India.* New Delhi: Prachi Prakashan.

Beekan, R.J., A.E. Simon, C. Wagner, K.L. Whitaker, and J. Wardle. (2011). Cancer fatalism: Deterring early presentation and increasing social inequalities. *Cancer epidemiology, Biomarkers and Prevention*, 20 (10): 2127-2131.

Conrad, M.E. (1996). Fatalism and breast cancer in black women. *Annals of Internal Medicine*, 125 (11): 941-942.

Hufford, David J. (1997). Folk medicine and health culture in contemporary society. *Complementary and Aternative Therapies in Primary Care*, 24 (4): 723-741.

Kishore, J., I. Ahmad, R. Kaur, and P.K. Mohanta. (2007). Beliefs and perceptions about cancers among patients attending radiotherapy OPD in Delhi, India. *Asian Pacific Journal of Cancer Prevention*, 8: 155-158.

Maclachan, Malcolm. (2006). *Culture and Health: A Critical Perspective Towards Global Health.* England: John Wiley and Sons.

Mahapatro, F., and S.R. Parkar. (2005). A comparative study of coping skills and body image mastectimized *vs*. lumpectomized patients with breast carcinoma. *Indian Journal of Psychiatry*, 47 (4): 198-204.

Mayo, R.M., J.R. Ureda, and V.G. Parker. (2001). Importance of fatalism in understanding mammography screening in rural elderly women. *Journal of Women and Aging*, 13 (1): 1-19.

Pelusi, J. (2006). Sexuality and body image. *American Journal of Nursing*, 106 (3): 32-38.

Phillips, J.M., M.Z. Chen, and G. Moses. (1999). Breast cancer screening and African American women: Fear, fatalism and silence. *Oncology Nursing Forum*, 26 (3): 561-571.

Powe, B.D., and A. Johnson. (1995). Fatalism among African Americans: Philosophical perspectives. *Journal of Religion and Health*, 34 (2): 119-125.

Price, B. (1993). Disease and altered body image in children. *Pediatric Nursing,* 2 (6): 18-21.

Rodin, G., C. Zimmermann, and A. Rydall. (2007). The desire for hastened death in patients with metastatic cancer. *Journal of Pain and Symptom Management,* 33: 661-665.

Rosman, S. (2004). Cancer and stigma: Experience of patients with chemotherapy induced alopecia. *Patient Education and Counselling,* 52 (3): 333-339.

Sontag, D. (1991). *Illness as metaphor.* London: Penguin.

Stahly, G.B. (1988). Psychosocial aspects of the stigma of cancer. *Journal of Psychosocial Oncology*, 6 (3-4): 3-27.

Strang, Veronica. (2009). *What Anthropologist Do*. Oxford: Berg Publishers.

Thomas-MacLean, R. (2004). Memories of treatment: Immediacy of breast cancer. *Qualitative Health Research*, 14 (5): 628-643.

Winkelman, M. (2009). *Culture and Health: Applying Medical Anthropology.* San Francisco: Jossey-Bass.

Index